W9-BYT-840

PROPERTY TO THE PEOPLE

Also from M. E. Sharpe

**HARD TIMES: IMPOVERISHMENT AND PROTEST
IN THE PERESTROIKA YEARS
The Soviet Union 1985–1991**
William Moskoff

PROPERTY TO THE PEOPLE

THE STRUGGLE FOR RADICAL ECONOMIC REFORM IN RUSSIA

LYNN D. NELSON
IRINA Y. KUZES

M.E. Sharpe
Armonk, New York
London, England

146215

Copyright © 1994 by M. E. Sharpe, Inc.

All rights reserved. No part of this book may be reproduced in any
form without written permission from the publisher, M. E. Sharpe, Inc.,
80 Business Park Drive, Armonk, New York 10504.

Library of Congress Cataloging-in-Publication Data

Nelson, Lynn D., 1943–
Property to the people: The struggle for radical economic reform in Russia/
Lynn D. Nelson and Irina Y. Kuzes.
p.   cm.
Includes bibliographical references and index
ISBN 1-56324-273-7 (cloth)—ISBN 1-56324-274-5 (pbk.)
1. Russia (Federation)—Economic policy—1991–
2. Privatization—Russia (Federation)
I. Kuzes, Irina Y.
II. Title.
HC340.12.N45   1993
338.947—dc20
93-5692
CIP

Printed in the United States of America

The paper used in this publication meets the minimum requirements of
American National Standard for Information Sciences—
Permanence of Paper for Printed Library Materials, ANSI Z39.48-1984.

Photograph by Lynn D. Nelson
"Lenin Burning"
November 7, 1990, in Palace Square, St. Petersburg

∞

BM (c) 10   9   8   7   6   5   4   3   2   1
BM (p) 10   9   8   7   6   5   4   3   2   1

To the memory of Sergei Shvedov

Contents

Acknowledgments

Our fieldwork in Russia was carried out by a staff of more than seventy capable interviewers and office workers in Moscow, Ekaterinburg, Voronezh, and Smolensk. Their exemplary participation made possible the successful completion of the research projects codirected by Lynn Nelson and Liliia Babaeva from which we draw so heavily in this book. We are especially indebted to Liliia Babaeva, who participated in designing the 1991 and 1992 projects and supervised data collection in Moscow; Rufat Babaev, general fieldwork coordinator and data-processing supervisor; our fieldwork directors outside Moscow, Sergei Khaikin in Voronezh, Svetlana Petrushina in Smolensk, and Boris Berzin in Ekaterinburg; Vladimir Meshcheriakov of the Smolensk regional administration; Eduard Yanbulatov of the Sverdlovsk Oblast property management committee; and Leonid Reznichenko and Anna Miskiniants, whose devoted work and valuable insights contributed in many ways to the 1992 project.

Several colleagues in Russia provided valuable suggestions and encouragement. Our debts to Grigorii Kaganov are numerous and varied. We also want to particularly thank Alex Levinson, Yurii Levada, and Inna Shpileva of the Center for Public Opinion and Market Research; Vladimir Yadov, Sergei Kuterin, and Olga Kryshtanovskaia of the Institute of Sociology (Russian Academy of Sciences) in Moscow; Boris Doktorov and Leonid Kesselman of the Institute of Sociology (Russian Academy of

Sciences) in St. Petersburg; writer Virginie Coulloudon; Oleg Pchelintsev of the Institute of Economic Forecasting; Vadim Sadovskii of the Institute for Systems Studies; and Sergei Shvedov, who was a researcher at the Institute of Socioeconomic Problems of the Population until his untimely death in October 1992.

In the United States, Christopher Clague of the Center for Institutional Reform and the Informal Sector at the University of Maryland was a valued supporter, critic, and contract administrator. He, along with John Robinson, provided valuable suggestions at critical times for our 1992 study. Eugene Trani, president of Virginia Commonwealth University, supported this extended effort from the beginning and provided critical seed money during its initial phase. Cynthia Graves of the International Research and Exchanges Board helped facilitate Lynn Nelson's travel arrangements. Ella Kagan and Pavel Ilyin provided much-appreciated personal support. We are deeply grateful to Patricia Kolb, executive editor at M.E. Sharpe, who supported our work unreservedly and offered thoughtful insights and suggestions at just the right times. All authors should have the good fortune to work with such a talented editor!

We gratefully acknowledge research support provided by the Center for Institutional Reform and the Informal Sector (IRIS); the International Research and Exchanges Board (IREX), with funds provided by the Andrew W. Mellon Foundation, the National Endowment for the Humanities, and the U.S. Department of State; a Grants-in-Aid award for faculty from Virginia Commonwealth University; and funds from the Institute of Sociology in Moscow. None of these organizations is responsible for the views expressed in the book.

Lynn D. Nelson
Irina Y. Kuzes

A Note on Transliteration

For the sake of readability, we have eliminated soft signs from people's names in the narrative but have retained them in end-note citations. We have generally followed the Library of Congress transliteration system, but in many cases we began proper names that are referred to in the narrative with *Ya* and *Yu* rather than *Ia* and *Iu*. In most cases we retained *ii* and *ia* name endings.

PROPERTY TO THE PEOPLE

1

Introduction

The Gorbachev era ended with only polite notice at the end of 1991, and Boris Yeltsin's path was suddenly clear, for the moment, to radically redirect Russia's economic course. Elected president of the USSR's Russian Republic by a large margin earlier in the year, his public support had been further enhanced by his compelling challenge to the leaders of the August coup. Yeltsin's approval ratings were impressive, his backing among legislators extraordinary, and his team of advisers talented and determined to pursue rapid economic reform. Repeatedly, during the months that followed, Yeltsin's cabinet members emphasized their aim of dealing a fatal blow to the command system in the process of fashioning a market economy.

A year later, the Russian economy was on the verge of collapse according to most indicators; it appeared that Yeltsin had lost much of his public support; and the Congress of People's Deputies, which had earlier handed him broad administrative powers to pursue his program for radical reform, removed his chief economic adviser from office and was decidedly unhappy with Yeltsin as well. The following March he narrowly escaped impeachment, and in April 1993 he was fighting for his political life.

The issues that had precipitated the August 1991 coup were predominantly *political*. Gorbachev's opponents did not want the central command structure to be gutted by the new Union Treaty, which would have decentralized authority among the republics of the Soviet Union. It was scheduled to be signed on August 20, 1991. The coup intervened.

The chief issue that began eroding Yeltsin's authority in 1992 and produced the crisis of early 1993 was *economic* reform. The government's program called for massive and comprehensive changes that would have profound implications for every aspect of Russian society. No country had ever before tried to reorient such a large and complex industrial economy so decisively and quickly. In the course of pursuing these objectives, legislated and decreed from the center, officials began uprooting mainstays of the Soviet way of life—from the economic security provided by the state to the ideology of classlessness promoted by the party. Even the collectivistic thinking which had predated communism in Russia was exposed to critical scrutiny.

The principal players on this stage were often suspected of camouflaging their true intentions with misleading gambits and of working against the people's interest. When Yeltsin heatedly proclaimed "democracy," he was sometimes accused of maneuvering to acquire unbridled personal power. When "centrist" Arkadii Volskii calmly insisted that "a single leap" to the market was a utopian dream, critics charged that he wanted to take two steps backward for every step toward dismantling the state planning system.

Before the end of 1992, Yeltsin's increasingly vocal opponents were charging that he was approaching the Russian economy with a bludgeon when a scalpel was needed, and that a continuation of his radical reform program would be ruinous. Yeltsin countered that his detractors wanted to restore the communist system and that he was Russia's only real hope for democratic and economic reform. The drama that would revive the specter of a revitalized communism in Russia and pit Yeltsin against the supporters who had recently hailed him as a hero began to unfold with the November 1991 announcement of price liberalization. This study is a critical narrative and analysis of the 500 days that followed.

The Study's Analytical Focus

The period of Yeltsin's brief tenure as the indisputable leader of Russia, with unique authority to fashion a new economic course, was charged with significance for the country's future. Yeltsin had a mandate to initiate broader and more comprehensive changes than any twentieth-century world leader had ever enjoyed in peacetime. No Western heads of state in the 1990s had so much power relative to other branches of their governments. None were so free to carry out their political agendas. In some ways, this period was one of those times Charles Tilly speaks of, when it seems that "what we need most is a clear understanding of the singularities of a particular historical experience."[1]

Agreeing with Tilly that "there is no such thing as social change in general,"[2] and sharing Theda Skocpol's "respect" for "the inherent historicity of sociopolitical structures,"[3] we also recognize along with Tilly and Skocpol that specific events beg for some measure of theoretical coherence, and that explorations of uncharted societal terrain can benefit from familiar conceptual guideposts. Such markers, however, could not be definitive. We were persuaded that hypothetico-deductive explanations, which impose rigid theoretical order on complex historical phenomena, would be unsatisfactory for the research problem at hand.[4] Recognizing a "strong tension between the demands of doing justice to the explanation of a particular case and the search for generalizations,"[5] in Barrington Moore's words, we found Paul Feyerabend's solution to this dilemma appealing. An explanation "has to have *some* content," he notes, ". . . otherwise it would be useless. But it must not have *too much* content, or else we have to revise it every second line."[6] Fernand Braudel's work *Civilization and Capitalism* exemplifies the fruitfulness of maintaining this fine line. His preference is for interpretation that aims at making sense of historical developments without, at the same time, introducing serious distortions: "I have . . . tried to see things and to present them in such a way as to understand, that is to verify. But I have done so with some insistence."[7]

A useful frame of reference for our study was the research tradition that attends to *the primacy of the state* in initiating some types of social change. A key concept in this stream of inquiry is "state autonomy," which is typically conceived as the significance of class relations to political decision making in a country.[8] Our concern was both with the extent of state autonomy—recognizing, of course, that autonomy is always relative—and with "the embeddedness" of Russia's economy "in changing transnational relations."[9] In addressing external challenges to state autonomy, we focused particularly on influences of Western consultants and financial institutions on the Yeltsin government's economic reform program and the course of reform in the country.[10]

It is clear that the Yeltsin economic reform program and the pattern of its implementation were "not simply reflective of the demands or interests" of powerful constituencies in the society.[11] The degree of a government's insulation from such interests is always relative, however, and the new struggle over power and privilege in Russia was intense. As sociologist Tatiana Zaslavskaia framed the problem, "There is one line of thought" that the new class of entrepreneurs "should be formed from the *nomenklatura,* and then there is another line—a democratic one. This latter view is fighting for the class to be made up of the most energetic and talented people, regardless of the social group to which they belong." This, she concluded, is "a real struggle for absolutely real assets," a struggle "for property and power."[12]

"The new class" of which Yugoslav communist Milovan Djilas had written in the 1950s—bureaucratic elites who controlled and enjoyed the "fruits of the revolution" because of their administrative positions[13]—was being challenged, it seemed, by one of its own. Among Yeltsin's chief declared objectives was to *break up* the expansive state bureaucracy, which had brought him to power and where most power had resided since the beginning of the Soviet period. It is sometimes argued that governments always enjoy a significant degree of functional autonomy,[14] but the purposive *enhancement* of governmental autonomy in Russia during this time, for the explicit purpose of transferring assets controlled by the state into private hands, was unique in its magnitude and scope. In requesting, and receiving, special powers that insulated him from legislative oversight in critical areas to facilitate implementation of his reform ideas, Yeltsin's team was orchestrating from the center a program they claimed would sharply reduce the center's monopoly control over the Russian economy.

In describing prominent features of reform programs in communist countries, Robert W. Campbell states that they "do not start out being advertised as the abandonment of socialism and the restoration of capitalism."[15] In Russia, however, Yeltsin and the Russian legislature came very close to doing just that, beginning in 1990. Yeltsin proclaimed his economic "shock therapy" intention even while the Soviet flag still waved above the Kremlin, and only four days after the USSR officially ceased to exist, a Yeltsin decree outlined the principal features of his program to accelerate the dismantling the command system now administered by his own government.

In exploring Russian economic reform in this study, we wanted to illuminate structural connections and clarify decision-making processes that could inform our understanding of state-directed change under conditions quite different from those that have characterized several other inquiries into the state as a causal force. The economic reform initiatives of the Russian government in the early 1990s illustrated several features of the process Ellen Kay Trimberger describes as *"revolution from above,"*[16] but this characterization is not entirely appropriate. Most obviously, the Yeltsin government's actions in 1991 and 1992 do not qualify as an "extralegal takeover of political power"; nor is Trimberger's focus on military bureaucrats in radical top-down change appropriate for the Russian case.

The momentous transformation under way in Russia at the beginning of the decade has some components of the *"charismatic breakthrough"* described by Reinhard Bendix, following Max Weber's analysis of revolutionary charisma in *Economy and*

Society.[17] The movement set in motion by radical reformers in Russia proposed to disrupt "rational rule as well as tradition altogether"[18] by interjecting alien visions of economic and political organization. We do not want to overstate, however, the strength of the radical reform movement or the similarity of perspectives among reform supporters. As Vladimir Mau points out, there were conspicuous "contradictions in people's thinking about the rationale and purposes of market-oriented reform."[19]

Revolutionary charisma need not be inspired by a single leader,[20] and Russia's was not. It is true that Yeltsin's populist tendencies meshed well with the profound restiveness among Russian people at the time, and the ideas he articulated about economic reform comfortably fit the growing public support for a market economy. Although Yeltsin was the most prominent public representative of this new mood, especially after the August 1991 coup, he was more a symbol than a bellwether. Indeed, the height of Yeltsin's public support would not come until a year after economic reforms in the RSFSR began noticeably outpacing those in the USSR.

Weber points out that "it is the fate of charisma, however, to recede with the development of permanent institutional structures";[21] and in the *routinization* that characterizes this new stage of change, self-interest considerations tend to predominate.[22] In the case of Russia, the permanent institutional structures were already in place, and the plan of radical reformers was to use those structures, plus some new ones that had been recently added, to strip away much of the power that these same structures had commanded for most of the Soviet period.

In *Bringing the State Back In,* Skocpol hypothesizes that one "feature of all autonomous state actions will be the reinforcement of the prerogatives of collectivities of state officials."[23] If her hypothesis should be broadly supported in the Russian situation, then Russia's program for top-down redistribution of resources was doomed to deviate sharply from its announced course. Exploration of this question is a central focus of our study.

Two periods within the eighteen-month span of Yeltsin's pre-referendum reforms are important to this part of the analysis. In the reform program's first phase, reforms were approved and started with the encouragement of many officials whose personal control over resources was threatened by the measures. In the second phase of Yeltsin's administration, a substantial number of officials began voicing increasingly urgent opposition to the program. Can the pronounced shift in the perspectives of these leaders, which reached a crisis point in December 1992, be better explained as a consequence of the reform program's failures or as confirmation of Skocpol's hypothesis? We trace interrelated aspects of this question in several chapters that follow.

Although Yeltsin's economic reform program was unprecedented in its scale and scope, in some ways the course of change from 1991 to 1993 was not new to Russia. This most recent attempt to encourage entrepreneurship and legislate privatization was not Russia's first experience of spinning radical change out of conservative tradition and drawing creative energy from the ashes of tired ideologies. Forced analogies with the past, however, would be misleading. Likewise, the upheavals throughout Eastern Europe can be usefully compared, if not too closely. The differences here are instructive—a subject to which we will return in the fifth chapter.

Data

We drew material for this study from a variety of sources. Research projects carried out at the Moscow Institute of Sociology in 1991 and 1992 (codirected by Lynn Nelson and Liliia Babaeva)[24] provided valuable interview and questionnaire data. In addition, these studies facilitated the identification of themes for further inquiry.

For research on political and economic issues in the post-Gorbachev era, Russian periodicals are a valuable source of data, provided that researchers carefully follow adequate guidelines for assessing the evidentiary status of such documents.[25] Periodicals were a rich source of data for this study, as were government publications that include texts of pertinent laws and statistical information. In the mass media, as in many other areas of Russian life, the early 1990s were a time of radical departure from past practices; the censorship that had been a familiar feature of Communist Party control virtually evaporated. As media analyst and former BBC correspondent David W. Benn describes the situation in 1990, "*de facto* media freedom had largely arrived."[26] The *de jure* phase dates from USSR legislation in August 1990 and Russian legal protection in December 1991.

Although the Russian Supreme Soviet was attempting to establish control over *Izvestiia* again in late 1992 and early 1993, the effort had not succeeded at the time our research for this book was completed. Newspapers and journals without historical roots in the state mass media system, such as *Delovoi mir, Nezavisimaia gazeta, Kommersant,* and *Delovie lyudi,* were entirely free of state censorship during the period of this study. Older and highly regarded journals such as *Ekonomika i zhizn* and *Literaturnaia gazeta* were also useful. It is clear from the contents of prominent Russian periodicals that, from 1990 onward, many editors and journalists did not shrink from exploring controversial issues and airing minority opinions. The masthead of *Kommersant* illustrates the changing fortunes of the press in Russia and the Soviet Union during this century: "Started in 1909. Not published from 1917 to 1990 due to circumstances beyond the control of the editors."

From 1991 through April 1993 we systematically extracted a large volume of material from Russian journals and newspapers. These sources reflected a broad spectrum of perspectives and interests. Especially useful were texts of key governmental planning documents, decrees, and laws; programs of political parties and coalitions; economic reform proposals developed by the government and other groups; detailed discussions of legislative proceedings and of developments in a wide variety of administrative units; interviews with public officials and specialists; results of public-opinion surveys conducted by a variety of organizations;

and analytical articles by scholars and decision-makers concerning narrowly focused questions.

We often worked with several published sources' treatments of a single topic or event—an address by Boris Yeltsin to the Congress of People's Deputies, for example. As any specialist who works with Russian materials knows, the entire text of an important speech is often available in newspapers, as are analyses and responses by specialists and interest group spokespeople. Frequently, divergent interpretations are provided in different periodicals as well as within a single periodical.

We were selective in our use of survey-research material, knowing that the value of survey research is partially a function of the adequacy of the research design and that in Russia public opinion studies vary widely in quality.[27] We avoided telephone surveys entirely, and for most themes of the research we preferred national surveys over studies in a single locale, such as Moscow or St. Petersburg. Often, results of several surveys were available for a certain question at a specific point in time. In such cases, we searched for divergences among results and attempted to identify characteristics of the different studies that would give us a sound basis for judging their relative merits. Our assessments also benefited from personal experience with several of the more prominent organizations in Russia where survey research is carried out. We report significant details about surveys we cite in either the narrative or the notes: the organization that conducted the survey, the sample size and population from which the sample was drawn, and the date(s) of the survey.

We incorporated in this study results of our 1992 research on privatization and entrepreneurship in four Russian cities: Moscow, Ekaterinburg (Sverdlovsk Oblast), Voronezh, and Smolensk. We selected these research sites to reflect regional, economic, and demographic diversity in Russia. In each city we collected data from active and influential *privatization decision-makers* (DMs), who were members of property management committees, privatization commissions, or property funds ($n =$ 171); *directors and owners* of state, privatized, and private enterprises ($n = 966$); and *nonmanagerial workers* in the three types of enterprises ($n = 4{,}645$). In Moscow we also interviewed several members of the Russian Supreme Soviet and Yeltsin's government who were involved in the economic reform program, and specialists whose work had contributed significantly to government policy. Our 1992 project followed a smaller 1991 Moscow study of 101 owners and managers of private-sector firms which are also included in parts of the analysis conducted here.

Details about the main topics we addressed in the interviews and surveys, brief descriptions of the research sites, the research design for the four-city study, and sampling procedures are presented in Appendix A, along with a discussion of control variables in the study. All tables referred to in the text are in Appendix B.

2

From NEP to Yeltsin

The state had monopolized economic decision making in the Soviet Union since the end of NEP—the New Economic Policy, which lasted from about 1921 until roughly 1929. In fact, even under NEP, in the mid-1920s, the state's role in the economy was greater than it had been prior to World War I, and the market was more closely regulated. R.W. Davies describes five "major instruments of control" wielded by the state in the NEP period that had not been available to it before 1914. First, wholesale industrial prices were fixed by the state, as were an increasing number of retail prices. Further, credit was regulated by the state. Additionally, the state regulated wages and attempted to bring income differentials in line with its ideological objectives. Fourth, the state possessed a monopoly of foreign trade and controlled all imports. Finally, a state plan, developed annually, was introduced to try to control economic development. There was no recent European precedent for the level of direct economic planning that was found in Russia by the mid-1920s.[1]

Yet NEP included many characteristics of a market economy. More than 40 percent of organized retail sales, and almost all "informal" sales by peasants, were private. Neither price controls nor attempts at wage controls were very effective. As Davies describes it, "The wage and price policies of the state were very largely attempts to manage what was still fundamentally a market economy."[2] Private ownership was never a major factor in large-scale industry, however. In 1923–24 only 2.7 percent of all industrial workers were employed in private enterprises. Wholesale trade included a larger proportion of nonstate activity, but in 1925–26 private wholesale sales amounted to only 7.3 percent of the total.[3] Nonstate enterprise in the 1920s was most prominent in retail trade, small-scale industry, and agriculture.

Lenin frequently justified a mixed economy as consistent with the goals of Bolshevism. In April 1921, just as NEP was beginning, he asked, "But need we fear this capitalism if we control the factories, transportation systems, and foreign trade? ... I think it is incontrovertible that we need have no fear of this capitalism."[4] NEP had been necessitated, Lenin argued, by the deteriorating economic conditions that followed the War Communism period, which lasted from June 1918 through 1920. The outlawing of private trade and broad nationalization of industry during this period had had disastrous effects. Production in 1920 was less than 20 percent of its prewar level, and privation was severe and widespread. Justifying the policies of NEP, Lenin said in October 1921 that "by attempting to go straight to communism, we suffered an economic defeat ... more serious than any defeat at the hands of Kolchak, Denikin, and Pilsudski." NEP, for Lenin, was another "severe defeat and retreat,"[5] but a necessary one.

Even with NEP, however, the Soviet economy toward the end of the 1920s still lagged far behind those of the advanced Western countries. Although the USSR's population was substantially larger in 1927 than that of the United States, Soviet national income was probably no higher than the national income in the United States fifty years earlier. Total per capita consumption of energy in the USSR at that time was 41 percent of Germany's and 13 percent of that in the United States; and even per capita paper consumption, in a nation with abundant forest reserves, was only 14 percent as great as in Germany and 6 percent of the U.S. level.[6] The Bolsheviks' uneasy accommodation to limited capitalism under NEP came to a swift end in the wake of the grain crisis late in 1927. Earlier that year, worsening international relations—most dramatically signified by the breaking of diplomatic relations with Great Britain—led to panic buying and depletion of stocks in shops and markets. The most alarming development for the state, however, was the disruption of grain supplies. Bread was the most important item in the people's diet, and the Bolsheviks wanted grain surpluses to secure the country against the potential disruptiveness of a bad harvest. Beginning in 1926, the tension between the government, which wanted a dependable supply of grain at low prices, and the so-called Nepmen, or private traders, who offered peasants higher prices for grain than the government wanted to pay, led to newspaper articles complaining about the activities of Nepmen in the agricultural sector and to state initiatives that reduced private grain trade.

This tension reached a crisis point in November–December 1927, when state collection of grain fell to only half of the 1926 year-end levels.[7] The party's response was to invoke "emergency" and "extraordinary" measures. Grain was confiscated from peasants who refused to accept the state's prices, and many prosperous peasants were tried in court for hoarding grain and realizing excessive profits from grain sales. Stalin and his lieutenants formulated the idea that the grain-procurement problem was caused by a "grain strike," described by Stalin as an "expression of the first serious action, under the conditions of NEP, undertaken by the capitalist elements of the countryside against the Soviet government."[8]

In his study of Nepmen, Alan Ball suggests that the conflicting interests of the state and the grain traders "was undoubtedly one of the factors that prompted Stalin and his allies to launch their momentous collectivization drive and ban the free trade of grain."[9] By the spring of 1928, after having used "extraordinary" measures to circumvent the market in grain procurement, Stalin could declare at the April plenum of the Central Committee that the state had "scored a signal victory" on the grain issue. "We have," he said, "put our procurement and party organizations in the localities on a sound, or more or less sound, footing."[10] He was speaking approvingly of the purges earlier that year of local party and Soviet institutions—purges aimed at replacing "degenerate elements" in the party with "new, revolutionary cadres" who would more effectively carry out Stalin's policies at the local level.[11] Before 1928, Stalin had wavered between those party economists, led by Nikolai Bukharin, who believed that the peasants should have even greater freedom, and the group who agreed with Leon Trotsky that rapid industrial growth should be the USSR's top priority. Now Stalin was convinced that the peasants threatened to stand in the way of the Bolsheviks' economic ambitions, and the grain-collection campaign quickly gave way to all-out collectivization of agriculture.[12]

The position of private-sector entrepreneurs had been worsening even before the grain crisis as taxation and other state regulations were used to limit their activities; now, with the government's pressure on the peasantry, came a broad attack on all private business. Early in this assault, Stalin spoke of the dangers from those within the party who, he asserted, favored a "broadening" of NEP. Later, he argued that Bukharin and those who shared his views would, if not challenged, "improve the chances for restoration of capitalism" in the Soviet Union.[13] Executions of "counterrevolutionaries" began in the summer of 1929, and widespread purges were undertaken to expel from the party those who had, among other offenses, been too strongly influenced by kulaks and Nepmen.[14] On November 12, Bukharin, who represented for Stalin the right wing in the party and support for private enterprise, confessed his errors in a joint statement with A.I. Rykov and M.P. Tomskii. A resolution adopted by the plenum denounced the Bukharin group, and Bukharin was removed from the Politburo. Another resolution highlighted the "transition to comprehensive collectivization of districts and okrugs" said to be under way.[15] In sum, the November 1929 plenum made decisive the agricultural policy shift that had already begun taking shape.[16] The state soon completely controlled almost all economic activity in the Soviet Union. Private entrepreneurship would not again find legitimacy in the USSR for nearly sixty years, except for the direct sale of produce grown on private plots by collective farmers.

Foreign Investment, Joint Ventures, and Foreign Technology

Foreign investment in Russia was widespread during the last part of the nineteenth century. Foreign capitalists saw opportunities in Russia's vast resources and huge potential markets; and added incentive was offered at the end of the century by the minister of finance, Count Witte, who spearheaded a multifaceted effort to attract foreign entrepreneurs. Witte offered foreign investors subsidies, credits, and profit guarantees. As he saw it, foreign participation would provide the critical capital, technology, and entrepreneurial "spirit" that Russia needed to catch up with the West economically.[17] By 1913 as much as 33 percent of the capital of private companies may have been foreign-owned.[18] (In the United States, by contrast, foreign capital accounted for about 10 percent of investment during the mid-1880s, when U.S. dependence on foreign investment was at its highest.)[19]

The October 1917 revolution only temporarily halted foreign investment. At the first All-Russian Congress of Councils of the National Economy in December 1917, it was agreed that Western investment would again be sought by granting concessions, through which foreign or mixed-ownership companies would receive surpluses or profits if they agreed to exploit and develop a specific opportunity. Negotiations were under way with French, German, British, and American investors before the Allied Intervention and the Civil War. In 1920 Lenin decreed that concessions could be granted to foreign capitalists, and throughout the decade of the 1920s many were.[20] Two kinds of concessions were common under NEP: the "pure" concession, in which the foreign firm invested stipulated sums of money and equipment for a specified period, without acquiring property rights;[21] and the "mixed" company concession, in which Soviet and foreign involvement were nearly equal[22] and a Soviet citizen chaired the board of directors with the deciding vote in cases of dispute.

The first American concession that actually came into operation, a "pure" concession, was worked out by Armand Hammer
for the Allied Chemical and Dye Corporation, to operate asbestos
mines at Alapaievsky, in the Urals. Hammer subsequently obtained a concession to organize the pencil factory which he credits with having made his name a household word in the Soviet
Union (". . . the name Hammer, stamped on each one, became
familiar to every Russian").[23] The first U.S. company to agree to
build a plant in the Soviet Union was the Gillette Safety Razor
Company, as part of the terms of its 1928 concession. This was
the last pure concession any foreign company concluded with the
Soviet government, and the razor blade factory was never built.[24]
By 1925–26 there were 330 "pure" and "mixed" concessions in
the USSR, but by the early 1930s most of these foreign opera-
tions had been taken over by the Soviets—usually without com-
pensation to their former foreign owners.[25] Concessions to
foreign firms, however, were of slight overall importance to Soviet industry, accounting for less than 0.5 percent of industrial
production in 1926–27, at the height of foreign concession activity.[26]

Beginning in the late 1920s and after, the Soviet government
often negotiated technical-assistance contracts with foreign firms
and individual specialists for technological designs, training, and
individual work agreements. This activity expanded rapidly after
the November 1929 plenum of the party's Central Committee,
which urged "the maximum utilization of foreign technical assistance and foreign specialists."[27]

This policy shift was born out of recognition that Soviet industry had been slipping ever further behind that of Western nations
in the years following World War I. The gap in production per
capita between the USSR and the advanced countries of the West
was as wide in the mid-1920s as it had been in 1913; even more
ominous, technological advances in the West were markedly
greater than in the Soviet Union during this period.[28]

The height of technical-assistance activity was from 1929 to

1932, when many of the Soviet Union's largest industrial facilities were designed and started up through technological support and equipment purchases from Western companies.[29] The best-known architectural firm in the United States, Albert Kahn, Inc., was commissioned to design more than two billion dollars' worth of buildings—all industrial facilities projected in Stalin's First and Second Five-Year Plans. This huge project was two and a half times greater than all the work Kahn had undertaken for U.S. firms from its beginning in 1903 until 1939.[30]

Other technical-assistance projects contracted with American and European businesses created a wide range of industrial, mining, weapons, communications, and energy facilities in the Soviet Union during this period. The Ford Motor Company agreed to provide technical assistance in the construction of a facility in Nizhnii Novgorod capable of producing 100,000 automobiles per year.[31] The KhMEZ turbine plant in Kharkov, designed by General Electric, had a capacity two and a half times greater than the main General Electric plant in Schenectady, New York; the iron and steel plant in Magnitogorsk, an enlarged copy of the Gary, Indiana, plant of U.S. Steel, was the largest of its kind in the world.[32] In 1936 the Soviet Union reported that 6,800 foreign specialists had been working in its heavy industry in 1932.[33] As R.W. Davies puts it in his study of the Soviet economy during this period: "Foreign engineers were employed on almost every major project of civilian industry and in almost every new factory; in major new factories, ... foreign foremen and skilled workers helped to train the Soviet workers."[34]

Because of the increase in imported industrial and agricultural machinery in 1929–30, total imports increased by 28 percent in just one year. Exports did not keep up, and the favorable foreign trade balance that the USSR had achieved in 1928–29 was reversed.[35] With the acquisition of the latest production technology during the late 1920s and early 1930s, however, the Soviet government was prepared to pursue its goal of rapid industrial growth; indeed, production output increased almost ninefold from 1928 to 1950. Growth in production of consumer goods, however, was much more modest, only doubling during the same period, and farm output on a per capita basis remained nearly constant.[36]

Starting with the Second Five-Year Plan (1932–37), the USSR gradually reduced its imports, so that by the late 1930s it had again achieved a trade balance.[37]

During World War II the Soviet Union amassed heavy debts, which were paid largely with credits from the United States through the Lend-Lease program and through short-term loans. The debts were quickly repaid after the war, however, largely thanks to Soviet economic involvement with East European countries. A new era in Soviet trade relations had begun, as the USSR became an investor nation in Eastern Europe.

By 1952, 83 percent of the USSR's total foreign trade volume was with other socialist nations.[38] Stalin pointed out that the international economy was now composed of "two parallel world markets . . . counterposed to one another." He continued: "There can be no doubt that with such a high tempo of industrial development, these countries will soon reach the point where they will not only have no need to import goods from capitalist countries but will themselves feel the need to dispose of the surplus of goods they produce."[39] What Stalin failed to note, however, was that foreign technology had been crucial to the industrialization carried out by his government.[40]

The "seeds of destruction" already firmly rooted in the Soviet production system would ultimately bring down not only the economic but also the political system. In a 1954 analysis completed just as the Stalin era was ending, Donald R. Hodgman observed that the USSR's impressive industrial expansion during the first two five-year plans "relied to an important extent upon the introduction of modern production techniques from abroad." Hodgman then warned: "But some aspects of both the technical and human organization of industry, especially the latter, are likely to prove too subtle for import. . . . Unless Soviet industry succeeds in developing substitute organizational methods and attitudes through its own experience, it may find the gap between Soviet and American industrial performance increasingly difficult to close."[41]

Hodgman could not have known how accurate his assessment was. That the Soviet Union did not successfully "indigenize" the technologies it had imported from the West is indicated by the increasing volume of foreign trade with nonsocialist countries during the Khrushchev years and beyond. By the early 1980s nearly half of the USSR's foreign trade was with capitalist countries.[42] Soviet imports had disproportionately become manufactured products and agricultural goods, with a high percentage of exports consisting of raw materials.

By now the trend was clear. Rather than having established a relatively autonomous "socialism in one country," what the Soviet leaders had fashioned was an economic system heavily dependent on the capitalist world for nonmilitary technology but lacking an infrastructure that could supply many consumer goods that could be marketed successfully in the West. Part of the problem was in the priorities of the production system. Heavy industry received the greatest attention. Production for the consumer sector, which could have both improved living conditions inside the Soviet Union and furnished much-needed export commodities, was neglected. The practical consequences of this policy seem not to have been even imagined by the leadership. The country's hard-currency debt escalated, and productivity declined markedly. By 1982 labor productivity had dropped to less than one-third of its 1966–70 level.[43] Average annual GNP growth from 1975 to 1985 was only half that of 1960–1975. Total factor productivity (efficiency in utilizing inputs) from 1981–85 was half that of the previous five-year period.[44]

The system worked against the introduction of new designs and production methods in the domain of consumer goods. The aggregated indicators of output that were developed for many products in response to overcentralized administration produced a conspicuous mismatch between supply and demand, and often wasted effort and resources.[45] (For example, as even Khrushchev jokingly observed, chandeliers were often very heavy because the plans for production measured only tons.) An undesired effect of this process was that new designs and methods often were not utilized because, as Alec Nove observes, "the resultant temporary disruption of established practices would threaten the fulfillment of quantitative output targets."[46]

Unfortunately for the Soviet economy, the world market for heavy chandeliers was not strong, nor was that for the state-of-the-art space technology that resulted from the high priority of defense and space innovations in the USSR's research-and-development program.[47] Near the end of the Soviet period, only 0.23 percent of the USSR's exports were of high-tech goods, while 80 percent of its hard-currency income came from the export of such raw materials as oil and natural gas.[48] Unintentionally, the path had been prepared for a major change in the Soviet Union's economic relations with capitalist countries. The shift was signaled in the program adopted by the Twenty-seventh Party Congress in early 1986, which acknowledged that "the Soviet share in world trade does not correspond to . . . the requirements of its economic growth."[49] Gorbachev would seek to strengthen the economy as Lenin had 65 years earlier, by encouraging entrepreneurship and foreign investment.

First Steps Toward Economic
Restructuring Under Gorbachev

Gorbachev departed from communist orthodoxy at the Twenty-seventh Party Congress by speaking positively about market relations, particularly cooperative activity, thereby setting the stage for internal economic reform. Yet, the decree on unearned income that was issued in May 1986[50] was widely regarded as threatening to both legal and illegal production in the private sector.[51] Although the Law on Individual Labor Activity adopted in November 1986 (effective May 1987) articulated rules for the operation of private enterprise, its general thrust was no more encouraging toward entrepreneurship. In addition to authorizing cooperatives (with the qualification that these enterprises could not make use of hired labor), it specified that private activity was to be part-time only, and not an alternative to state-sector work. It also required that participants be licensed.[52] These licenses were often difficult to obtain, and because they were valid for only five years, the requirement underscored the long-term uncertainty of nonstate enterprise in the Soviet Union.[53] Further, while the February 1987 decree On the Creation of Cooperatives in the Service Sphere for the Population authorized the establishment of cooperatives, a significant restriction was the provision that cooperatives could be created only under the authority of local government commissions or state enterprises or organizations.[54] The 1988 Law on Cooperatives had been more supportive of nonstate enterprise, but it maintained a distinction between socialist cooperative activity and capitalism.[55] Subsequent legislation restricted entrepreneurship in other ways—forbidding or limiting cooperative enterprise in some sectors of the economy, allowing local soviets to fix maximum prices for cooperative products, and levying special charges on cooperative purchases.

Ambivalence about capitalism among Soviet decision-makers both in the 1980s and during the NEP period is an extension of a theme that is familiar in Russian history before the October Revolution. As Gregory Guroff notes, "Private entrepreneurship had been the dream of very few Russians during the nineteenth century."[56] Tsarist Russia's skepticism about capitalist development was reflected in the marketplace by a lower level of capitalist enterprise than was prevalent in other countries of the Western world. Macroeconomic data tell part of the story. Russia's per capita income in 1900 was only one-third that of Germany, one-fourth that of the United Kingdom, and one-third that of the Balkans.[57] The evidence suggests that part of the reason for Russia's economic position was its lower level of the kind of industrial activity that in other Western nations was characteristically spearheaded by entrepreneurs. Teodor Shanin observes that 57 percent of Great Britain's labor force was employed in manufacturing and mining during this period, compared to only 5 percent of the work force in Russia; in Britain, only 10 percent were agricultural workers, while in Russia the corresponding percentage was 74.[58]

There were, of course, some Russian entrepreneurs before the Soviet period; but, as Alec Nove points out, "The traditional Muscovite merchants, rich and uneducated, were far from being the prototypes of a modern commercial capitalism." He adds that toward the end of the nineteenth century, "Russian entrepreneurs of a modern type began more and more to emerge";[59] but there never were many of them relative to their numbers in other Western countries. One reason was structural. The political system was, in Guroff's blunt assessment, "a major obstacle to industrialization."[60] Another, and perhaps the most important, reason was cultural. The values and lifestyles of entrepreneurs were out of step with mainstream Russian society. In a biography about one entrepreneur in Moscow, Ivan Sytin, who became a publishing giant comparable in stature and wealth to Joseph Pulitzer or William Randolph Hearst in the United States, historian Charles A. Ruud notes, "Sytin was an uncommon Russian—so much so that some contemporaries, whether praisingly or pejoratively, called him an 'American.'"[61]

The Break with the Past

The concept of a rapid economic restructuring in the USSR gained momentum during the summer of 1990 and then foundered before year's end; but the debate over reform saw the Russian Federation (RSFSR) begin an independent course which eventually produced the program for privatization administered by Anatolii Chubais's State Property Management Committee.

Three different plans were initially proposed. Soviet Prime Minister Nikolai Ryzhkov sponsored a plan for a "regulated market economy" which included many features of an economic reform proposal that had been presented by Leonid Abalkin the previous October. Ryzhkov introduced his plan in a speech to the USSR Supreme Soviet on May 24, 1990.[62] He called for "a one-time comprehensive revision of the entire price system" to begin early in 1991 and to be followed by the gradual introduction of market-based pricing. Many aspects of the plan continued to bear the stamp of central planning, and in the discussion that followed it was clear that a large number of deputies believed that it did not go far enough toward promoting radical reform.

A year later, Grigorii Yavlinskii, who was a principal developer of the Shatalin plan (discussed below), would call Ryzhkov's May 24 speech "unfortunate"; he saw in it the unleashing of forces that were to send the economy into a tailspin. Conditions were already severe at the time of Yavlinskii's assessment in 1991 and they deteriorated alarmingly thereafter.

According to Yavlinskii's reconstruction of the watershed period of mid-1990, inflation had been manageable before the end of May, although prices were rising. Income growth was being restrained, and a consumer market existed. "The decline in production was affecting basic industries even then," he noted, "but few could have imagined that the production of meat, milk, fabrics and so on would drop by 15 percent to 17 percent. All that," he added in June 1991, "is happening now."

The public response to Ryzhkov's May 24 speech was a harbinger of things to come. "In the twinkling of an eye," an *Izvestiia* report stated two days later, "throughout the country, even the few things left on the shelves—mainly food, salt and matches—began to disappear from the stores."[63] The significance of the Ryzhkov proposal, and the public reaction that followed, is underscored by sociologist and survey researcher Yurii Levada: "There was an explosion of mass dissatisfaction, and a rapid decline in the authority of the government and the leadership as a whole. . . . From that moment on," Levada wrote in 1991, "a majority of the population has consistently favored the resignation of the government, which it deems to be unable to overcome the crisis."[64]

In the year following Ryzhkov's speech, according to Yavlinskii, "the state has lost the main levers for controlling the economy, reserves have been 'eaten up,' and the very structures of control are collapsing. The economy, which has entered a phase of crisis, is hanging on for the time being through inertia and the force of habit of millions of people who continue to go to work every day and to receive in exchange pieces of varicolored paper that, again because of inertia, are known as 'money.' "[65]

Even before Ryzhkov's speech in May 1990, output had begun falling for the first time since the beginning of the first five-year plan more than six decades earlier. This was a striking illustration of Gorbachev's inability to rebuild a Soviet economy already in stagnation, a fact that was recognized by Ryzhkov in a speech to the USSR Congress of People's Deputies in December: "Perestroika in the form, and I emphasize this, in which it was originally conceived, has failed to be realized."[66]

Opposition to the Ryzhkov plan both in the legislature and among the public necessitated a new direction. Boris Yeltsin, then chairman of the Russian Supreme Soviet, argued vehemently that the government plan was too conservative, and in July Gorbachev and Yeltsin agreed to appoint a working group to develop an alternative plan for transition to a market economy, headed by economist Stanislav Shatalin.[67] The Shatalin plan was decidedly more radical, proposing a 500-day period during which prices would be rapidly decontrolled and large-scale privatization of industry would be carried out.

When the Shatalin plan was unveiled, Gorbachev at first favored it; and, according to Yurii Levada's public opinion research, the citizenry favored it by five to one over Abalkin's program, but significantly, the military and the "military-industrial complex" did not.[68] Perhaps due to Ryzhkov's threat that he would resign if the Shatalin plan were adopted, Gorbachev reversed himself.[69] A commission headed by economist Abel Aganbegian was charged with developing a compromise program. Levada characterizes this third variant, called "The Main Directions," as an "inconsistent, contradiction-ridden compromise program."[70] These three proposals were considered at the session of the USSR Supreme Soviet which opened on September 10, 1990, but no agreement was reached.

In the Supreme Soviet of the Russian Federation, however, the

Shatalin plan was passed by an overwhelming majority of 213 to 2. A month later, in a speech to the Russian parliament, Yeltsin accused the USSR leadership of sabotaging the Shatalin plan.

On October 19 the Supreme Soviet of the USSR, while unable to endorse concrete details of a reform plan, gave republics the freedom to take more specific actions to promote privatization. This "green light" encouraged Russia's accelerating divergence from USSR policy on economic restructuring; and before the end of 1990 the RSFSR Supreme Soviet approved laws that made private ownership legally equivalent to state or cooperative ownership,[71] specified the principal organizational and legal forms of enterprises, and guaranteed people's right to engage in entrepreneurship.[72]

At the beginning of 1991 Russia's Supreme Soviet decisively rejected the tentativeness that had characterized all previous overtures toward market relations since the Bolshevik Revolution. In the January 4 Law on Enterprises and Entrepreneurship, the term "private enterprise" was mentioned for the first time in such a context since 1917. According to this law, any person could now open a private business and own private property.[73]

Russia's path-breaking legislation in this area was followed in April by the Law on Principles of Entrepreneurship, approved in the USSR Supreme Soviet, which pointedly endorsed "initiative-taking and self-development by citizens that is intended to obtain income or profit . . . and is performed for oneself and at one's own risk and property responsibility, or is performed on behalf of and at the property responsibility of a legal person—an enterprise."[74] Then, on July 1, the Supreme Soviet of the USSR approved the Law on the Basic Principles of the Destatization and Privatization of Enterprises, which specified target dates for removing enterprises from state control; some of them would initially be leased and others converted into joint-stock companies.[75] According to the plan, about half of the fixed production assets of state enterprises would be shifted outside the sphere of direct state management by the end of 1992; this sector of the economy was expected to grow to between 60 and 70 percent by 1995.[76]

After Yeltsin's decisive election as president of Russia, which many took as a mandate for more radical reform than Gorbachev had favored, the RSFSR Supreme Soviet increased its pace on the road toward a market economy. On July 3, 1991, the Law on Privatization of State and Municipal Enterprises was passed.[77] According to this legislation, enterprises could be privatized in several ways. An entire enterprise could be sold through auction or competition (in which potential buyers would submit a plan for their use of the enterprise, and the relative merits of the proposals would be evaluated by a competition commission created for each individual enterprise). An enterprise could be transformed into a joint-stock company and its shares sold. (Workers of enterprises transformed into joint-stock companies had the right to buy shares for 30 percent less than their face value; the proportion of an enterprise's shares that could be purchased in this way was to be decided later in the state program for privatization, which would be reformulated each year.) Finally, leased enterprises could be redeemed by their managers and workers for a predetermined price, without auction or competition. A leased enterprise could be made into a joint-stock company if the option of buying the leased enterprise was not exercised, and in this case, employees could buy as many shares as they could afford, selling the remaining shares. This law also specified a procedure for applying to privatize an enterprise.

The same day, another law was passed in the RSFSR, On Personal Privatization Checks and Accounts,[78] which suggested that privatization "investment accounts" could be established in state banks for all citizens. With these accounts, citizens could buy property from the state. Over the summer of 1991, the Russian legislature issued a series of normative documents outlining privatization plans of different departments. By the end of the year, however, the government had decided that the idea of privatization "investment accounts" was premature. It would soon be reintroduced by Anatolii Chubais.

During the spring and summer of 1991, while Russia was going its own way toward a market economy, the Soviet government was forging plans for a political and economic union comprised of most of the republics. Following a referendum to decide which republics wanted to remain in the Soviet Union, the "Nine-Plus-One" agreement was ratified by the nine participating republics on April 23.[79] (The "One" was Gorbachev, who had proposed the agreement.) The pact included a structure for new, less centralized, political relations and suggested that a new constitution would soon be approved. Thus, the freedom of republics to leave the Soviet Union on demand was being openly acknowledged.

Concurrently, two economic reform plans were being developed —one by Ryzhkov's successor as prime minister, Valentin Pavlov, and another by Yavlinskii. Pavlov's would have preserved key elements of a command economy, while shifting more power away from Moscow to the republics and injecting limited market reforms at the beginning. Pavlov wanted the state to supervise the move to a market economy through the existing administrative structures. Yavlinskii favored an across-the-board reduction in the state's role in the economy. His proposal further included provisions for participation of Western governments and financial institutions, including aid from the West during the period of price liberalization. The principal goal of Yavlinskii's plan was to create an active class of entrepreneurs who would spearhead the transition to a market economy.

For the Soviet Union in 1991, it was a new day not only for politics but also for the economy. Timidly at first, but with clear resolve by midyear, the USSR had moved dramatically to facilitate development of the nonstate sector. New legislation between January and July showed that the ideological center of the country had shifted. The state was now encouraging the establishment of new private businesses as well cooperatives, joint ventures, and other economic forms that were developing out of individual initiative. By August more than 111,000 cooperatives were in operation,[80] and the cooperative sector accounted for 6 percent of the Soviet Union's gross national product for the year[81]—about seventeen times greater than the cooperative contribution in

1988.[82] Seven million people were working in cooperative enterprises[83] and the number of noncooperative private enterprises was growing rapidly.

These unprecedented developments were producing obvious strains as well as changes in the economic system. There was rancorous disagreement about the political and economic initiatives that were being considered. Pavlov asked the Supreme Soviet for extra powers to carry out his economic proposal and was denied. He had harsh words about Yavlinskii's recent consultations with Western specialists: "I know some of these gentlemen from Harvard University. I've met them. They have no idea about our way of life, our views about life. They have their own criteria and values, their own ideas, their own conceptions about how people should live and work. . . . That's why we should not expect them to explain what we should do. They would never understand why I *cannot* leave potato with gravy in my bowl. But I can't help it."[84] It was June 17, 1991.

On August 19, the day before the Union Treaty was scheduled to be signed, an "emergency situation" was announced. The August coup derailed progress on both political and economic reform. Events that followed would ensure that the year's earlier, unprecedented developments toward political and economic reform in the Soviet Union would be prevented from getting back on track.

Bold Reform or Forgone Opportunities?

The economic reforms that were under way in late 1991 were, in many ways, a patchwork of compromises stitched together in response to pressures from divergent sources. In this ferment, a new class of entrepreneurs had begun to emerge which posed the first serious internal challenge to the state economic monopoly since the days of NEP. Many Soviet economists had worked single-mindedly toward this milestone since Gorbachev's early days as party general secretary. Repeatedly, proposals for a transition to the market had been developed and then reworked after

LIBRARY
BRYAN COLLEGE
DAYTON, TENN. 37321

being deemed either too theoretical or too advanced for the realities of Russian society. Now, however, reformers were presented with the opportunity to weave into one comprehensive cloth the most promising lines of reform thinking.

After the failed putsch, democratic forces in both the USSR and the Russian republic were riding a gigantic wave of public support. They now had leverage to widen the fissure in the Communist Party apparatus that had been plainly exposed by the coup attempt. It would have been naive to believe that the USSR's command system could have been brought down overnight, but at this time the country's democratic forces had a clear opportunity to carry out sweeping reform at every level of the administrative structure and to hobble, perhaps permanently, the familiar pattern of *nomenklatura* privilege.

It seems clear that they could have been swept to electoral victory and control of both the legislative and executive branches of the Soviet and RSFSR governments. New elections could have been held during the fall and many members of the Communist Party apparatus could have been removed from powerful administrative positions, with approval from a broad spectrum of the citizenry.

Yeltsin failed to take advantage of this political momentum or to move forward with economic reform plans that had already been worked out and approved. Instead of calling for early elections in Russia, Yeltsin chose to use the RSFSR parliament as a forum to publicly humiliate Gorbachev[85] on the occasion of Gorbachev's first meeting with Russia's popularly elected lawmakers (August 23, 1991). Although he had consistently endorsed the Yavlinskii reform program, which was embodied in the Treaty on an Economic Community that was signed by the leaders of eight republics on October 18,[86] he sabotaged it by announcing the imminent "freeing of virtually all prices."[87] With a nearly unimaginable opportunity to nurture both political democracy and economic freedom within the framework of the Soviet Union's historical experience, Yeltsin chose instead to demolish the Union and announce his own radical economic program, the guiding principle of which was a single-minded monetarism that had been imported from the West.

"If we embark on this path today," Yeltsin declared on October 28 in announcing the introduction of his "shock therapy" proposal, "we will obtain real results by the autumn of 1992."[88] In rapid sequence, Yeltsin then appointed Egor Gaidar to head the RSFSR Ministry of Economics and Finance and signed a package of ten decrees and resolutions intended to get his new reform initiative started. *Komsomolskaia pravda* labeled these documents "10 Decrees That Shook the World," and went on to say: "Thus, at a single stroke, Yeltsin has taken full economic power into his own hands."[89] It was November 15, 1991.

On December 8, Yeltsin and the leaders of Ukraine and Belarus signed an agreement, initiated by Yeltsin, which stated that "the USSR is terminating its existence as a subject of international law and as a geopolitical reality."[90] On December 25, the hammer-and-sickle flag was lowered from the Kremlin. Price liberalization began in the newly independent Russian Federation eight days later—a dramatic signal that Yeltsin's reform program was under way.

Later, Yavlinskii would charge that, in creating his new plan for radical reform, "Boris Nikolaevich and his close circle had very clear political aims." They wanted, he emphasized, to effect "immediate[ly]—in one day—both political and economic disintegration of the Union and elimination of all economic structures . . . and to completely isolate Russia from the other republics."[91] Further, in Yavlinskii's view, the Gaidar team began their reforms with a strong "dislike, and even hatred of their own country. They said, 'Everything here is bad; everything here is *sovok*; everything here is filthy. And now, we are starting the cleansing fire of inflation. We will demolish everything here, and then we will start building.' "[92]

Sergei Vasilev, the head of the Russian government's Center for Economic Reform, which worked closely with Gaidar during his tenure in Yeltsin's cabinet, underscored Yavlinskii's perspective in an April 1992 interview. "The program for dismantling the Union and creating the CIS was worked out by Gaidar. . . . And now it is necessary, using Yeltsin's charisma, to provide an economic mechanism for Yeltsin's political program."[93]

3

Russian and Western Voices on Radical Economic Reform

Addressing the RSFSR Congress of People's Deputies on October 28, 1991, Yeltsin emphasized that the country was at a critical historical juncture—that the future of Russia in the coming years and decades was being decided at that very time. Egor Gaidar had developed the main themes of Yeltsin's landmark speech. Parts of the address were predictable—Yeltsin's call for financial stabilization, budget cuts, and tax reform, for example. Then came his main point. There would be a "one-time change-over to market prices," with the goal of stabilizing the economy.[1] This was a bold move. It signaled decisive action, and it produced a series of aftershocks that sent the country's economy spinning out of control.

At the beginning of November, the Congress gave Yeltsin the authority to undertake this "shock therapy" plan by voting him special powers to issue mandatory decrees on a variety of subjects. Price liberalization went into effect the following January 2. The Åslund–Sachs perspective in Western economics had prevailed over mainstream Soviet economic thinking.

The Åslund–Sachs Approach

In a Stockholm conference held during the summer of 1991, Anders Åslund, director of the Stockholm Institute of Soviet and

East European Economics, had emphatically advocated the prescription Yeltsin would write for Russia four and a half months later. "In the USSR, there is a nearly universal belief in the necessity of gradualism in the transition to a market economy," Åslund wrote in his conference paper.[2] He made it obvious that, as he saw it, Soviet economists were not as qualified as their Western counterparts to evaluate the workings of a market economy. "*Even reasonably knowledgeable* Soviet reformers have great difficulty understanding what a market economy actually entails," he stated. "It seems that travelling abroad is necessary but not sufficient to give reformers such insights."[3] Hammering home his point, Åslund described the customary view among reformist Soviet economists as "an unfounded belief in gradual transition." He insisted that, since "the current Soviet price structure is utterly distorted in all aspects," the only response that could work would be rapid price liberalization. Decrying the fact that "every programme under consideration [in the USSR] is in favour of a gradual liberalization of prices," he argued that "any partial alteration will only lead to new distortions."[4]

In the same paper Åslund highlighted his respect for the economic thinking of Academician Egor Gaidar, whom Yeltsin would soon put in charge of the government's fledgling economic reform program. "The Soviets should focus on the experiences of Poland," Åslund urged, *"to which Egor Gaidar in particular has given appropriate attention."*[5]

Then Åslund both stated the empirical basis for his proposition and provided the challenge Yeltsin would present to the Congress the following October 28, in his call for economic shock therapy: "In short, *capitalism has to be declared* and to become a basis of the new rule, as it was in the East-Central European countries before they launched a true shift to a new economic system."[6]

A year later, Gaidar explained why he had favored the strategy of price liberalization. "The Russian government had no choice remaining," he reasoned. "It had to become the initiator—to start the transformation. . . . We realized very clearly that price liberalization by itself would not provide even the minimum prerequisite to make the market work." People had money, but there were few things to buy. Price liberalization was intended to make profitable production possible, which would get goods into the stores so that people would put their money in circulation.[7]

Gaidar's defense is familiar to anyone knowledgeable about Åslund's point of view. He called forth the same historical examples Åslund had referenced a year earlier at the Stockholm conference. "The East European countries used the same procedure in reforming their economies," Gaidar emphasized, quoting Åslund almost directly.[8] Had Gaidar's ideas been aired in Stockholm, however, some other participant might have pointed out that none of Åslund's East European examples offered much clear guidance for the Russian case. Early reforms had been more successful in some East European countries than in others, and so many changes were taking place almost simultaneously that no objective analysis could have definitively identified the most important reasons. Moreover, all of these countries were very different from Russia on key economic and social dimensions.

For the men who would become Yeltsin's closest economic advisers, however, the way Åslund framed the problem had *political* appeal. It would unambiguously show, as Gaidar later explained, that the government was finally doing *something*. With clear, clean strokes, Åslund had crafted a daring vision for economic leadership. Yeltsin would find out whether or not it was good economics.

There were several other Western economists among the Russian and Soviet governments' cadres of advisers during this period. Along with Åslund, Jeffrey Sachs, a Harvard University professor who had also been an adviser on economic policy to Poland, was one of the most influential. Sachs also was a participant at the 1991 Stockholm conference. "The successful transformation of the socialist economies," Sachs wrote, "has to be based on three fundamental factors." Among these factors he named "truly radical economic reform."[9] In Poland, the overnight price liberalization that was tied to the reform plan was called "the big bang."

A few weeks after Yeltsin's announcement of shock therapy, economist Vladimir Popov offered a succinct assessment of the plan: "Boris Yeltsin proclaimed the imminent liberalization of prices on October 28th. By the beginning of November, all shops were stripped bare of all products, including bread. On November 5th, the rouble dropped to an all-time low"; and, Popov continued, prices in 1992 would probably increase "by tens of times."[10]

Within a month after price liberalization, the verdict was already in from many analysts. "Market prices should be determined by competition between private producers and retailers, and not on the whim of monopolistic manufacturers and those who deliberately withhold products which are in short supply," Aleksandr Zaichenko wrote in January. "Unfortunately," he continued, "this glaring truth has passed the Russian authorities by."[11] The Central Bank had proposed that prices should be freed only in sectors of the economy where competition could hold the lid down on prices, but this suggestion was ignored. "As a result," Zaichenko pointed out after two months of experience with the new initiative, "monopolies compete with each other only in raising prices."[12]

During the summer of 1992, our research team explored the government's reasoning in putting price liberalization ahead of demonopolization in its economic reform program. We wondered why, in light of widespread opposition among Russian experts, Yeltsin's proposal to loosen the grip of command economics with one swift stroke had met with little resistance. According to a nationwide survey that had been conducted by the Center for Public Opinion and Market Research (CPO) just before the January price liberalization, only 26 percent of the respondents said they supported price liberalization; 18 percent said they did not know; and 56 percent stated that they definitely opposed the idea.[13] Yet those skeptics never congealed into an organized opposition. As the Bolsheviks had stormed the Winter Palace decades before to find no enemy braced for a fight, so Yeltsin initiated this economic revolution with relative ease as the hammer-and-sickle flag still waved atop the Kremlin.

By February 1992, another national CPO survey found that 45 percent of the respondents would support a general strike against the price increases of January 2.[14] Three months later, 70 percent of the respondents in another nationwide survey said they did not believe that price liberalization would help lead the country out of its economic crisis.[15] In an interview that same month with Dmitrii Vasilev, a vice chair of the State Property Management Committee, we asked whether, with the benefit of hindsight, he believed it had been a good idea to liberalize prices before widespread privatization. He quickly responded, "It was not an *idea.* It was a necessity. Do you remember that in December 1991, several times there was no bread in Moscow and Leningrad for as long as four days? We definitely had no choice."

We did remember. We were in Moscow at the end of 1991, and we knew the apprehension that hung heavily over this city of 10 million as food in near-empty stores grew scarcer by the day. On the one hand, it was nearly inconceivable that millions of people in this mighty nation could soon find their stores entirely emptied of food. On the other hand, ever-lengthening lines signaled less food—not more—with no certain solutions in sight. There was talk of famine. Such concern was not, as economists Michael Ellman and Vladimir Kontorovich emphasize, "just idle chatter from people who could not distinguish between food shortages and a famine. There are people alive today in the USSR," they continue, "who have known four famines. . . . These famines, especially the first two, were major catastrophes in which millions of people died. Hence in the USSR," they conclude, "people do not use the word 'famine' lightly."[16]

There was just one problem with Vasilev's explanation. The serious food supply problems had developed in December. The price liberalization had been announced as imminent at the end of October. Thus, price liberalization was not a *response* to the December scarcities. It undoubtedly exacerbated them, as retailers held goods in anticipation of huge markups in January.

Some of Gaidar's predictions about the positive effects of price liberalization were realized. Goods *did* begin flowing into the stores again within several weeks. People spent their money. And the pace of economic change accelerated. But there were other effects that Yeltsin and Gaidar had not expected. Money quickly lost most of its value because of inflation; and production, rather than increasing, continued to decline.

Vasilev's argument was repeated by Sachs in March 1993. Sachs was attempting to shore up the Clinton administration's strong defense of Yeltsin, following his power struggle that month with the Russian Congress. Sachs argued (against the views of most members of the legislature): "If Yeltsin can stay the course on economic reform, Russia will prosper."[17] Again like Vasilev, Sachs seemed not to understand that the acute food shortages in December 1991 had at least in part been *caused* by the announced price liberalization for the new year: "When Yeltsin began his radical reforms in January 1992, Russia was plagued by food shortages, empty shops and the real fear of hunger in major cities. Russia has passed its second winter without mass hunger because free-market prices have allowed for normal trading. Like the rest of the world, Russia now manages to get goods to the market."[18]

What Sachs failed to add was that, in 1992, *with* price liberalization in effect, agricultural production had declined, along with production in almost every other sphere of the economy. Agricultural output in 1992 fell 10 percent below 1991 and was expected to decrease another 6 to 7 percent in 1993. Predictably, average diets had been slimmed. In an intended defense of price liberalization, Yakov Urinson of the government's economic ministry admitted, late in 1992, that "living standards dipped by 20 to 25 percent compared with 1991." But, he added in weak encouragement, "Even so, *about 100 million people,* or the bulk of the population, *maintain consumption at an acceptable level.*"[19] Implicit in that statement is the admission that a third of the population were underfed by year's end. Yet Sachs insisted: "Make no mistake: Where reforms have been implemented, they are working."[20]

Princeton's Stephen Cohen stood almost alone in March 1993

when he deplored "the many U.S. intrusions into the cauldron of Russian politics" and pointed out that, because of the strong influence of U.S. advisers in the Yeltsin government's economic reform program, to many Russian citizens, "their misery seems to be 'made in the USA.'"[21]

Price Liberalization, Monopolism, and Inflation

Shortly after Yeltsin's price liberalization announcement, RSFSR Minister of Labor Aleksandr Shokhin described the thinking of the planners who had developed the price liberalization strategy. He first summarized the "ideal" scenario for economic reform, set forth in the "classic" "500-Days" plan: First, stabilize the financial system, eliminate the budget deficit, and demonopolize the economy with privatization. Only then, liberalize prices. But, Shokhin continued, a year ago "it became obvious" that it would be impossible to eliminate the budget deficit and monetary surpluses without unfreezing prices. "Now we have been forced to make a second exception from this ideal plan," Shokhin explained: "to set prices free without making systematic transformation in the economy, without conducting its privatization, without creating a competitive market, and without smashing the socialist monopoly." Underscoring the undesirability of the scenario that was being set into motion by Yeltsin's price liberalization decree, Shokhin added, *All of this is being done under duress. . . .* Whereas a year ago we had at least some possibility of getting out of the crisis stage by stage and, hence, more smoothly, now that possibility is gone; *we blew it.*"[22]

Grigorii Yavlinskii agreed. As the chief architect of "500 Days," he was its strong advocate; and he believed, along with Shokhin, that the opportunity that had existed in 1990 for "rapid and relatively painless stabilization" had passed by 1991.[23] Yavlinskii's recommendations diverged markedly from the path Gaidar's team chose to follow. To achieve short-term financial stabilization, which had been a promise of Gaidar's reform program, would be too costly and would threaten to create additional imbalances. In Yavlinskii's view, the best way out of the 1991 situation was to orient economic policy "toward long-term financial stabilization," rather than to adopt the "neoliberal-monetarist" doctrine Gaidar had embraced, which necessarily assumed "the presence of a functioning market economy." Since that requirement could not be met in Russia, the government's program, as Yavlinskii saw it, meant "playing by market rules even before the game itself starts." His prognosis was bleak. The government's course, he suggested, would lead not to accelerated development of a market economy "but to its destruction, including the destruction of the few spheres that could have formed the framework of a future effective market economy."[24]

Yavlinskii's position on price liberalization was shared by many Russian economists. In the autumn of 1992, ten months after price liberalization was initiated, Vladimir Tikhonov, an economic adviser to Yeltsin, reflected back on the chain of developments that had further damaged an economy already weak at the beginning of the year. Tikhonov could not "understand the government's logic in starting reform with so-called liberalization of prices. . . . Instead of liberalized prices, we got the same monopoly, but with higher prices that were decided by the producer." By that time, prices had increased an average of twenty times over their level at the beginning of January.[25]

Yavlinskii's description of the situation was only slightly different. The Russian government had "eliminated state *control* and passed it to state *monopolies* and local authorities," Yavlinskii emphasized. "There was no *real* liberalization. . . . There was just *decentralization* of price controls. . . . Earlier, Moscow fixed prices; now the monopolist does it."[26]

Leonid Abalkin, who had developed a much-discussed economic reform proposal in 1989, spoke against price liberalization in a context of monopolism, saying that it not only would generate staggering inflation, but also could exacerbate the productivity decline. "There is no need for output to be increased," he pointed out, when profits can be boosted simply by raising prices; indeed, "producers are even prepared to reduce it."[27]

Nikolai Petrakov, an economic adviser to Gorbachev who supported the development of a market economy, wrote in March 1992 that the government's decision to liberalize prices could have only two explanations: either the government "does not realize the processes under way now or it is deliberately ruining the economy." He went on to argue that key industries had been severely hurt by price liberalization, and added, "This policy has no future and will spark off political instability."[28]

These criticisms were not afterthoughts offered by detractors of Gaidar's program who now had the benefit of hindsight. Yavlinskii had insisted from the beginning of his work on reform that price liberalization without demonopolization would be a serious mistake.[29] Similarly, Petrakov had emphasized during the Soviet period that "before the liberalization of prices, we need to form the basic market structures and get rid of monopolism."[30] Abalkin's 1989 proposal had called for price liberalization only after privatization was well under way and demonopolization had been achieved in key sectors. This perspective was a prominent feature of Russian economic thinking from the beginning of discussions about sweeping economic reform in the Soviet Union under Gorbachev.

When we talked with economist Larisa Piiasheva, then the leading privatization planner for Moscow, she was quick to voice her judgment on the policy of price liberalization. "It was their [the Russian government's] most serious mistake. Privatization," she emphasized, "was the first necessary step. Then, liberalized prices for private enterprises. . . . But *they* first liberalized prices, partly, . . . and that started the inflation engine."

A prominent radical economist, Piiasheva was known for her proposal to privatize all state enterprises within a few months by turning them over to their employees with no restrictions. There would be no charge and no competition for the property. Possession, which in this case meant employment, would constitute ownership. Unlike the state program, which focused on small enterprises for the first several months of the country's privatization effort and would require at least three years to achieve, Piiasheva's proposal would have permitted the privatization of both large and small enterprises very quickly. She told us in May 1992 that she wanted to privatize 80 percent of state property in one year.

Pace was important for Piiasheva, because she believed there needed to be a significant number of private enterprises before prices were decontrolled. With enough nonstate enterprises, there would be competition; and competition would help prevent drastic price increases as prices were liberalized. "We gave Yeltsin our program to consider," she said. "If he continues to act according to his own scenario, I would expect failure very soon."

In the Yeltsin government, however, the voices of Yavlinskii, Tikhonov, Abalkin, and Piiasheva were largely ignored.

The Russian Privatization Program

On December 29, 1991, only four days after Gorbachev resigned as president of the USSR, Yeltsin issued a decree On Accelerating the Privatization of State and Municipal Enterprises,[31] which approved the main points of the 1992 privatization program that had been developed by his cabinet. The program authorized by Yeltsin's decree deviated on several points from the one that had been outlined in the July 3, 1991, legislation of the RSFSR Supreme Soviet discussed in chapter 2. A critical difference was that Yeltsin decided not to allow state property to be sold for personal privatization checks in 1992. With the urging of Gaidar, Yeltsin had agreed to authorize auctions and competitions in which the state would receive money for property, rather than distributing state property among all the citizens. Privatization checks would be redeemable for property beginning in early 1993 (this date was later moved up to December 1992).

In the interim, according to Yeltsin's decree, workers would be given, at no charge, shares representing 25 percent of the fixed capital of privatizing enterprises where they were employees. These were to be nonvoting shares. Workers could buy an additional 10 percent at a 30 percent reduction. Five percent of the shares were tagged for the managers of enterprises, who could also buy an additional 5 percent. The Russian government would own 60 percent of an enterprise's shares at first. Ten percent of that amount had to be sold within a month and the remaining 50 percent within six months.

Why was the free distribution of state property, which had been promised on July 3, postponed for a year in Yeltsin's December 29 decree? Anatolii Chubais, the chief architect of the government's privatization program, answered this question in a year's-end *Moskovskie novosti* interview. "When I got this position, I realized immediately that we couldn't keep this promise." The cost would have been too high. "We decided that it was necessary to postpone issuing privatization accounts until 1993."

The interviewer observed, "Spontaneous privatization, with no regulations, started a year ago [late 1990] or even earlier. The local privatizers have been hurrying to catch the largest fish in these murky waters. Purchasing state property was the 'catch.' What do you think about it?"

Chubais answered, "Until today, the situation you have described was absolutely unavoidable. . . . Now the legal basis for privatization is being established to catch up with the spontaneous process."[32]

Yeltsin's December decree was the first step in creating the "legal basis" Chubais mentioned. According to the program elaborated in the decree, during the first nine months of 1992 the privatization effort was to be concentrated on wholesale and retail trade, public catering, consumer services, and food processing. The second stage, which was to begin in July, would include privatization of transportation, repair shops, construction and related industries, and light industry enterprises with fewer than 200 workers. Later, an additional goal was added to the 1992 program—to privatize about seven thousand large industrial organizations before the end of the year.[33] Russia's privatization program for 1992 included the provision that local governments should develop more detailed privatization plans for the specific kinds of enterprises in their jurisdictions. This directive was carried out by property-management committees below the federal level. (This decision-making structure is described in chapter 7.)

Gaidar was appointed on November 6 to the office of vice prime minister. The following August, on the occasion of a tribute to those who stood against the coup, he recalled the "total disaster" of the economy and the "increasing chaos" in the political system that had preceded the putsch. Following the coup, Gaidar said, Russia inherited total responsibility for the unstable conditions of the Soviet Union. The Russian leaders had had no time to develop a detailed *plan*. The planning system had broken down, and stores were empty. The only reasonable course of action, in his view, was to create economic connections that would replace the ruined political control apparatus—to breathe to life a market system not yet developed, and thereby to get food into the stores. The government hoped to achieve this goal with an instantaneous freeing of prices. "We realized that price liberalization alone was inadequate for creating market relations," but we had to take the first step, Gaidar insisted.[34]

And so the market was pushed to center stage with no time for rehearsal. Food appeared immediately, but stabilizing the ruble and developing an economic reform plan acceptable to the legislature would prove to be more elusive.

The Moscow Program

Economist Gavriil Popov became mayor of Moscow in June 1991, almost half a year after the Moscow city government had created the first property management committee in the USSR with the goal of developing a plan for privatizing municipal property. Popov had his own ideas for carrying out privatization, however, and he asked economist Larisa Piiasheva to help him develop a center for privatization which would operate separately from the property management committee.

When we interviewed Piiasheva in 1992, she spoke excitedly about the advantages of her approach over the government's program. Under Piiasheva's plan, the privatization process would be rapid, and the old system of state ownership would be destroyed. It would be fair, she insisted. Every worker would be able to reclaim property confiscated decades before by the state. When Piiasheva joined Popov in the Moscow city government, she modified her general proposal for privatization throughout Russia to fit the Moscow case. In November 1991 her program had been approved by the Moscow Soviet, with the qualification that privatization should begin with small enterprises (*malaia privatizatsiia*).[35] The plan was to privatize more than 90 percent of municipally owned small enterprises (retail, public catering, and consumer services) in one year.[36] When we talked with her in May, Piiasheva was generally positive about the Moscow program, except for one detail: "The officials decided to stop privatization of the largest enterprises for two to three years. They want to privatize only small enterprises now. But the process *should* be carried out in *all* enterprises. I don't divide into large–small."

Because of the Moscow government's early privatization initiatives, the same day that Yeltsin outlined the main points of the state program (December 29), he issued a decree supporting Moscow's pioneering course and affirming its right to develop its own privatization plan. The following month, after studying the Yeltsin–Gaidar proposal, the Moscow Property Management Committee rejected several elements of the state program on the grounds that it was "too unwieldy," and several city officials publicly underscored Moscow's intention to deviate from the state program in several ways.[37] The most critical difference between the two approaches was that in Moscow, the plan was for most small privatized enterprises to be owned entirely by their personnel; but according to the state plan, most of these enterprises would be sold at auction or through competition.

In Moscow, about 70 percent of these types of enterprises were leased. Seeing this as an opportunity to speed up privatization, the Moscow government hoped that the leased enterprises would quickly privatize if their workers were allowed to become owners for a low price. These enterprises had been given an assessed value at the time they were leased, and to facilitate leasing for a price the workers could afford, the assessments were typically lower than their actual market value. To encourage rapid privatization among enterprises that were not leased, the Moscow program added that *all other* enterprises of the type eligible for privatization in the first stage could also be bought by their personnel if they applied for privatization before January 6, 1992. Thus, many workers in Moscow had a more attractive privatization opportunity than workers anywhere else. This example undoubtedly encouraged workers in other areas to press for benefits not provided under the proposed state program.

The Moscow committee was soon embroiled in controversy about how to proceed, however, and 1992 saw fewer successes than had been expected. City officials had believed that when enterprises were privatized, their productivity would increase and the quality of output would improve. It was thought that worker ownership would provide the incentives necessary to bring about these positive changes. Also, rapid privatization in the sphere of consumer goods and services had been expected to reduce inflationary pressures, thanks to increased competition.

There were several reasons why the Moscow approach did not produce the anticipated results. First, the Moscow experiment eventually convinced the city government that workers often were not the best managers. We learned that this view was widespread among the privatization decision-makers (DMs) in Moscow during the course of our mid-1992 interviews with 68 members of the Moscow Property Management Committee and several privatization commissions. By this time, the Moscow program had been in effect for half a year. Many of the DMs told us that workers were "not prepared for ownership" and that they "did not know how to engage in independent market activity."

The view that workers often lacked the skills necessary for ownership of enterprises was deeply rooted in the thinking of privatization planners at the federal level, and it was an important reason for their resistance to Piiasheva's proposal that enterprises throughout Russia be turned over to their employees. Shortly after our first interview with Dmitrii Vasilev, a vice chair of the State Property Management Committee, he outlined the Russian government's privatization proposal at an international conference. In discussing the "Russian conceptualization" of privatization, he strongly criticized the "Moscow variant." After noting that more than a thousand small enterprises had already been privatized in Moscow, and pointing out that this activity was being presented "as a big achievement," Vasilev said that "there have been no positive changes" in work performance as a result. "People who became owners without any cost did not thereby become better workers."[38]

In response to growing criticism of the Moscow approach, several commissions were created at both municipal and federal levels to study the Moscow program. A prominent question was whether the Moscow method of turning enterprises over to workers was producing the intended results. The Moscow experiment was providing a good testing ground for one of the most popular theories about how privatization throughout the country should be realized.

One outcome of this inquiry was the finding that by summer's end only a third of Moscow's privatized enterprises had made any improvement in the availability of goods or the quality of service. Many privatized enterprises had begun practices that were unfavorable to consumers—selling the goods they had obtained through the state supply network to speculators for above-retail prices, dealing dishonestly with their customers, and failing to maintain acceptable sanitary conditions, for example. One commission report stated that seven out of every ten privatized stores studied had been found cheating customers.[39]

After the Moscow program was abandoned in August 1992, a deputy of the Moscow Soviet, Galina Burmistrova, evaluated part of the program: "In keeping with Lenin's dictum, 'Factories to workers,' Moscow authorities developed the principle, 'Shops to shopkeepers.' I hope shopkeepers will forgive me for this observation, but our shopkeepers do not have highly developed professional qualities. The results of [the Moscow program for] privatization proved this point. It turned out that the majority of enterprise personnel were not ready to act by themselves under market conditions. They were not able to find goods; they were not able to succeed."[40]

A second reason the Moscow program was faulted stemmed from perceived inadequacies of the privatization decision-making process there. An overarching defect many critics found was that DMs sometimes seemed to be enhancing their own power through the process; adequate safeguards to prevent abuse had not been built into the structure. More specifically, commission members were repeatedly charged with having benefited themselves and their friends through specific privatization decisions. In Moscow, unlike in Russian cities that followed the state plan, members of privatization commissions often had backgrounds in the fields they were now overseeing and thus often had a personal interest in privatization outcomes.

Further, although the program was intended to transfer property to *all* personnel in an enterprise, in many cases an enterprise's director or state officials who wanted ownership in a particular enterprise paid most of the sale price. Because workers sometimes did not know the established procedures for privatization, they could easily be deprived of the ownership to which they were entitled. Twenty percent of the Moscow DMs we interviewed told us that, although workers were ostensibly the buyers of municipal enterprises, "behind them" were "high administrators," "*nomenklatura*," "black marketeers," or "mafia structures."

Moscow DMs were more likely than decision-makers in the other cities we studied to indicate that other players in the privatization process were exerting undue influence on workers. A contributing factor to this situation undoubtedly was Moscow's unique privatization program and the opportunities for self-benefit that elites could find in it.

Interestingly, of the 68 DMs we interviewed in Moscow, all were able to specify to us who the buyers of privatized property were, but in Voronezh 26 percent and in Ekaterinburg 29 percent of the DMs said they did not have any information about buyers. In Smolensk 64 percent lacked this knowledge. "I don't know. We aren't interested in it," one Smolensk DM told us. Perhaps not surprisingly, then, when asked to describe the most typical discrepancies between program requirements and reality, 64 percent of Smolensk DMs answered that there were none, but only 21 percent of Moscow decision-makers expressed that view. One of the principal inconsistencies they identified in mid-1992 was "uncertainty about workers' rights in the privatization process."

In Moscow the push to privatize property quickly was sometimes urged by elites who wanted to realize as much profit as possible before flaws in privatization procedures could be corrected.[41] In our research among Moscow workers, we found that many did not even know that the enterprises they were working in had been privatized—this in a city whose privatization program had been designed to make workers the principal owners. This was unambiguous *nomenklatura* privatization.

In extreme instances, enterprises that had been privatized without full participation of workers were subsequently "closed for repairs" and their equipment sold by the management. In other cases, an entire enterprise was sold by its director or an outside buyer and the profit pocketed. In these situations, the workers not only were deprived of ownership but also lost their jobs. Such flagrant violations were illegal and probably did not occur very often, but they were widely discussed among Muscovites close to the privatization initiative as examples of how privatization could benefit only top management or government officials.

Aleksandr Osovtsev, a deputy in the Moscow Soviet, provided a blistering assessment when we interviewed him in May. "As a rule directors don't even *buy* enterprises now," Osovtsev charged. "They just appropriate, and then lease them." He gave several examples of this formula for making profit under the new system. "The biggest department store in Russia was almost privatized yesterday without any governmental approval. It *can* be done. In Moscow, privatization isn't an economic procedure. It's a political one."[42]

The feature of Moscow's program that made corruption more likely there than in other cities was the absence of any "watch-dog" organization in Moscow's privatization decision-making process. In the *state* program the *property fund* represented the interests of the state (the owner before privatization). When an enterprise was privatized, the fund sold it, and the fund received the proceeds of the sale. Since each fund was under the authority of the corresponding soviet (of a municipality, for example), the fund was under legislative authority. With property management committees under the supervision of the executive branch (e.g., the mayor's office in the case of municipal property), there were built-in checks to help prevent abuses; the legislative branch "looked over the shoulder" of the executive branch.

In Moscow, however, this separation of powers did not exist in practice—because of Moscow's special privilege to structure its privatization program differently from the state blueprint. The Moscow Property Management Committee, which had sole authority for privatization decisions—including the workings of privatization commissions—was under the administrative control of Moscow's executive branch; and no other branch of the state structure participated in the process. Thus the Moscow Fund had no role in privatization. The Moscow Property Management Committee performed all functions that, in other places, were the responsibility of the appropriate fund. We interviewed several Moscow Fund members in 1992, and a consistent theme in these interviews was the complaint that the fund was "out of the loop" of decision making. All of the fund members we talked with recognized the potential for abuse of the Moscow system and wanted to play the role that was assigned to them in the state program.

With the Moscow Property Management Committee free to privatize according to its own scheme, not only were there many abuses involving enterprises, but prime residential property in Moscow's center also became an object of exploitation by high officials. Over the summer, Piiasheva had more and more conflicts with the Moscow government about the way privatization was proceeding. She charged city and federal officials with taking advantage of their positions to acquire especially desirable property.[43] A special commission was created by the Presidium of the Russian Supreme Soviet to investigate charges of corruption. Its findings were published in August 1992. "Uncontrolled arbitrariness of the highest officials in Moscow was shown in monopolistic, hidden decisions about the best land," the report stated. "They made arrangements with joint ventures and other commercial structures, in which they were co-owners, to lease the property and the land, ignoring rights and interests of Muscovites and workers in enterprises."[44] That month, the Moscow Soviet passed a resolution stating that, since Moscow's privatization program had encountered serious difficulties, privatization in Moscow would henceforth follow the guidelines of the state program.[45]

By August, however, the most desirable small enterprises in Moscow had already been privatized. This situation presented a problem for Muscovites when vouchers were distributed later in the year, because the prime enterprises could not at that point be purchased for vouchers. (Vouchers are discussed in chapter 4.) In an *Izvestiia* interview with Dmitrii Vasilev, reporter Igor Karpenko asked whether voucher auctions in Moscow could be held for any enterprises except those ready for bankruptcy, since "all the profitable and prestigious enterprises have already been privatized by the mafia and the party *nomenklatura.*"

"That's a problem," Vasilev responded. "The situation in Moscow is fairly complicated, but it is not typical for the whole country. In Moscow we are seeing the fruits of Piiasheva's privatization."[46]

Yurii Luzhkov became Moscow's new mayor in June, and one of his early priorities was to change the Popov–Piiasheva privatization policy. He had disagreed with the pace Piiasheva had set for privatization and had established one of the commissions that investigated the activities of privatized enterprises. Before the end of the summer, the Moscow government decided to reclaim some of the enterprises that had been privatized, based on commission findings that they had violated their privatization agreements. Included in the privatization agreements that had been executed between most privatizing enterprises and the city government were provisions that an enterprise would continue to offer the same kinds of goods or services as it had offered before privatization; that the level of output would not be lower than it was before privatization; and that workers would not be fired. These stipulations were to hold for one year after the privatization of an enterprise, but numerous enterprises had violated the terms almost immediately. In September Luzhkov dismissed Piiasheva and the head of the Moscow Property Management Committee. Moscow's distinctive privatization experiment was over.

Privatization in Nizhnii Novgorod

Russia's biggest privatization success story in 1992 and early 1993 was Nizhnii Novgorod. The third largest city in the country, Nizhnii Novgorod was the site of Russia's first public auctions, in April 1992. From the start, however, a fast pace was not Nizhnii Novgorod's principal emphasis. Instead, the chief concern of planners there was to work out a systematic approach to carrying out privatization as efficiently as possible while minimizing the negative consequences of the Yeltsin–Gaidar shock therapy program. The state program was followed for the most part, with several critical modifications that were approved by the Russian government.

When prices were liberalized in January 1992, the governor of the Nizhnii Novgorod Oblast, Boris Nemtsov, began working with Grigorii Yavlinskii and specialists from the International Finance Corporation (IFC) on a plan for economic reform. Yavlinskii's Center for Economic and Political Research (EPI Center) sent 15 specialists to Nizhnii Novgorod for three months during the summer to develop a program for reforms in the region. The approach of Yavlinskii and IFC was to consider the Nizhnii Novgorod economy in its totality, and to tailor an economic strategy that would take into account specific features of the Nizhnii Novgorod situation—such as the high concentration of large industries there. (In 1992, 20 percent of Nizhnii Novgorod's production was military equipment, and defense enterprises employed a quarter of the work force.)

To facilitate entrepreneurship, Yavlinskii developed a procedure to streamline the start-up process for new firms. As we shall discuss later, the Yeltsin–Gaidar program did not facilitate the creation of new businesses; but partly because of Nizhnii Novgorod's two-pronged approach—which encouraged both privatization and new businesses—city officials predicted at the end of 1992 that half of the work force would be in the private sector within a year. To break the cycle of inadequate training, low morale, and low productivity, a small enterprise (fewer than 200 workers) that was about to be privatized was first shut down to permit the new owners to hire employees of their choice. To encourage commitment to their work, enterprises were *sold* instead of being given to employees at no cost, as was the case in Moscow. (About a third of the enterprises privatized in Nizhnii Novgorod in 1992 were bought by their workers.) To promote modernization of privatizing enterprises, buyers were permitted to deduct the cost of upgrading their firms from the amount they were charged for leasing the buildings and grounds. To help offset the devastating effects of inflation on family budgets, a network of "food banks" was created, which made it possible for shareholders to buy food throughout the year at fixed prices. To help farmers to obtain loans, a land bank was created, which allowed them to use privately held plots as collateral. Such reforms, each modest in scope, combined to stimulate Nizhnii Novgorod's economy during a period when most Russian cities were caught in the viselike grip of a moribund economy.

The Nizhnii Novgorod experiment showed such achievements in its first year that Gaidar, Chubais, and several other federal officials studied it. Impressed with what they found, they began highlighting Nizhnii Novgorod as illustrative of the government program's potential for success. At an international conference in

May 1992, Dmitrii Vasilev made a point of criticizing the Moscow plan and showcasing the Nizhnii Novgorod approach as a superior alternative. "In Nizhnii Novgorod, where enterprises were bought for a price, the efficiency of work increased a great deal," he said.[47] In July, Chubais urged that cities throughout Russia begin following the "Nizhnii Novgorod model" in mass privatization of small enterprises.[48] But Yavlinskii, who had masterminded the Nizhnii Novgorod variant of economic reform, suggested, "The main meaning of our work in Nizhnii Novgorod has been to smooth the negative consequences of errors in the government's reform program."[49]

4

April–December 1992

Following the guidelines of the earliest privatization legislation,[1] 174 enterprises were privatized during 1991.[2] In 1992 the pace of privatization increased rapidly. By the end of the year, about 40,000 enterprises had been privatized—comprising, according to Chubais, 17 or 18 percent of the total number of enterprises in Russia. The most demanding challenge of the program, the privatization of large industrial enterprises, was beginning. By the end of 1992, more than 5,000 of these were at various stages in the privatization process, and half had already been transformed into joint-stock companies and were ready to begin selling their shares.[3] Among small enterprises, where widespread privatization had begun, another 36 percent of the total were privatized during the year.[4] This was a dramatic change from the beginning of 1992, when only about 50 small stores and restaurants were in private hands.[5]

In the process of implementing these reforms, however, the Yeltsin government found itself increasingly alienated from a Congress that would remove his chief reformer by the end of the year and then go after, and nearly impeach, Yeltsin himself.

The April Crisis

In April the Congress of People's Deputies rejected the 1992 privatization program that had been worked out under Chubais's direction and which followed, for the most part, the main points elaborated in Yeltsin's decree the preceding December.[6] Russia's economy had seriously deteriorated by then, however, and life for most citizens had worsened in nearly every way. Gaidar had warned that price liberalization would cause hardships, but he had seriously underestimated the scope and magnitude of the negative effects that would be visited on Russia in the wake of this action.

Yavlinskii's Center for Economic and Political Research (EPI Center) assembled a damning set of statistical correlations to pinpoint some specific hardships since the January price liberalization.[7] During the first quarter of 1992, earnings in Russia increased by an average of 590 percent in comparison with the first quarter of 1991; but prices for goods and services surged 1,020 percent. Most people now spent a larger proportion of their income for food than ever before, but average daily caloric intake had fallen to a level inadequate even for a preadolescent child (2,100 calories per day). Not surprisingly, in light of the food situation, there was an increase in malnutrition-related diseases among infants. The first quarter also saw an alarming increase in crime. Compared to the corresponding months in 1991, crime in the first quarter of 1992 rose 24 percent in January, 36 percent in February, and 43 percent in March.[8]

The Russian people were becoming skeptical of the government's reform program. A national survey at the end of March, just before the Congress began its April session, found that a minority (46 percent) were positive, even "to some extent," about the results of the first three months of reform. Price liberalization, which had been initiated on January 2 as a critical first step toward economic reform, came under heavy fire from the public. Only 22 percent favored it, and nearly half (47 percent) said that they "strongly" opposed it.[9]

Another study conducted at about the same time reported nearly the same percentage opposing Yeltsin's overall activity (42 percent) as supporting it (43 percent); the corresponding figures for Gaidar's team, which was directly in charge of economic reform, were markedly less favorable, with only 27 percent supporting Gaidar.[10]

The previous October 30, Yeltsin had appealed to the Congress for special executive power to carry out radical economic reforms. He asked for a grant of authority until December 1, 1992, to, among other things, "issue mandatory decrees . . . even if they are technically at variance with laws of the [Soviet] Union or Russia." He had justified this request by stating that the program he was proposing to introduce "is simply impossible to conduct without sufficiently tough actions by the entire system of executive power in the RSFSR."[11]

Before Yeltsin made this bold appeal, which at the time "seemed not only excessive but dictatorial"[12] in the minds of many deputies, the Russian legislature had approved all the major themes of Yeltsin's reform program. In July 1991 they had authorized selling enterprises at auction and creating joint-stock companies. They had even passed a law for the issuing of privatization "investment accounts," which Yeltsin then delayed including in the government program for nine months. In short, Russia's deputies seemed as determined as Yeltsin was to *begin* the process of radical economic transformation. And in early November 1991, they had voted Yeltsin the special powers he had requested to implement his program.[13]

By April 1992, the Congress, along with a substantial proportion of the population, was beginning to question the path they were traveling at the behest of the republic's president. Their dissatisfaction was growing in the face of increasing signs that his reforms were not proceeding as smoothly as he had said they would. Real personal disposable income in April was 71 percent lower than it had been the previous December, and personal deposits in savings banks had lost 82 percent of their value.[14] The stage was set for confrontation, and at the April 8 meeting of the Sixth Congress, the Rising Generation/New Policy faction distributed a statement judging the progress of economic reform to have been unsatisfactory, proposing that Yeltsin be deprived of his special powers, and recommending that a new economic reform program be developed.

The Congress approved a resolution on April 11 which followed the spirit of the Rising Generation/New Policy statement. It stated that the government's reform program was unacceptable and rescinded the earlier agreement to allow Yeltsin to head and form the government until December 1. (Yeltsin was his own prime minister at that time.) Because the resolution authorized the Supreme Soviet to replace cabinet members as early as July, the cabinet, justifiably viewing this development as a threat to the continuity of their work, announced that they would resign. Their statement included a charge that would be leveled repeatedly against the Congress in the months ahead as relations between the executive and legislative branches worsened: "the Congress of People's Deputies is blocking the possibility of continuing along the chosen course."[15]

This time, the Congress backed down. On April 15, it approved a resolution affirming its commitment to the government's course of economic reform and, in effect, allowing Yeltsin's emergency powers to stand, including his authority to appoint his own cabinet without approval.

Why did the Congress reverse itself during the April session? According to analyst Aleksandr Bekker, "Despite the dramatic tension visible on the outside, the outcome of the duel was predetermined: The government had a big material advantage in the form of the West's promise of $24 billion in credits and a stabilization fund for the ruble. Ruslan Khasbulatov [the chair of the Congress and speaker of the Supreme Soviet] and the comrades close to him in mind-set could not offer anything remotely similar."[16] A large part of the promised $24 billion was not forthcoming, however; and the following December Khasbulatov would not let the Congress forget it, claiming that the unfulfilled promise of aid had been a Western scheme to further weaken the faltering Russian economy.

Overall, the Congress's mood in April 1992 seems to have been more skeptical than intentionally obstructionist. During the April session, 505 deputies were polled about their opinions regarding the sharing of power between the legislative and executive branches and the progress of economic reform. At that time, more deputies believed that the course of the government's reforms was right than were comfortable with Yeltsin's success in achieving his aims until that point. When asked, "What do you think of the government's economic reforms in general?" a majority (53 percent) said that they supported the general direction of reform, at least in part, although most of these deputies now believed that major modifications were needed. Yet, to the question, "How would you evaluate the results of the first three months of the economic reform?" only 29 percent gave Yeltsin's program a favorable rating.[17]

Growing uneasiness about Yeltsin's economic policies was, therefore, a major reason for the critical shift in the Congress's center of gravity that was manifest in April. Perhaps there was also another reason—one that underscores the delicacy of Russia's nascent political democracy. Support for Yeltsin's radical reforms had been broad-based partly because he had successfully stared down the powerful Soviet machine; but after the dissolution of the Soviet Union, the strains in this coalition became increasingly pronounced. And the legislators now found themselves in a very different position. Among the majority who supported Yeltsin's early proposals, a veneer of solidarity had masked conflicting interests and loyalties that might have remained suppressed had Yeltsin's reform initiatives produced the results he had promised, but they surfaced with the first sign that Yeltsin's heroic image was no longer unassailable.

Yeltsin's majority in the Congress during the early days of reform had come from a bloc of liberal reformers and a substantial number of deputies from a larger "centrist" group who generally would have preferred more gradual reform but were willing, if often grudgingly, to give Yeltsin's idea a chance. A minority of the Congress, perhaps between 33 and 40 percent, comprised a "red–brown" coalition of old guard communists and fervent nationalists. An important unknown, from the beginning, was whether the large center would ultimately press its own agenda— possibly picking up critical support from the factions nearer the extremes—or whether enough centrists would back Yeltsin and his liberal democrats to allow them to pursue their program. At first, Yeltsin's perspective prevailed, but by April the center was asserting its reservations more pointedly. To rekindle diminishing support for the government program, the Gaidar team resuscitated the idea of distributing vouchers to all citizens. This action would prove, however, to create its own set of problems.

The Voucher Plan

The proposal to issue privatization vouchers, or investment checks, to all citizens who were permanent residents of Russia was introduced as part of the government program at the April session of the Congress. These vouchers would be distributed free of charge, and they could be used to purchase shares of many large or medium-sized enterprises, or else sold at their market value. If the plan were approved, property ownership would begin to be shifted back to the people for the first time since the beginning of collectivization early in the Soviet period.

The idea to issue "investment checks" for the purchase of state property had been introduced by Larisa Piiasheva in 1990.[18] Her proposal, however, was to transfer enterprises to the people who worked in them—not to all citizens. This notion was controversial from the start, and proponents of privatization vouchers disagreed among themselves about whether all citizens or only workers in enterprises should be given vouchers. Most opposition to privatization vouchers took a procedural and pragmatic rather than an ideological path. Privatization, it was generally agreed, was inevitable. The question was who the beneficiaries should be. If privatization were to be carried out so that it was just another method of state "distribution," lawyer Sergei Alekseev argued, it would not work. "People's privatization," he said, would be a repetition "of the October slogan 'to steal what was stolen,'" permitting the privileged to acquire a disproportionate share of property.[19]

In 1990, at the same time that Piiasheva was proposing that

property be transferred out of state hands by means of investment checks, Prime Minister Ryzhkov's government believed that the most reasonable way to privatize industries was to *sell* state property, not to distribute it without charge among workers or the citizenry, an approach that was also fundamental to the Shatalin "500-Days" proposal. Many officials continued to prefer selling state property rather than distributing it without charge to the Soviet citizens who were theoretically its real owners. Property sales would bring the state much-needed revenue, while voucher redemption would not.

Gaidar's team, too, had originally favored the selling of state property for currency over the idea of free distribution. They believed that to distribute state property without charge would do nothing to improve efficiency in state enterprises. Their reasoning was that when people acquire something without cost, they do not value it. Chubais, who led the team that developed the Yeltsin–Gaidar privatization proposal, stated this position clearly: "What blows in with the wind will fly with the wind." It was the winter of 1991–92.[20]

People who had become private entrepreneurs during this period tended to show strong support for the position the government held at that time, for two primary reasons. First, as investors and risk-takers themselves, they placed a high premium on *earned* ownership over *bestowed* ownership. Second, as citizens outside the state production system, they wanted a privatization program that would also benefit them. They argued that outside investors would be more concerned with the health of an enterprise and would plow profits back into the firm to foster its growth, whereas directors and workers would be more likely to use profits to increase their own salaries. Put differently, these entrepreneurs were developing a rationale that would justify their becoming active participants in the government's privatization program.[21] Both lines of reasoning made them supporters of the government's position that efficiency considerations should take precedence over distribution concerns.

Gaidar's planning group changed its position in the spring,

however, in response to the swelling trend of public opinion for citizen ownership of state property—an idea deeply rooted, of course, in communist ideology. People had worked throughout the communist period for low salaries with the understanding that they were building their society, their "common house." The Gaidar team believed—perhaps incorrectly—that their earlier plan to sell enterprises would meet with strong protest among the general population. Indeed, they were under intense fire for this initiative from the Congress, labor unions, and other interest groups. The economic suffering of Soviet people during the Stalin years and after had always been rationalized with the promise that the people were sacrificing for the future, and that some day life would improve. By 1992, life had not improved, and the idea of continuing to sacrifice for the purpose of building socialism had lost most of its appeal. Lenin's dictum "Land to peasants; factories to workers!" was now being scrutinized from a different vantage point. And if factories went to workers and land to farm workers, what would teachers and doctors receive in return for their years of work and austere living?

As Gaidar's team considered these points, they decided that at least a substantial part of "the people's property" should be distributed to citizens free of charge. There was also a practical consideration here. With the liberalization of prices on January 2, savings were largely wiped out; most people did not have enough money to buy property and at the same time adjust to the rapidly rising prices of necessities. Thus, the architects of Russia's reform ultimately incorporated the concept of free distribution of property to citizens as a keystone of their program.[22] This was a critical development that had broad implications for the way the privatization effort evolved during 1992 and early 1993.

The voucher program represented a compromise between those who wanted all state property to be shared among all citizens and those who believed that enterprise personnel should own the places where they worked. It also took the side of those "radical" democrats whose chief objective was the *relatively equal distribution of property,* and against those who believed that the primary goal of privatization should be to increase productivity and efficiency. The radical democrats did not often speak about efficiency. Instead, they assumed that productivity would not suffer if owners were able to acquire enterprises without competition from other would-be buyers and if they were not required to invest *real, preexisting assets* into their enterprises.

Although the second aim listed in the 1992 State Program for Privatization was "to increase the productivity of enterprises,"[23] it was clear by the time the Congress approved the program that the primary focus of privatization was now the distribution of property to the people. Whereas in the previous winter Chubais was concerned about "what blows in with the wind," now he defended the government's new position: "The politics of the State Property Management Committee is not to further the stratification of society but to let everyone take part in people-oriented privatization."[24]

The government's chief concern had shifted to dismantling the state control system and replacing it with privatized ownership as quickly as possible. Along the way, questions about efficiency were largely ignored. The possibility of disruptions during the rapid shift to decentralized planning was now seen as less sinister than the threat that opposition forces might halt the process entirely if given enough time. Thus, time and equity considerations predominated over concerns about efficiency and productivity.

To ensure that a large volume of property would be available for free distribution, the proposed program specified the kinds of enterprises to be earmarked for *obligatory* privatization as joint-stock companies, with the provision that stocks could be obtained with personal privatization checks (vouchers) that would be distributed to citizens. These would be large enterprises with many workers. Many smaller enterprises, according to the plan, would be sold for money, to bring much-needed revenue to the state.[25]

The issuing of privatization vouchers to *all* citizens, of course, would bring outsiders into the ownership of enterprises, and thereby reduce workers' potential shares in the enterprises where they were employed. Chubais addressed this point by arguing that to restrict ownership to workers would be a new "dictator-ship of the proletariat." Workers had already been given many privileges, he said, and they should not receive more.[26]

A Preliminary Verdict on Gaidar's Reform Program?

Taking into account the objections that had been raised by the Congress in April, Gaidar revised his team's program and sub-mitted it to the Supreme Soviet in May. The voucher plan was now its centerpiece. After a short discussion, the Supreme Soviet delayed any decision on the proposal and decided to create a commission to study it. Enterprise directors and trade unions were demanding more privileges for themselves than Gaidar's plan called for, and the Supreme Soviet was sympathetic with their perspective.

Because of their type of activity, many of the enterprises slated for early privatization were leased enterprises. According to the July 3, 1991, legislation, workers in leased enterprises could buy their enterprises directly from the state for the value specified in their lease agreements, without an auction or any competition. To make it possible for workers to lease enterprises, many had been evaluated at a very low price. Indeed, more than 5,000 enter-prises had been privatized in this way by May 1992.[27] The state privatization program approved by Yeltsin's December 29 de-cree, however, stated that personnel in leased enterprises would have no special privileges that had not already been granted by existing agreements. (This provision was not applicable in Mos-cow, which had developed its own privatization program, dis-cussed in chapter 3.)

Another change from Yeltsin's December 1991 plan which *did* give workers additional privileges, however, was a provision that allowed enterprise employees to become majority stockholders of enterprises being transformed into joint-stock companies. Ear-lier, employees' only choice was to receive 25 percent of the nonvoting shares without charge, with the option of buying an additional 15 percent that would carry voting rights.[28] In many enterprises, employees were unhappy about the prospect of losing control of their companies to outside owners who would control at least 85 percent of the voting rights. Now, in addition to that possibility, enterprise personnel could choose to buy 51 percent of a firm's voting shares. This concession to workers helped to satisfy some of the objections that had been voiced by trade unions and directors' lobbies. As events continued to unfold later in the year, however, it would become clear that one concession to directors and workers would generate demands for additional benefits.

The month of May saw a significant change in the composition of Gaidar's team. Organized opposition to the government program had intensified after January, especially among directors of large state enterprises. During the first quarter of 1992, the government's financial support of these enterprises had diminished to the point that many workers could not be paid and productivity was declining. In an effort to find a workable compromise between Gaidar's program and its detractors, Yeltsin appointed additional vice premiers to work with Gaidar.[29] Many Russian observers believed that these appointments significantly diluted Gaidar's leadership of the reform program. This sense was shared by several members of Gaidar's staff, who described the process as "Abalkanization," after Leonid Abalkin who had developed a program for Prime Minister Ryzhkov during the Gorbachev period that had never been implemented. In a press conference shortly after the appointments, Chubais characterized these new members of Yeltsin's inner circle as "representatives of the corps of directors."[30]

With Yeltsin's new appointments in May, it became evident to people outside the government that even Yeltsin now agreed that Gaidar's reform strategy had to be modified. Yeltsin was bringing new blood into the planning group to appease adversaries of the program. In response, Gaidar's staff, "one after another" in the words of one observer, carried the message to the mass media that "these new appointments from the industrial lobby" would lead to tactical changes only, and not weaken the overall thrust of the reform effort. One of the new vice premiers, however, Vladimir Shumeiko, had already expressed his opinion that the plan to privatize large industries should be postponed. It was widely believed among analysts that all three of the new appointees would want to slow down reforms.[31] The Congress obviously believed that about Viktor Chernomyrdin, who was appointed a vice premier in May, and in December was elevated to the position of prime minister with the expectation that he would redirect the economic reform program.

Before Yeltsin's May appointments, the government had said that it would liberalize energy prices and stabilize the ruble in July, changes that did not come about. Further, the "industrial lobby" succeeded in getting a person who shared their ideas to become the new director of the Central Bank. The new chairman, Viktor Gerashchenko, promptly approved additional credits for industrial enterprises to help keep them in operation, and many debts that state enterprises owed to each other were canceled.

Yeltsin's advisers now found themselves being pulled simultaneously in different directions. The industrial lobby wanted more favors; the radical democrats wanted more fairness. Judgments about what was fair, however, clearly depended on one's position in the social order. Besides feeling pressures from outside demands, government planners also were forced to confront the demands of problems inherent in the program, but some of the demands called for contradictory solutions. Continuing to subsidize unprofitable industries, for example, would further weaken the ruble and increase inflation, but allowing industries to fail would create massive unemployment and might produce serious social backlash. Price liberalization and rapid privatization offered the hope, advocates believed, of irreversibly crippling the state's economic monopoly, but the dislocations and hardships that these procedures entailed risked further alienating large numbers of people.

June Approval, with Reservations

On June 11, the Russian Supreme Soviet approved the Gaidar–Chubais privatization program for 1992.[32] The main points of

Russia's new program had been outlined eleven months before, in the July 3, 1991, legislation. The intervening period had seen an aborted coup, the jockeying for position among republic and USSR officials, and the ultimate collapse of the Soviet Union. Privatization-by-decree had been proceeding, following Yeltsin's order of the previous December 29, but months had been lost in developing privatization legislation. During the debates over economic reform, animosities had been heightened, bringing a quick end to Yeltsin's honeymoon period following the coup.

By this point, many deputies must have been finding it difficult to continue supporting Yeltsin's reforms. Public opinion about the legislature had never been strongly favorable, and the deputies were acceding to reform initiatives that were getting ever lower marks from the population. From the time Gaidar first proposed the voucher program to the Congress in April until they approved it two months later, Yeltsin's approval rating dropped eleven points, to a shaky 32 percent. Gaidar's support among the general public, always a better indicator of public opinions about specifically *economic* reform, dropped to 19 percent. By this time, only 17 percent of the public endorsed the Russian Supreme Soviet's performance—practically the same approval rating as Gaidar's.[33] Undoubtedly, many members of the legislature believed that their low approval rating was tied to their compliance with the government's reform initiatives. Unless the reforms soon began showing more favorable results, the stage was inexorably being set for a confrontation. Yet apparently, only a quarter of the deputies were willing to consider asking for resignations from Gaidar's team at that time.[34]

Anders Åslund was not so generous. One of Yeltsin's prominent foreign consultants who had helped to fashion Gaidar's reform program, Åslund took the role of political as well as economic adviser. In Åslund's view, reforms could be pursued more aggressively with a different group of deputies. He complained in an article written for *Izvestiia* that reform had been hampered by the legislature. "Democratization is the life blood of successful economic reform," he argued, and went on to maintain that it was essential to hold early parliamentary elections because "87 percent of the current Supreme Soviet are former communists. A new parliament will create a reformist government."[35]

Åslund knew, as we found in our four-city study, that most people favored at least the *idea* of privatization while the government program gathered momentum in 1992. Only 12 percent of enterprise personnel in our study thought it was not needed. Not only did the vast majority of Russians apparently favor privatization, but more than half of our respondents indicated dissatisfaction that it was not proceeding more quickly by midyear. As we shall see, however, public opinion on this subject took a sharp turn before year's end. Åslund had caught the high point of public support, but it would soon be obvious that he had badly misjudged the level of shock his "therapy" would yet inflict on both macroeconomic trends and people's personal lives. His hope for a more reform-minded legislature would soon give way to the realization that, with the foundering of Russia's economy, the deputies would become aggressively more conservative.

A New Phase Begins and the Voucher Program is Evaluated

As the public became increasingly restive over the summer, Yeltsin offered modifications designed to restore the public's waning confidence in his reform program. He issued a decree on August 14 that outlined for Russian citizens the procedures for redeeming state property with vouchers. Besides using them to buy shares of enterprises, people could now use them to invest in funds which in turn would invest in a large number of privatizing enterprises, thus reducing the risk of investing in a single firm. Vouchers could also be sold on the open market.[36]

According to the decree, only 35 percent of the shares of privatizing enterprises being transformed into joint-stock companies could be sold for vouchers. The 1992 program specified that voucher distribution was to begin during the last quarter of the year. The government decided to begin issuing vouchers on the first day of the last quarter, because they feared that continuing opposition from conservative members of the Supreme Soviet might somehow succeed in stopping the plan before it could get under way.

"People's privatization" (*narodnaia privatizatsiia*) began the first of October with the distribution of vouchers carrying a face value of 10,000 rubles (R10,000). These could be used to acquire shares of privatizing enterprises from December 1, 1992, until their expiration date of December 31, 1993. (The vouchers' market value was lower than their face value from the beginning— R6,000 to R7,000 in December 1992.)[37] Additional voucher issues were planned for the future, but the government was equivocal about details. When would more vouchers be distributed? "First, we need to see the results of this wave of privatization," a vice chairman of the State Property Management Committee responded.[38]

Voucher distribution had enormous symbolic significance, as well as serving the practical function of providing a means to privatize state property. With vouchers in the hands of the people, the total control of property by Russia's power structure had been broken. But the beginning of this metamorphosis was not promising. The public's early reaction to the voucher plan was largely negative. In one survey taken in September, only eight percent of the respondents believed voucher distribution to be "a step toward private ownership." Most thought it would benefit only the wealthy or that it would not have any overall effect.[39] Not surprisingly, then, only a small proportion of the people claimed their vouchers when the program began. The voucher program was also widely criticized by analysts. Aleksandr Zaichenko, for example, argued that it permitted too much property to remain under government control. He concluded that the plan "suited both plant managers and all state bureaucrats" because it "would enable them to convert their former power into the rich assets now available, by giving them control over property."[40]

The program was also criticized because there was not enough property for voucher holders to buy—a particularly worrisome situation in light of the December 31, 1993, expiration. Further, it was often claimed that most of the enterprises available for purchase with vouchers were not desirable—that they had outmoded equipment and other liabilities. Economist Vasilii Seliunin estimated that only 10 percent of large industrial enterprises could be considered attractive investment opportunities.[41]

Moreover, the expanding privatization privileges being afforded to industrial employees resulted in a backlash from people whose jobs were not in industry—teachers, health-care professionals, retail trade personnel, and others. These people wanted opportunities to use their vouchers in ways that would offset the favorable terms that had been conceded to workers in the industrial sector. For many nonindustrial workers, municipal property was of more interest than property controlled by higher levels of government, but municipal property was not part of the voucher program.[42]

Rural and small-town people, too, were seen as having been slighted in the formulation of the voucher plan. Few large enterprises were located in many of their locales, and residents often did not have access to information about enterprises in distant cities that were undergoing privatization. Yeltsin had proposed that farm land be sold for vouchers, which would largely have solved this problem, but the Russian legislature had not agreed.

The government's response late in 1992, through two decrees by Yeltsin, was to allow individuals to buy twice as much state property as originally planned, to allow land to be purchased for productive enterprises, and to allow the purchase of apartments, all with vouchers. According to the new program, special voucher auctions were to be held for state, federal, and municipal property, and the previous limit of 35 percent of an enterprise's shares that could be sold for vouchers was increased to an average of 80 percent for different types of enterprises.[43] Furthermore, all middle-sized industries with assets of more than R1 million and less that R50 million were free to privatize, if the employees chose to, in any of several ways—one being through the creation of joint-stock companies whose shares would be purchased with vouchers.[44] The question of land sale, however, remained a controversial issue.

Yeltsin's modifications were a hastily drawn substitute for the opportunity to buy stock in the privatizing enterprises that the government had intended to make available by that time. Most of the 7,000 large enterprises that had been targeted earlier for transformation into joint-stock companies by the end of the year were still firmly in state hands, and prospects were not good that the process of privatization would accelerate quickly enough to prevent loss of confidence in the voucher program.[45] If that happened, not only would more vouchers be sold for money, but their market value would decline. Chubais's team wavered from the start about the implications of selling vouchers for money. On the one hand, such transactions demonstrated that vouchers had real value to people; on the other, sales of vouchers threatened to increase inflation.[46] With the new alternatives created by Yeltsin's decree, it was hoped that people would have more attractive alternatives for converting their vouchers into property ownership. By November, only 3 percent of the population were willing to sell their vouchers for less than their face value, according to a nationwide survey of 3,000 people carried out by the Center for Public Opinion and Market Research (CPO).[47] Vouchers being sold on the street and in kiosks at discounted prices, however, were attracting media attention. Even the tiny percentage of people willing to sell was quite visible in Moscow and St. Petersburg, but this activity clearly did not reflect the value most citizens placed on vouchers.

In late 1992, Ekaterina Vasileva wrote in *Delovoi mir,* "Critics of the government's reforms have denied the clear evidence that the voucher program has broad social support."[48] Her conclusion, however, is contradicted by survey data from Moscow at the beginning of 1993. The Independent Opinion Service reported that 64 percent of their respondents complained that privatization was not being carried out fairly. Only 7 percent had a positive attitude about the process. About 55 percent believed that the average person was being cheated in the voucher program.[49] As of late January 1993, however, more than 90 percent of the Russian population had claimed their vouchers.[50]

The government's attempt to make the voucher program more attractive underscores its importance to Yeltsin's reform plans in late 1992.[51] Yeltsin argued that the principal objective of the voucher system was to divide state property among the citizens, and in this way to give all people an opportunity to be active participants in the transition to a market economy.[52] "We don't need a few millionaires," he said. "We need millions of owners."[53]

Even after the voucher distribution program was revised, many remained skeptical about it. Several analysts recommended that the uses of vouchers be broadened, although it was obvious that allowing vouchers to become a substitute for money would ensure additional inflation; and unfortunately, other critics added, vouchers could never replace money for some critical purposes. The governor of the Nizhnii Novgorod Oblast, Boris Nemtsov, complained in a *Literaturnaia gazeta* interview, "Vouchers make no economic sense at all. . . . Enterprises need real money to modernize their facilities, not a stack of paper vouchers."[54] The most pointed criticism of the voucher program came from Yavlinskii. He had been involved in planning for economic reform since the Gorbachev period, and he believed from the start that the Yeltsin–Gaidar program was ill-conceived. To him, the voucher program was one of its more conspicuous failures. He found only one justification for the plan: "They think that if they distribute property in small pieces, then it won't be possible to stop reform." A committed reformer himself, Yavlinskii quickly added, "I appreciate their *emotions*, but professionally I can say what I think. Vouchers have only two destinies. They will either completely lose their value or, more likely, they will be transformed into money, which will add 1.5 trillion rubles to the consumer market. And all prices will increase."[55]

Even before the privatization program for 1992 was finally approved in June of that year, Gaidar's team had begun working on a program to deepen overall economic reform. The plan went through several revisions, the last of which was presented to the Supreme Soviet on October 5.[56] In the introduction, the governmental working group admitted that the results of reform until that point were not encouraging. "Pathological processes in the economy are too deep," they said, "deeper than had been expected." Financial stabilization, one of Gaidar's main objectives, had proven to be impossible. There had been some good results, however. The population was more active in economic activity, and, increasingly, people were asking for "freedom to make their own fate" instead of for money and social guarantees.

On December 8, *Izvestiia* published an interview with Dmitrii Vasilev, a vice chairman of the State Property Management Committee. "Our first task was to overcome the psychological barrier to private ownership among the people, and we have almost achieved it," he said. "In late 1991, a clear majority of the population were against privatization. Now, the visible opponents of privatization are very few. To achieve such a great change in people's consciousness, away from the negative attitude about private ownership which had required decades to develop, is a great success."[57]

The People's Consciousness

Vasilev had overstated the effects of the government program on people's attitudes in two ways. First, his perception that "a clear majority of the population" opposed privatization as recently as late 1991 is not supported by available data. Several other interpreters of Russian public opinion have made the mistake of assuming that attitudes among Russians about cooperatives, which were often negative, reflected similar attitudes about private enterprise and privatization. Vasilev may have fallen into this same trap. In an earlier study, Nelson et al. showed that attitudes about cooperative work, which is what most public-opinion studies in the area had emphasized through 1991, were often very different from judgments about other forms of nonstate enterprise. That study of workers in Russia's state sector found that while most respondents were not enthusiastic about cooperatives at the time, an overwhelming 85 percent favored a transition to a market economy.[58] Months before the time Vasilev mentioned, most by far said they would prefer nonstate over state employment. Had the public *not* shown enthusiasm for expanding the private sector, the deputies probably would not have given Yeltsin the authority to pursue his privatization program.

Vasilev likewise ignored the difference between public support for the government's economic program and the broader issue of support for privatization. Although it is clear that in 1992 most Russian citizens supported a transition to a market economy, it is also apparent that, in December, the Yeltsin–Gaidar program lacked broad and unqualified support. In chapter 5, we address the apparent inconsistency between the unambiguous evidence of public disaffection with the government's reforms and the vote of confidence handed to Yeltsin the following April to continue on his economic reform course.

The Fall of Gaidar

According to the Program for Deepening Reform, the transition from the present crisis to a period of economic growth was projected to take three years. The program outlined procedures for achieving the goals of financial stabilization, reform of state expenditures, and economic growth. Rather than discussing specifics of the proposal, however, the Supreme Soviet concentrated on criticizing Yeltsin and his advisers and blaming the current economic crisis on the government's reform strategy.[59] It was at that point that Yeltsin distanced himself from the Gaidar program for the first time by declaring to the Supreme Soviet that the "big jump" was a mistake from the beginning. "There turned out to be too much macroeconomics in [Gaidar's] economic politics," but not one of the macroeconomic tasks was realized.[60] The reform program needed to be revised, Yeltsin added, and "useful ideas" needed to be included from other political movements. He specifically mentioned the centrist coalition Civic Union *(Grazhdan-*

skii soiuz).[61] Yeltsin closed his speech with a quotation from Arkadii Volskii: "The market itself is not the aim, but the means to restore the Russian economy."[62]

On November 26, following the Supreme Soviet's directive, Gaidar presented a government "anticrisis program" which, as Yeltsin had ordered, took into account suggestions from the Civic Union, the Supreme Economic Council of the Russian Supreme Soviet, and several academic institutions. It focused on inflation and decline in productivity, and it outlined a system of state credits and expenditures to support production over the following four months. The parliament approved the proposal in principle, asking for a more detailed plan. The revision was to be presented to the Congress of People's Deputies, which would convene on December 1.[63]

By the time the Congress met in December, both Yeltsin and his reform program were clearly in trouble. Yeltsin's approval ratings had peaked in the summer, and had gradually fallen since then.[64] In October, nearly half (47 percent) of the respondents in a CPO survey described the country's situation as "unbearable."[65] By November, 49 percent of the respondents in another CPO survey thought it was "quite likely" that there would be "mass action against the government's economic policy . . . over the next few months," while another 20 percent thought it was "hard to say" whether or not public rejection would be this pronounced.[66] A national survey conducted by CPO in November found that, while more favored Yeltsin over anyone else to be the leader of Russia's government, he was actually supported by only 27 percent of the people interviewed. Second place went to Vice President Aleksandr Rutskoi (13 percent), who would be one of the first to speak out after Yeltsin signed his "decree of special rule" on March 20, 1993.

When he took the floor to describe the revised plan to the Congress in December, Gaidar emphasized that the most important task of economic reform was to maintain momentum away from the command economy. Attempts to stop the privatization (*privatizatsiia*) process now, he said, could only open the way

to piratization, or theft of state property (*prikhvatizatsiia*).[67]
Gaidar was on the defensive, fighting for his political life and a
reform program delegitimated by persistent and accelerating economic decline.

The Congress's disaffection with Gaidar's economic approach is
not difficult to understand, in light of the optimistic predictions both
Yeltsin and Gaidar had made earlier in the year and the worsening
of Russia's economy after that time. When price liberalization was
introduced on January 2, Gaidar predicted price increases of 3.5
times, but by September they had jumped by more than 20 times.
Economist Vladimir Tikhonov, an adviser to Yeltsin, attributed this
huge discrepancy to the monopolistic character of the Russian economy[68]—no excuse for Gaidar, who should have been well versed in
the workings of monopolies. To gain support for their program,
both Yeltsin and Gaidar repeatedly predicted that the economic
picture would soon improve. When Yeltsin introduced his economic proposal in late 1991, he announced that the economy would
begin to improve in the summer or fall of 1992.[69] By the spring,
all indicators had worsened and public dissatisfaction was rapidly
mounting; and Gaidar stated that by the end of 1992 "inflation
will slow down to a few percent, the rouble will stabilize and the
necessary preconditions will be created to attract foreign investment."[70] In June, improvement was nowhere in sight; that month
Yeltsin told an interviewer from *Komsomolskaia pravda*, "I expect prices to stabilize by the end of the year. People's lives will
start to improve then."[71] By December, however, Russia was
"begging the world for humanitarian aid."[72] The "carrots" offered by Russia's government may have been necessary to secure
acceptance of the hardships they knew would be created in the
near term by their policies. But not all of the people, or all of the
people's deputies, forgot all of the promises. "The people feel
deceived," Yavlinskii wrote near year's end, and "trust in reformers and reforms has gone completely or is close to doing so."[73]

A study conducted after the close of December's tumultuous
Seventh Congress by the All-Russia Broadcasting Company
(VTRK) Ostankino inquired into public opinion about Yeltsin

and the Congress. When asked, "Who would you charge to lead the country out of the current political and economic crisis?" the percentage of respondents who were uncertain or uninterested (48 percent)[74] topped the percentages favoring the legislature (7 percent) or the Russian president (31 percent).[75] More people in this study said they did not "approve the economic and political course of the government and the president" (34 percent) than that they approved (23 percent). The most frequent answer was "difficult to say" (43 percent).[76]

Yeltsin's strongest support at the end of 1992 came from entrepreneurs (with 39 percent favoring him), young people (35 percent), and pensioners (32 percent).[77] Entrepreneurs supported Yeltsin because there was no other national leader with the potential they saw in Yeltsin to work for their interest. Yet, this hope was based on little that was tangible. Gaidar's program had focused primarily on *privatization* of state enterprises. Private entrepreneurs were remembered in the program primarily as sources of tax revenue. Among people in the army and the militia, Rutskoi received the most support (33 percent). He was also more popular than Yeltsin among middle-aged people.[78]

Disappointment with Yeltsin's leadership at year's end was to be expected, given the rapid deterioration of Russia's economy during 1992. Russia's 1992 GNP was 20 percent below its 1991 level.[79] The buying power of salaries shrank alarmingly over the course of the year: average prices increased at more than twice the rate of salary increases. Not surprisingly, the structure of spending changed. Food accounted for an ever-increasing proportion of most families' budgets (45 percent of average family incomes, up from 34 percent in 1991). Pensioners spent 81 percent of their income for food. The total volume of spending for *all* types of consumer goods, including food, was also different in 1992. People bought 39 percent less in 1992 than they had the year before, including 13 percent less meat, 20 percent less milk, 30 percent fewer shoes, and 54 percent less clothing.

It would be one thing if these abrupt changes could be explained by the new dynamics of a rapidly growing private sector, which might suggest that the strains of 1992 could be eased as the system adjusted; but in actuality, the effect of the much-discussed privatization was slight. By year's end, 72 percent of all consumer goods were still being sold in the state sector, down only 5 percent from 1991. Most nonstate sales were made by cooperatives—not newly privatized enterprises or other private businesses. Only 8 percent of the goods sold in retail enterprises were sold in the private sector, although retail enterprises were primary objects of the government program's first stage of privatization.

Consumer goods were not 1992's only production disappointment. In almost every category, production was down from 1991. Production of steel declined 14 percent, tractors 25 percent, industrial equipment 25 percent, and plastics 80 percent. In short, under Yeltsin's leadership the economy was in free-fall with no turnaround in sight. On the positive side, the reformers emphasized, mass privatization was proceeding: shops were well-stocked; the ruble was still in demand in spite of its declining value; and orders for manufactured goods were on the rise.[80] But the Congress wanted a change. On December 9 Gaidar was denied confirmation as prime minister. Ironically, that same day Moscow's first voucher auction was held.[81]

Organized Responses to the Government Program

The Civic Union

The most powerful organized group that took issue with the Yeltsin government's reform program was the Civic Union, led by Aleksandr Rutskoi, Arkadii Volskii, and Nikolai Travkin.[82] Volskii's theoretical views significantly shaped the Civic Union's approach. Volskii was a member of the Central Committee of the Communist Party for twenty years, and he had succeeded in rising through the party bureaucracy under leaders with widely divergent styles. An economic adviser to Andropov and Chernenko, Volskii was no stranger to large-scale planning, and through the years he had developed close relationships with many influential people in government and industry.

Volskii had been speaking against rapid economic change before Yeltsin took strong steps in the opposite direction. In 1991, before the April and July laws on entrepreneurship and privatization were passed, Volskii had written: "I think the perfect strategy would be to encourage the different sectors to adopt market principles progressively, rather than all at once."[83]

For Volskii, several months of experience with the Yeltsin–Gaidar program underscored his earlier reservations about that kind of approach. In November 1992 he observed, "None of us, realizing very clearly the scale of changes that are required, expected reforms to proceed easily and without pain. But no one guessed that the economic situation would worsen so quickly, that the slide in production would be so steep and that the quality of life would decline so dramatically."[84]

Volskii objected especially to the government's reliance on Western consultants. His perspective was that Russia could not forge a workable path to a market economy by trying to duplicate procedures used in other countries. "A real transformation to the market is not possible without considering national traditions and specific features of our country," he argued.[85]

On this point, his position was identical to that of Leonid Abalkin, the mastermind of the 1990 reform proposal sponsored by Ryzhkov. "Market relations cannot be declared by decree or created through a referendum," Abalkin cautioned. "A market economy was never created that way anywhere. . . . It has always been the result of long historical development. It always takes time to create market structures, to develop appropriate legislation, to change cultural values and individual motivations for behavior." Obviously referring to the government program in force when he was interviewed in October 1992, Abalkin continued, "To expect fast, instantaneous transformation means that one does not realize the inner logic of market development—or, alternatively, that he chooses to ignore it."[86]

During the period of transition to "market-based regulation,"

Volskii emphasized that it was "urgently necessary to strengthen state influence on the economy, an approach," he insisted, "that has been tested and found suitable at the world level in global crisis situations (for instance, during the implementation of F. Roosevelt's New Deal), with a subsequent gradual cutback in the sphere of state intervention as the stage of crisis development ends and the stage of economic revival begins."[87]

On this point, too, Volskii's perspective paralleled that of Abalkin. Comparing the Russian situation in 1992 with the Great Depression in the United States, Abalkin reasoned that Roosevelt had used the vehicles of state regulation and subsidies to help overcome the crisis of that period in the United States. Similarly, in Russia today, "the only kind of market that could work would be a regulated, socially oriented market. Only that kind of market could guarantee a stable sociopolitical system."[88]

The Civic Union was organized in June 1992 as an umbrella organization for three political parties. The People's Party of Free Russia headed by Aleksandr Rutskoi represents a group of reformists, many of whom are former party officials. Nikolai Travkin heads the Democratic Party of Russia, which is committed to a policy of gradual reform. The party Volskii helped to create is the All-Russian Renewal League (ARL), headed by Aleksandr Vladislavev. ARL was organized with the intention of representing the interests of "productive forces"; among its members are directors of more than 2,000 large enterprises, many of them engaged in military production. ARL clearly reflects a management viewpoint and its agenda for the Russian economy aims to attract "authoritative industrial executives."[89] Along with encouraging market relations, ARL emphasizes a need to keep state industries in operation and to modernize them, under the assumption that they will be the core of the country's economy for a long time to come. Support for private entrepreneurship would be a priority of the state. In writing about this point, Volskii emphasized that the support provided by the state would be "decisive," and, he continued, "I emphasize *state*."[90]

During 1992, the Civic Union developed a proposal for economic recovery that was intended to be an alternative to the government's plan. It began by emphasizing that "a transition to the market is not the goal but the means" of social improvement and aimed at doing this by first returning "to the system of state procurement" and broadening wage and price controls. Prices for energy, transportation, and principal foodstuffs would be frozen. The transition to the market would be slowed to minimize dislocations and allow time for the system to adjust to economic restructuring. The proposal was not to reduce the state sector to the smallest size possible, but to consciously work toward a "two-sector economy, such as exists in China." Large enterprises would not soon be transformed into joint-stock companies. Other possibilities for using vouchers would be developed.[91]

Volskii was dismayed that many people formerly employed in the state sector had left to work in "different kinds of centers, funds, agencies, joint ventures," and other jobs that serve no productive purpose. He called these kinds of jobs "parasites on the sick body of the Russian economy." While underscoring Russia's need for foreign investment, he added, "We must get rid of the myth that 'the West will help us.'"[92]

The Civic Union became a political force to be reckoned with in 1992. By September the organization claimed to have the support of 30 to 40 percent of the deputies of the Russian legislature.[93] According to Åslund, it was the Civic Union that got Viktor Gerashchenko appointed to chair the Central Bank. Gerashchenko's policy of continuing to subsidize unprofitable enterprises and his decision to cancel the debts of many enterprises during the summer "was the last hit," Åslund lamented, "to the program of macroeconomic stabilization."[94]

The Party for Economic Freedom

Konstantin Borovoi's Party for Economic Freedom (PEF) claims to represent the interests of both the business community and "those who associate their future with the private sector." Borovoi, a former mathematics professor who became a successful entrepreneur before getting into politics, believes that the party's potential constituency, which he characterizes in broad strokes, is huge—perhaps 40 million people. While Russia's entrepreneurs and would-be entrepreneurs are an admittedly diverse aggregate of people, in Borovoi's opinion they share the goals of his party: "stability, the free market, democracy and human rights."[95] Borovoi organized PEF out of frustration at the legal roadblocks he had encountered to his own business activity—obstacles that he insists were unnecessary and harmful. "Today in Russia it is not possible to achieve economic freedom without political organization," PEF's economic reform proposal states.[96]

PEF published its proposal in December 1992. In agreement with the government program, PEF favored rapid privatization of state property. In general, it supported "the proposals and activity" of the government during late 1992 but suggested "some corrections to make the process more successful and less painful." Specifically, PEF wanted the most profitable state-owned retail and service enterprises to be sold through auction and only for vouchers, instead of being turned over to their employees. This proposal would give those not employed in state enterprises the opportunity to participate more fully in the reallocation of state property. Vouchers would have expanded uses under the PEF plan. They could be invested in pension funds, medical insurance programs, and other insurance funds. Further, PEF called for legislation that would support the creation of smaller businesses and proposed that taxes on profits and production be reduced. At the same time, it urged that subsidies to unproductive enterprises be eliminated. PEF also highlighted the immediacy of ecological problems and the necessity of taking strong measures to promote environmental improvement.

The Party for Economic Freedom thus stands in clear contrast with the Civic Union. Whereas the Civic Union favors an expansion of state control, PEF favors an economy as independent of government control as possible. The Civic Union opposes the voucher program; PEF proposes that the role of vouchers in the economy be broadened. Another key difference between the two movements is that, while the Civic Union was well represented among the deputies, at the end of 1992 PEF was a fledgling party with little legislative clout.

The Supreme Economic Council

The Supreme Economic Council of the Russian Supreme Soviet has ideas about economic reform that are at variance with the government program. Philosophically, the Council's position is somewhere between those of the government program and the considerably more conservative Civic Union. "The idea that in two or three years state property could be transformed to fit the Western model is utopian," Vladimir Ispravnikov (chair of the Supreme Council) suggested when we interviewed him in May 1992. "During the transition, which will take considerable time, Russia needs to develop 'mixed' types of property ownership. In several West European countries, the share of state property in some sectors of the economy is 50 to 60 percent. We should be able to approach this 'mix' in about five years, not sooner. The state sector has to be reduced; there is no alternative to that. But our approach should not be so much to *eliminate* state property as to *transform* it into other forms of ownership. That means being sure to promote *horizontal* integration at the same time that we reduce *vertical* integration.

"Practically all of the programs for economic transition proposed until now have the transition to a market economy as their main aim," Ispravnikov observed. "We [the Council] are sure that this is a strategic error. Key questions for the people, which also have to be key questions for the government and the Supreme Soviet, are: What is the purpose of destroying the existing management structures? What is the purpose of destroying existing economic structures? For what purpose are we changing the ideological basis of the society?" The government has not answered these questions, Ispravnikov said. It has not sketched out even a preliminary image of what kind of economy or what kind of society Russia will have once the "transition" has been accomplished.

By the time we interviewed him, it already seemed apparent to

Ispravnikov that Russians were tiring of governmental reform programs, including Gaidar's. "I think we have to create a program for privatization that a majority of the population will support," he said. "Now, the people are fed up with different programs and suggestions. Words such as 'market' and 'perestroika' are just annoying to them."

It is not only people in the state sector who are upset with the government, Ispravnikov added. Through heavy taxation, Gaidar's reform program threatens to strangle many smaller private businesses that were started on personal initiative. "Such enterprises broaden competition and provide employment opportunities, and they need to be encouraged. There is no government support now for businesses of this type, and there should be."

By November, the Supreme Economic Council believed that it saw how to overcome some of the defects it had identified in the government program. The Council's proposal emphasized measures designed to stimulate productivity and minimize the dislocations of privatization. They believed that enterprise personnel should have first claim for ownership and management of enterprises slated for privatization. In this, their position was similar to Piiasheva's. They took strong issue with the government's voucher distribution plan, arguing that the cost of administering the program would be enormous, and that ownership through vouchers would not ensure that the people working in an enterprise would have adequate incentives to improve productivity and quality. They found no offsetting advantages to voucher distribution, maintaining that the average citizen would not greatly benefit from owning a voucher and that releasing vouchers into the economy as money surrogates would increase inflation. The Council's proposal also included provisions to support new private businesses through favorable interest rates for loans, opportunities to lease and buy essential equipment with specially created funds, and tax incentives.

5

"The Smooth Reformist Period Has Ended . . ."

Referendum Politics

If 1992 had ended badly for Yeltsin, the first quarter of the new year found Russia's president and his reforms facing a mounting crescendo of criticism. Inflation was a staggering 27 percent in January 1993, and wholesale prices surged that month by 32 percent. Production continued to decline. The standard of living fell to 63 percent of its December 1992 level, and only 30 percent of its December 1991 mark.[1]

Relations between Yeltsin and the legislature continued to deteriorate in early 1993. Yeltsin's sole victory in the combative Seventh Congress was an agreement from the deputies to hold a referendum the following April; but by early February, the chair of the Congress, Ruslan Khasbulatov, was trying to back out, charging that "the idea of a referendum belongs to our ultra-radicals."[2] After that, Yeltsin's position eroded rapidly.

At the special session of the Congress in March, the tension that had been building between the executive and legislative branches erupted into an unvarnished power struggle. Each side accused the other of obstructionism and betraying the interests of Russia. By the time Chernomyrdin addressed the legislators on March 11, their earlier approval of him had largely evaporated and confrontational politics had driven out any clear possibility of compromise. That day the Congress voted by an overwhelming majority to curb Yeltsin's powers sharply and introduced a measure to scuttle the planned April referendum on executive and legislative power. Yeltsin countered by underscoring his resolve to hold a referendum and also threatened unspecified "additional measures."[3] The next day, an unfazed Congress voted itself the power to suspend Yeltsin's decrees and spoke of impeachment if Yeltsin violated the constitution. "The smooth reformist period has ended," said Deputy Prime Minister Sergei Shakhrai. "Unfortunately, we are now at the brink of revolution."[4]

The Brezhnev-era constitution, to which Yeltsin was chained in his confrontation with the Congress, was a relic of another era. By now it was an unwieldy document—so often amended (more than three hundred times) that it was laced with contradictions. During the Soviet period, the Congress had been a rubber stamp for party decisions, although constitutionally it was the country's supreme power. In its special March session, the Congress repeatedly asserted its constitutional authority vis-à-vis Russia's popularly elected president. Yeltsin's team hoped for help from Valerii Zorkin, chief justice of the Constitutional Court; but during the special session of Congress Zorkin told the deputies that he believed the constitution to be valid.

On March 12, Yeltsin briefly and calmly addressed the Congress once again. In a brief presentation devoid of emotion, he stated, "I came to the Congress hoping that the spirit of concord would prevail here in spite of everything. Nevertheless, the Congress has turned toward still greater confrontation."[5] After Yeltsin left, his spokesman Viacheslav Kostikov remarked, "The president has said his last word to the Congress. He understands he has only one partner left with whom he can talk. That is the people."[6]

But the next day, the Congress was still speaking. With unrestrained exuberance over its success in humiliating the country's most recent national hero, it accused Yeltsin of causing "chaos and the disintegration of Russia." Yeltsin's economic reforms had "backfired against a majority of the people," the statement continued.[7]

By March 16 Yeltsin was on the offensive again. "I see that democracy and the reforms are confronted with a very great threat," he said, with visiting French President François Mitterrand by his side. "There is clearly an attempt afoot to restore the Communist regime of the Soviets."[8]

Amid mounting alarm that Russia might be on the verge of disintegrating, or that the military might step in to strip away the last remnants of his rapidly dissipating authority, Yeltsin declared "special rule" on March 20 and stated that the referendum that had just been rejected by the Congress would be held on April 25.

In his March 20 speech, Yeltsin continued and broadened his charge that the Congress was dominated by reactionaries. "The Eighth Congress reverberated with an imperialistic tone," he charged. "If this theme were to become the basis of our politics, Russia would certainly be involved in military conflicts with its neighbors. . . . In his final speech, the speaker [Khasbulatov] actually called for renewal of the cold war."[9]

The Congress reacted quickly. They called an emergency session, and on March 28 decided to seek Yeltsin's impeachment—a vote that would require a two-thirds majority. Yeltsin's foes fell short by only 72 votes. The tally was 617 *for* and 268 *against* impeachment. Failing the impeachment initiative, Congress voted the next day to include in the referendum ballot a question on support for Yeltsin's economic reforms, which was designed to undermine his leadership.[10] The Congress clearly thought that most people would vote no to that question; public displeasure with the economic reform program was well known. They believed that, with this question, they were striking Yeltsin's most vulnerable position.

Yeltsin's supporters in the Congress tried to keep this question off the ballot, but they failed. Expecting the vote to embarrass Yeltsin, his supporters immediately began trying to weaken the impact of a negative response. Viacheslav Volkov, a vice chair of the presidential administration, insisted, "The second question is totally absurd. We are not going to pay any attention to it. Such wording actually makes no legal or social sense. Let's say that a majority of voters say 'no'—that they don't approve of Yeltsin's reforms. What would it mean? Could it mean that the people were not satisfied with the reforms because they are not radical *enough?*"[11]

But on April 25, Yeltsin and his reforms swept to an unexpectedly decisive victory. "Do you have confidence in Russian President Boris Yeltsin?" the first question read. Fifty-eight percent of the voters said yes. Even more surprising than the landslide proportions of this vote of confidence was the 53 percent support registered for the economic reforms.

Not only did a majority in all age groups vote for Yeltsin, according to an exit survey conducted for U.S. news organizations, but Yeltsin garnered 70 percent of the vote even among those who believed that Russia's economy would not improve within the next five years. His support was broad-based, the poll found. As might be expected, an overwhelming majority of voters whose lives had improved during the past two years voted for Yeltsin, and even among those who said that their lives had been better under communism, 43 percent favored Yeltsin in the April referendum.[12] (Among eligible voters, 64 percent turned out for the referendum.)

Yeltsin's greatest support came from large cities, especially Moscow and St. Petersburg; in some rural regions, he received less than 50 percent of the vote. For the most part, however, both Yeltsin and his reforms were approved across Russia.[13]

Displeasure with the legislature was also plainly evident. About 70 percent of voters supported early parliamentary elections, while just under 50 percent favored early elections for president. (The Constitutional Court had ruled earlier, however, that more than 50 percent of *eligible* voters would have to approve these two proposals for them to be binding.)

Yeltsin's referendum victory represented the most dramatic turnaround of his political fortunes since the August 1991 putsch.

Only a few weeks earlier, it had appeared that more people would stay away from the polls than would cast their votes for Yeltsin. On March 13 and 14, right after the Eighth Congress ended, the Center for Public Opinion and Market Research (CPO) conducted a national survey of 1,280 people to tap public opinion about recent political developments. Only 26 percent of the respondents said they would support Yeltsin's position in a referendum; 12 percent opposed him; and 43 percent indicated that they would not vote. Nineteen percent were undecided.[14]

But Yeltsin had struck a responsive cord with his March 20 declaration of "special rule." Through that swift challenge, he had underscored the image of an unyielding, indomitable leader, and his approval rating soared. It seems not to have mattered that the statement he issued later omitted essential points of his challenge to the legislature. Yeltsin had spoken with force. As in August 1991, he symbolized resistance to entrenched power and an old way of life. Our evidence suggests that *this,* above all else, captured the loyalty of a country that was weary of economic reversals and high-level bickering but powerfully drawn to the promise of radical change.

Before the end of March, another CPO survey found that 43 percent planned to vote for Yeltsin; 19 percent were against him; and 26 percent said they would not vote. Twelve percent were undecided.[15]

Thus, Yeltsin's support had jumped by nearly two-thirds in two weeks—to the point that 58 percent of the people who expected to vote indicated that they would support Yeltsin. That was exactly the percentage he received in the referendum on April 25. He actually garnered a slightly higher percentage of the vote in April than he had received when he was elected president of the Russian SFSR two years earlier.[16] Exuberant, Yeltsin declared on April 28, "The people's support for change is the meaning of the referendum."[17]

It is clear that most voters in the April referendum were voicing their preference for an unexplored path *away from* the all-too-familiar planning system. More than being a vote *for*

Yeltsin's economic program, which was obviously unpopular, the majority were voting *against* the Soviet-style approach now represented in most people's minds by Khasbulatov and many other deputies.

Sociologist Yurii Levada offered the same interpretation on the eve of the election. Levada first cited recent survey results on economic issues, such as an April CPO survey in which two-thirds of respondents said that, if elections were held for the legislature, they would support speeding up the economic reform. "One of the paradoxes" of public opinion, Levada concluded, was that criticism of Yeltsin's *specific reforms* was fairly high, while support for Yeltsin as *the country's leader* was also high. Even more telling was the fact that his overall ratings as a leader soared when his position as president of the country was threatened. "Voting for Yeltsin, people are actually voting against a return to the old system of power," Levada concluded. "Most of the population think of Yeltsin today not just as a person with strong and weak qualities, but as a symbol—as representative of those changes which most people do not want to lose."[18]

Leon Trotsky's analysis of the sources of mass mobilization in his 1930 preface to *The History of the Russian Revolution* offers, we think, an enduringly persuasive interpretation of the recurring struggle of Russians to redirect their historical course. "The masses go into a revolution not with a prepared plan of social reconstruction," Trotsky wrote, "but with a sharp feeling that they cannot endure the old regime."[19] We think Trotsky's observation about the revolutions of 1917 helps to explain the Russian people's April 1993 vote to press for demolition of the command economy. The most feasible alternative available, in the view of most voters, was the Yeltsin government's economic reform program.

Moreover, the promise of *strong* rule had widespread appeal. A Cable News Network poll in January 1993 asked people in several cities to evaluate different kinds of leadership for Russia. Fifty-one percent believed that authoritarian leadership would bring economic and political stabilization.[20] Yeltsin consistently played to that sentiment throughout his referendum campaign, emphasizing repeatedly that his victory would mean the establishment of a "presidential regime."[21] Starting April 26, he promised, he would issue a package of proposals to speed up reform and stabilize the economy. "If there is support for the president in the referendum," Yeltsin declared two weeks before the vote, "the president will take more decisive action."[22]

The Western Aid Component of Russia's Economic Reform Plan

Developments in 1992

The Russian government needed to gain membership in the International Monetary Fund (IMF) in order to be eligible for Fund-provided resources.[23]

In January 1992 Russia applied for full membership in the IMF, and on June 1 the Articles of Agreement for full membership were signed. In the meanwhile, Russia was engaged in discussions with the Fund on economic policy issues.[24] In February the Russian government had approved an Economic Policy Memorandum document for negotiations with the IMF which outlined the principal directions of the reform program for the year. The most prominent features of Russia's plan concerned financial stabilization. The proposal called for the budget deficit to be slashed by the end of 1992, for the monthly inflation rate to be lowered, and for the decline in production to be halted.[25] When Gaidar presented the government's privatization program in June, he stated that the revised program should reduce inflation to a monthly rate of 3 percent and strengthen the ruble.[26]

Russia also suggested that energy prices would be liberalized in April, although the IMF had not initially insisted on that action. This point became the focus of controversy in the ensuing months within Russia, and with the government's failure to implement the plan, its energy policy also became a major issue in the international community.[27]

American economist Jeffrey Sachs provided three arguments for large-scale assistance to Russia. First, he said, Russia needed help with its balance-of-payments crisis, which limited Russia's ability to purchase imports from other countries. (Responding to balance-of-payments problems among member nations has long been an important function of the IMF.) Second, Sachs noted that Russia's fiscal crisis was being exacerbated by the burden of foreign-debt servicing as well as the social spending required in the 1990s to promote economic transformation. Finally, Sachs cited "an urgent need to help cushion the shocks coming from the collapse of the old system and the emergence of a new market economy. Foreign aid can give hope to the population and thereby provide a key to political and social stability during the transition to democracy and a market economy."[28]

In 1991, Sachs, in consultation with Yavlinskii among others, had proposed that the Soviet Union begin negotiations with the IMF for membership in October of that year. Fund membership, along with an arrangement for radical economic reform, would open the door, Sachs believed, to financial assistance from both the IMF and Western governments. As Sachs had envisioned the scenario before the breakup of the USSR, "this general proposition would be put on the table by the West, that there would be meaningful assistance in the event of radical political and economic reform. The Soviet Union would respond with the intention to move forward in that direction."[29] Sachs had not been speaking of token aid from the West. He had emphasized that to create the "Grand Bargain" of which he spoke for the USSR would require "a scale of commitment of over 100 billion dollars." He added, "This is such a difficult, excruciating process of transformation right now, that to do it peacefully will require outside help."[30]

Writing about the kind of political transformation in the Soviet Union that might allow his vision to be realized, Sachs had cautioned, "There may be a 2 percent chance of something like this happening in fact, but given the possible 2 percent chance of this actually going forward, given the number of man-hours that went into it, this will still be a very good bargain even if there were a 0.1 percent chance."[31]

After the "2 percent chance" was realized in Russia following the dissolution of the Soviet Union, international financial institutions and the seven advanced market nations comprising the Group of Seven (G–7) advanced industrial nations[32] agreed to grant Russia aid in the amount of U.S. $24 billion. As was usual in such situations, this was a conditional agreement—dependent on Russia's achievement of economic objectives as negotiated with the IMF.

Gaidar's unenviable job was to tiptoe a jagged course in this mine field. If subsidies to state industries were sharply reduced, production would surely suffer, which would increase the budget deficit and might well lead to social turmoil as workers lost their jobs by the thousands. But the IMF had made deficit reduction a condition for receiving badly needed loans and credits. Liberalization of energy prices, an idea the IMF had welcomed, would add fuel to the fires of inflation; but the Fund insisted that the inflation rate be reduced.

Shortly after the Gaidar–Chubais revised 1992 privatization proposal was presented to the Congress in April, Gaidar was interviewed by a reporter from *The Economist*. The reporter asked, "How useful *politically* would the [much-discussed] financial aid be from IMF and the G–7 countries? Doesn't it weaken your position that you are allowing foreigners to dictate your economics?"

"We really need this aid," Gaidar answered. "This aid could help us avoid long-term economic decline . . . and we could then make some real structural changes."[33]

Gaidar actually understated the extent to which his reform program depended on aid from the West. The government, in a published explanation of its economic strategy that appeared a month before Gaidar's interview, had acknowledged, *"We can achieve the objectives proposed here only with foreign aid, and it must be granted very quickly to prevent spiraling inflation. . . . We would not make this proposal if we had not been confident that the aid to be provided in the very near future would be more valuable both to us and to the West than aid provided later."*[34]

Western aid was to be used to stabilize the ruble, to reduce Russia's international debt, to subsidize the import of materials needed for production, and to provide humanitarian help for people especially affected by government reforms.

In the end, aid from the West turned out to be only a fraction of what had been expected in 1992 and early 1993, although even the amount promised was hardly generous. As American economist Marshall Goldman noted, a $200 billion German investment in the former East Germany yielded unimpressive results. "By comparison," he added, "it is hard to see how the much smaller $24 billion pledged by the West to Yeltsin can be more effective."[35]

"The $24 billion aid package announced on April 1 has simply vanished," Sachs observed. "Loans have basically stopped since July. The IMF money has been essentially non-existent; the first World Bank loan has not even been finalized. The EBRD [European Bank for Reconstruction and Development] remains a small player on the scene, partly because its mission has not yet been made clear." Sachs further emphasized that while the IMF was understaffed and thus overwhelmed by the job it was supposed to do in working with Russia, "Western governments have simply stood by and done virtually nothing."[36]

Not all of the promised aid actually vanished. The $6 billion approved "in principle" to stabilize the ruble "is still there on a shelf, waiting for better times," according to IMF director Michel Camdessus.[37] Russia received about $1 billion. An additional $12 billion was provided in short-term credits, a substantial portion of which began to come due in 1993. Seven billion dollars more in debts to Western creditors was deferred.[38]

Western Responses in 1993

The Congress's assertiveness against Yeltsin and his reforms succeeded where all other warnings had failed in jarring Western powers into fashioning a more urgent response to Russia's economic decline. Before the Congress ended its fiery Eighth Session on March 13, 1993, Western leaders had finally decided to act. For more than a year before then, as historical events had unfolded in the wake of the 1991 coup, the West had had adequate time to act in the interest of democratic forces within Russia and in its own self-interest; yet this unprecedented opportunity had been lost.

Part of the problem with aid to Russia was that mechanisms were not in place there to ensure that the aid would be used properly. As IMF director Camdessus put it in early 1993, "There is no reason for international society or for IMF to use the few resources we have available to support [Russia] if we are not positive that [Russia] has taken necessary measures to . . . keep the money inside Russia, and for it not to be immediately transferred to bank accounts in Zurich, Paris or London."[39]

At the beginning of March, less than two weeks before the Congress's decisive moves to derail Yeltsin's economic reform program, analyst Fred Hiatt vividly highlighted the West's seeming inability to respond to the window of opportunity in Russia, which had, at that point, been open for more than a year:

> As to any bustling Third World capital, consultants and World Bank specialists are streaming into Moscow. They lodge at the finest hotels, rent apartments once reserved for the Communist elite and work in skyscraper suites where Czechs and Cubans once reigned.
>
> Yet despite their ballooning presence, the rescue operation has stalled. The result is frustration, resentment and a growing fear that the historic opportunity emerging from the end of the Cold War is being squandered.
>
> "The situation in our country is worsening, and this harsh crisis easily could lead to fascists or Communists coming to power," said Boris Nemtsov, governor of Nizhny Novgorod and a leading reformer. "If the West wants this, then, fine, it should do nothing."[40]

But with Yeltsin on the ropes, almost impeached by a now-surly Congress and facing an uncertain referendum with a restive electorate, Western political leaders rushed to bolster Yeltsin's shaky leadership at home. U.S. President Bill Clinton quickly arranged a summit meeting to show "the President's support" for Yeltsin, as U.S. Secretary of State Warren Christopher put it,[41] and the German government quickly drafted a statement saying that Yeltsin represented "the unhindered continuation of democratic and free-market reforms" in Russia.[42]

In mid-March, members of the G–7 gathered in Hong Kong for emergency discussions about Russia's political and economic situation and invited Russia's new minister of finance, Boris Fedorov, to participate. Several leaders of the G–7 democracies were urging quick support for Yeltsin.[43] The plan that rapidly began to emerge was to provide aid that would be highly visible to the people of Russia. This strategy was articulated by Fedorov at the meeting and quickly accepted by its participants. The Russian government's proposal was for the G–7 countries to give assistance that was "visible, so that people feel that this contribution really helped." *Visibility,* Fedorov insisted, was more critical than the *amount* of aid. This assistance would be more a political tool than a major stimulus to economic recovery.[44] An aid package totaling $28.4 billion, with another $19 billion from individual countries and relief through debt rescheduling, was worked out by the G–7 nations in April.

Aid would be conditional, however, on reductions of credits to state enterprises and restraint in the printing of money. The first $1.5 billion, which would come from the IMF, would be delivered when the Yeltsin government got a firmer grip on the Central Bank. Following that, $2.6 billion more would be provided as Russia's inflation rate dropped. (The March 1993 inflation rate was 12 percent, down sharply from its 25 percent level in both January and February.)

Several conditions that the IMF usually imposes on assistance were eliminated in its long-term "loan" of $4.1 billion, and the $6 billion approved in 1992 to stabilize the ruble was carried forward to 1993. Additional funds were to be provided by the World Bank, the European Bank for Reconstruction and Development, and G–7 member nations. Also in April, in an action separate from the G–7 initiative, the Paris Club, a group of 15 nations to which Russia owed about $80 billion in outstanding debts, agreed to defer Moscow's payment obligation.[45] An additional U.S. contribution of $1.8 billion was proposed, which would be above the $1.6 billion pledged by Clinton at the April summit.

Western financial specialists were unabashedly delighted with Yeltsin's strong showing in the referendum. "The clear sense is that now is the time for the Russian government to take the necessary steps" if it is to make the G–7's aid package "maximally effective," a senior U.S. Treasury official stated at an April 29 G–7 meeting.[46] A *New York Times* writer covering the meeting observed that "the tone of the meeting" was far less rancorous than that of G–7 sessions a few years earlier when "the seven nations often bickered because the United States was reluctant to cut *its* deficit."[47]

East European Applications of the Theoretical Model

The Case of Poland

"The Soviets should focus on the experiences of Poland," Anders Åslund insisted in a June 1991 conference at the Stockholm School of Economics.[48] Jeffrey Sachs agreed. "As former advisers to the Polish government and current advisers to the Russian government, we are struck by the similarities of broad trends in the two countries," Lipton and Sachs declared in 1992.[49] "Poland alone [among the countries of Eastern Europe] enjoyed a resurgence of overall industrial growth in 1992," Sachs wrote early in 1993.[50]

The familiar argument that Russia should follow Poland's example is inadequate on three counts. First, the differences between these two countries on dimensions that are important to the economy are so great as to cast serious doubt on any but the most general of comparisons. Additionally, Poland in 1993 was not the success story for radical reform that it is often pictured it to be. Finally, the reforms instituted in Poland were based on a controversial economic theory that lacked empirical confirmation.

Poland and Russia are vastly different in many ways that have major implications for interorganizational economic relations and economic connections between people and social institutions. But the generalizing perspective that prevailed in the early 1990s among top foreign advisers to Russia, as well as among officials of such international financial institutions as the IMF, found a willing adherent in Poland's prime minister, Hanna Suchocka. Responding to Arkadii Volskii's contention that the Russian economic situation is different from Poland's, Suchocka said, "Economics, as well as physics, cannot be American or Polish or Russian."[51]

Suchocka's explanation was not satisfying to Arkadii Volskii in his role as a spokesperson for many directors of large industrial enterprises in Russia. Volskii realized that in Poland, military production played a minor role in industry; whereas Russia's industrial economy was centered on the military-industrial complex, which accounted for perhaps as much as 20 percent of industrial employment through the 1980s.[52] How could any adequate strategy for economic reform not take such differences into account, he wondered?

The Russian and Polish cultural and social systems were also quite different. Poland's experience with communism was much briefer than Russia's, and the private sector was much stronger in Poland than in Russia at the time economic reforms began. About half of the prices in Poland had been liberalized by January 1990, when shock therapy was instituted there,[53] and more than three-fourths of Poland's agricultural land was in private hands even before the communist government lost power. Before 1990, most wholesale trade, transportation, foreign trade, and construction enterprises were private, and most consumer services were in private hands. Poland thus entered its period of radical economic reform with a great deal more experience with nonstate enterprise than Russia. Further, the scale of production was enormously different in the two countries. In 1991 Poland had fewer than 8,000 state enterprises; Russia had more than 200,000.

The contrasts between Poland and Russia could be multiplied. Nevertheless, the proponents of a rigid macroeconomic stabilization policy for Russia largely ignored larger questions of cultural values and social traditions, as well as the thorny problem of how to take into account existing economic arrangements, while citing the Polish experience as proof of their position. For them, it was simpler to tear down and start over in Russia than to reform with the aim of minimizing social disruption.

Even if the Polish experience could be duplicated in Russia, the results in Poland after three years were not nearly as impressive as Western analysts often implied. During the last quarter of 1992 Poland's industrial production did experience an encouraging increase of 4.2 percent. After a drop of nearly 40 percent with the introduction of shock therapy in 1990, however, the 1992 gain left the country far behind its productivity level before price liberalization had begun. Even more to the point, only 30 percent of Poland's industrial output was outside the state sector by the end of 1992.

As would be the case in Russia later, and for similar reasons, the Polish government decided to issue massive credits to state industries within months after the inauguration of shock therapy. Because fiscal targets for 1991 were not met, the IMF suspended disbursement of expected funds.

By early 1993 the Polish economy was reeling from enterprise closures and other dislocations created by the economic reform program. Thirteen percent of the active work force were unemployed. There was an unemployed worker in every third family. Purchasing power had declined sharply.[54] Responding to the social hardship created by the reforms, the Polish parliament wanted to increase the government's budget for 1993 in order to provide additional social services. Lech Walesa, Poland's president, threatened to dissolve the parliament if it did not approve his more austere budget proposal. Walesa's budget had been designed to satisfy the International Monetary Fund. The parliament gave in, by a vote of 230 to 207; and the same day the IMF and the EBR announced that they would furnish additional credits to Poland.[55]

On March 18 the Polish parliament rejected a proposal to privatize 600 state companies. After two years of radical reforms, a majority of the country's legislators were ready for a change. Following the vote, Prime Minister Suchocka admitted that the parliament's decision was "a serious signal that there's a possibility of abandoning the road of reforms."[56] But on April 30 the lower house approved the bill, and it appeared to be headed for final approval in the Senate. "We are elated; it is an absolute breakthrough," said World Bank representative Christian Duvigneau after the vote.[57] The World Bank had threatened to withhold new money from Poland if the bill were rejected.

In 1992, David Lipton and Jeffrey Sachs wrote of "the steady, peaceful, and democratic progress of the Polish reforms."[58] To strengthen their claim, they referred to a November 1991 survey by Ammeter-Inquirer designed to gauge public response to the government's economic reforms. The results "demonstrated acceptance of the economic changes," Lipton and Sachs stated.[59]

The Ammeter-Inquirer report included one question that directly tapped the respondents' "acceptance of the economic changes": "Do you prefer an economy in which government is responsible for everyone's job and determines what shops can sell and sets all the prices, OR, an economy in which everyone is free to seek whatever job he or she likes, and shops offer at their own price whatever people want to buy?" Forty percent of the respondents choose the latter, "free economy," variant; 59 percent preferred a "controlled economy."[60]

The Ammeter-Inquirer results were duplicated early in 1992 by a Gallup International survey which found that 58 percent of a national sample were unhappy with the way the country was being run.[61] These public-opinion findings were consistent with the assessment at the beginning of 1993 by opposition leader

Aleksander Hall. "After three years of reform, opposition to the idea of a market economy has increased," he said, "and there is a longing for socialistic organization of work and social guarantees."[62]

"Popular support for the reform path has eroded over time," the 1992 *OECD Economic Survey* of Poland acknowledged, adding, "this erosion needs to be contained."[63] Another OECD report called "the weakening of public support for the reform programme" in Poland "one of the most disturbing aspects of recent developments."[64] For a large proportion of citizens in both Poland and Russia, however, what was most disturbing was the sharp economic decline that had been triggered by economic reforms designed according to monetarist principles.

In reality, there was no tested formula for successful economic reform in socialist economies. Advocates of macroeconomic stabilization furnished no strong evidence that more gradual reforms might not have served Russia and Poland better. Advocating decentralization as a vital early step in reform, they ignored the examples of Japan, South Korea, Hong Kong, Singapore, and Taiwan, which showed that central planning could be an integral feature of a successful economic reform strategy.[65] Urging lightning-quick economic reorganization, they ignored the experiences of West European economies in the period following World War II, a transition from wartime to peacetime structures that had required a decade or more even with the massive aid provided under the Marshall Plan. Russia had further to go in the early 1990s; it received less aid from the West; and Western financial institutions demanded that its transition be more rapid.

The Czechoslovakian Example

In 1992 Anders Åslund was calling Czechoslovakia "the ideal" example of economic reform, choosing to "disregard the problems of the dissolution of the Czech and Slovak Federation," which he preferred to "look upon as a separate issue."[66] Czechoslovakia was no better an example for Russia than Poland, however, and for many of the same reasons. To force comparisons between Czechoslovakia and Russia is to disregard a large number of critical differences. With no spiraling inflation problem or budget deficit, Czechoslovakia's economy was in markedly better health than Russia's when reform began there. A smaller number of Czechoslovak industries faced the formidable task that Russia confronted, either to convert from military to civilian production or to close. Regulated prices in Czechoslovakia were much closer to market prices than they were in Russia. The disparities are numerous. And Åslund's attempt to separate the breakup of Czechoslovakia from its economic reform program is analytically unsound. In a study of privatization in Central Europe, Frydman et al. summarize the obvious causal connection Åslund would like to ignore: "The cost of these transition measures has been much higher in Slovakia than in the Czech part of the country. This has strengthened the separatist and anti-reform forces in Slovakia, which resulted in the strong showing by the party seeking Slovak independence in the June 1992 elections."[67]

The IMF and Bulgaria

Bulgaria's minister of finance, Stoian Aleksandrov, suggested at the beginning of 1993 that his country probably would withdraw from the IMF soon if the Fund's stringent conditions for receiving credits were not relaxed.[68] Like Russia, Bulgaria was contending with rapid inflation, persistent declines in production, and a growing gap between prices and wages. The country's per capita gross national product had declined from $2,339 in 1990 to $957 in 1992.[69] Unemployment was already at a high level and increasing. "We suggested to IMF that they not impose such strict parameters," Aleksandrov recalled. "IMF imposes the same guidelines on all countries, but this standard formula does not work for Eastern Europe now. IMF is not taking into account the unique character of this post-communist transitional period."[70]

6

New Money, New Business

Fiscal and Monetary Policy

During the first quarter of 1992, the Russian government's goal of financing the budget without increasing inflation was largely achieved, and the ruble held up well on the currency market. By midyear, however, the overall picture had changed in several critical ways. Prices had risen more than had been expected—partly because sellers were trying to "hedge" against inflation. Sales volume was low because prices were so high. With declining demand, enterprises continued to raise prices, but production continued to drop. Writing in August about this violation of the law of demand, Gaidar attributed it to the population's lack of experience with a market economy.[1] The vice director of the Central Bank, Aleksandr Khandruev, added, "Our enterprises achieved freedom, but they were not able to change their way of thinking."[2] This social dimension had not been factored into the "shock therapy" equation.

With the drop in production, personnel were required to take unpaid "vacations" or to work fewer hours per week. Thus people had less money, but goods cost more. Inevitably, the state came under tremendous pressure from the directors' lobby and trade unions to do something about the crisis, and in the second quarter the government increased support to the most vital sectors of the economy—particularly agriculture and food processing, and energy. Pensions and student stipends were also increased, as well as salaries for state employees outside the production sphere. Consequently, the budget deficit began to grow. With the decline in production and sales, debts that enterprises owed to each other and to the state could not be paid. By the end of June the total amount of unpaid debts was 78 times more than it had been six months earlier.

Before June, the Central Bank had followed the government's plan to reduce the rate of increase in the amount of money in circulation. But by June, the threat of widespread production stoppages was real. The options were to let a large number of enterprises close their doors or else to keep them operating with subsidies. In June the Central Bank increased the amount of money in circulation by 26 percent, and in July and August by 32 percent per month. (From January through May the rate of increase had varied between 9 and 14 percent per month.)

Printing money was not the government's only action to help struggling enterprises during the summer. A telegram from the Central Bank to local banks on July 28 sent shock waves throughout Russia. *Komsomolskaia pravda* labeled the missive "explosive,"[3] and Gaidar interrupted his vacation and rushed back to Moscow to sort out the implications of Viktor Gerashchenko's order that banks grant credits to state enterprises to cover their debts to one another. Petr Filippov, chairman of the Supreme Soviet's Subcommittee on Privatization, wrote in *Izvestiia* that "this telegram marks a turning point in Russia's economic and political history." It meant, to Filippov, that Russia "is giving up the implementation of market reforms."[4]

From July to November the Central Bank issued twice as much currency as it had during the first six months of 1992. The printing of new money had a pronounced effect on prices. During the first six months, the monthly inflation rate averaged about 15 percent; from October through December, it averaged about 30 percent.[5]

However, with the "nonpayment crisis" ended, production began to increase and the budget deficit decreased. But in the fourth quarter of the year, inflation reached new heights, climbing from a monthly rate in August of 9 percent to 33 percent in November;[6] and the debts of production enterprises again grew because of low demand for their products. Again, salaries went unpaid, although the amount of money in circulation increased by 10 times during 1992. Officially, it was reported that in December wholesale prices had increased 34 times and consumer prices 26 times over the previous December.[7] Other analyses, however, pegged the increase in wholesale prices at 62 times the December 1991 level.[8] By December the value of the ruble had fallen precipitously from its midyear levels (Table B–6.1). Early in 1993, new credits were again issued.

Jeffrey Sachs blamed most of Russia's economic troubles in 1992 on growth in the money supply. He posited a strong causal relationship between inflation and money growth, noting that money growth had been about 10 percent per month during the first few months of 1992, and that "price inflation fell to around that rate by midyear." But with changes in the policies of the Central Bank in mid-1992, following the appointment of Viktor Gerashchenko as its chair, "monthly money growth climbed to around 30 percent per month. By October," Sachs continued, "monthly price inflation increased to around this rate as well."[9]

The real cause of 1992 inflation was not price liberalization in a monopolistic context, Sachs argued, but rather Central Bank credits—especially credits to state enterprises that were experiencing severe financial problems. Gerashchenko's predecessor at the Central Bank, Georgii Matiukhin, agreed. "In the current political situation, the Russian government cannot achieve any success in fighting inflation," he wrote in January 1993. The government cannot operate as it should "because it is not allowed to by the military-industrial complex. *They* are the main source of blame for the budget deficit."[10]

Gerashchenko responded that the main inflationary factor was the state budget deficit, and that bank credits, rather than making economic conditions worse in Russia, were the principal financial source for converting military enterprises to civilian production and for facilitating the structural reform of other industries as well.[11] Enterprises in the West could issue stocks and bonds, Gerashchenko said, and they could borrow money from banks. But in Russia there was not as yet a capital market. "There is just the banking sector, which can make credits available."[12]

Prime Minister Chernomyrdin, however, agreeing with Sachs, countered that unwarranted credits and subsidies were the main reason for 1992 inflation; and, he added, only 20 percent of all the credits were used to support production. The other 80 percent went to increase salaries.[13]

Of course, Gerashchenko's rebuttal could have been that salary increases were necessary because of inflation.

The issue of monetary policy was at the heart of Russia's struggle over economic reform in 1992 and early 1993. It divided radical reformers, who wanted to unleash market forces to restructure Russia's economy, from conservatives, whose top priorities included preserving Russia's industrial enterprises and keeping unemployment low. The conservative position was aimed, in large measure, at preserving the power of enterprise directors—many of whom headed large, and vulnerable, firms in the military-industrial complex. The directors "were confident," Erlen Bernshtein argued, "that their debts would be canceled, because the state is expected to take care of state enterprises."[14] The strategy of reformers, however, was to weaken the political strength of industrial directors; they believed that their goal of financial stabilization could not be achieved in any other way. In 1992 "inflation was only the most obvious symptom of the battle for power between Moscow reformers and the more reactionary forces which still control the economy," according to analyst David Bollz.[15]

Among the enterprises that were on the brink of closing in 1992, before government credits were issued, a substantial number produced goods that were in demand. There were also many, however, that had been chronically burdened with large inventories of unsold output even in better economic times—unsold because, as economist Vladimir Tikhonov explains, "Following

Soviet tradition [Russia] continues to produce goods which are not much needed, or even not needed at all. But someone has to pay for them. That is when the Central Bank enters the stage to help the state apparatus."[16] That was one of Filippov's principal complaints about Gerashchenko's July 28 order. "This kind of behavior by the economic *nomenklatura* has become a large-scale phenomenon," Filippov said, because state enterprise executives operate "with absolute certainty that the government will bail them out."[17]

"By the summer," observes economist Efrem Maiminas, "the government had lost its resolve to allow the total collapse of industry and mass unemployment" and capitulated to the directors' view that industries should be kept operating, in spite of the burdensome cost and the inconsistency of this approach with the government's emphasis on a restrictive monetary policy.[18] The result, to Tikhonov, was a serious setback for the government's program—"back to the beginning of January 1992."[19]

If Gerashchenko's credit policy was as damaging to the reform program as Filippov claimed, then the Civic Union may have achieved a partial victory, since, according to several observers close to the situation, Arkadii Volskii's coalition had been responsible for Gerashchenko's appointment to chair the Central Bank. This was just one manifestation of the new trend. "By the end of the year," Maiminas continues, "Gaidar's economic policy was derailed . . . by massive pressure from many sources."[20] Volskii agreed, noting that Gaidar had been unable to use his power effectively while in office, and adding that only a small percentage of the Yeltsin government's decisions had actually been implemented under Gaidar's leadership.[21]

In a March 1993 press conference, Minister of Finance Boris Fedorov charged that the leaders of the Central Bank were "returning to centralized methods of running the economy, and destroying commercial structures." Credits that the Bank had been issuing to former republics of the USSR were among the main reasons for galloping inflation, he said.[22] Overall, 1992 subsidies from Russia to other countries of the Commonwealth of Independent States, including credits from the Central Bank, totaled $18 billion.[23]

The next month, however, the Central Bank announced a new credit policy for the second quarter of 1993. In April it agreed to limit the growth of credits in the second quarter to 30 percent of the total amount of credits in existence at the end of the first quarter. Although this ceiling did not indicate the level of restraint the IMF would have liked, it was a move in the direction they consistently recommended, and Russian officials indicated that such pressure from the West had been a major determinant of the Central Bank's decision.[24]

The Attempt to Extend the Government's Administrative Control

At the Eighth Congress of People's Deputies in March 1993, Yeltsin proposed that authority be consolidated for activities related to economic reform. He wanted the executive branch to supervise the Central Bank and property funds. He also asked for authority to determine anticrisis measures without legislative approval. Acceptance of this proposal would nullify the provision in the July 3, 1991, RSFSR Law on Privatization of State and Municipal Enterprises, which had given the Supreme Soviet administrative control over these agencies; and it would afford Yeltsin special powers reminiscent of the authorization that the Congress had voted him in November 1991.[25]

Yeltsin's idea was that all matters pertaining to economics should be under executive control. He justified this by arguing that to overcome the severe economic crisis, exceptional measures were necessary, and "no one but the President can demonstrate the necessary decisiveness."[26] Chernomyrdin supported Yeltsin's proposal and added that the government's responsibility for economic reform could not be discharged unless the government were given more authority.[27]

Yeltsin's March proposal for additional authority grew out of the government's plan for 1993 to achieve two key objectives carried over from Gaidar's 1992 plan. Following Gaidar's agenda, the Chernomyrdin team emphasized the importance of financial stabilization and deficit reduction. They wanted the support of enterprises with credit to be selective, according to priorities established by the government. Carrying out this plan, however, would necessitate a change in the Central Bank's policies under Gerashchenko—specifically, his pattern of issuing large amounts of new money and granting massive credits to Russian enterprises and other republics. The change the government wanted could be assured only if Gerashchenko came under the administrative supervision of the Yeltsin government.

Minister of Finance Fedorov, explaining why he thought the executive branch should supervise the Central Bank, stated that he had "always believed that the Central Bank should be independent."[28] But recently it had been "sabotaging" the govern-ment's economic policy, Fedorov charged, as well as negotiations with the IMF. And, he continued, "we now face a situation in which the Central Bank wants to play the role of a state bank—perhaps because its leaders represent the old way of thinking. There is no other country in the world where the government has to explain to their national banks that the banks have to fight to make their national currency stable."[29] By the end of April, however, the Central Bank was still under administrative control of the Supreme Soviet, although Gerashchenko was now also a member of the Presidium of the Council of Ministers in the Yeltsin government.

New Russian Businesses

The flood of new money from the Central Bank that was intended to keep state enterprises in operation was not matched by a comparable effort to stimulate new business or to support existing private businesses.

Nonstate businesses had begun to establish a presence in Gorbachev's Soviet Union with the legalization of cooperatives; and, as we indicated in chapter 2, the early growth of cooperatives had been impressive.[30] The philosophy behind cooperatives was to preserve the idea of "socialist enterprise." The stream of legislation about cooperatives that was passed in the USSR legislature during the late 1980s had been justified as fostering a form of economic activity that was both true to the goals of communism and suited for the conditions of the time. This attempt to avoid breaking with party orthodoxy, however, soon ended. Most cooperative owners had actually wanted to be private business people; and workers, while preferring nonstate to state employment, had had a strong preference for a form of private business activity other than cooperatives—private firms or joint ventures, for example.[31] An RSFSR law approved on December 25, 1990, On Enterprises and Entrepreneurship, had outlined several permissible forms of property ownership, including private enterprises.[32] By 1991, most people who were beginning new businesses in Russia were starting private enterprises, not cooperatives.[33]

In Gaidar's economic reforms, however, the flourishing private sector was virtually ignored; and the introduction of price liberalization, along with higher taxes, drove many nonstate firms out of business. Ironically, the actual number of small businesses declined during 1992—the first (and only) year the Yeltsin–Gaidar reform program was in operation.[34]

Private businesspeople were frequently accused of engaging primarily in speculation during this period, and indeed, Vladimir Tikhonov notes, hardly any new production enterprises were started in the private sphere during the last half of 1991 or in 1992. For Tikhonov, the prime culprit at first was the inaccessibility of production materials, which were easier to procure in the state sector. Most of the capital of new entrepreneurs was therefore kept in the monetary sphere.[35] By the beginning of 1992, many private entrepreneurs thus had large reserves of capital that they were ready to invest in production enterprises,[36] but this capital had lost most of its value nearly overnight, due to inflation. Moreover, it was very difficult for private firms to borrow money for business development; when loans were available they were nearly always short-term (one to three months) and at very high interest rates (from 100 to 200 percent in the autumn). In March 1992, *Delovoi mir* editor Yurii Kirpichnikov described the most pressing problems of small businesses: "Because the state is not supporting small businesses, it did not make it possible for them to secure financial, material, and natural resources for production. Thus their main field is selling and buying—not production." In Kirpichnikov's view, this was the most serious problem in the Russian economy.[37]

"As soon as Gaidar came to power he became an opponent of entrepreneurship," according to Mark Masarskii, an adviser on entrepreneurship to the Moscow government.[38] Before joining the Yeltsin government, Gaidar the academician had written in glowing terms about the salutary role of entrepreneurs, Masarskii said, and he had been an active supporter of the Russian economy's entrepreneurial segment. Gaidar the decision-maker, however, had not taken into account the crippling effect of the government's price liberalization and tax policies on entrepreneurial activity. The Council on Entrepreneurship, an independent think tank made up of domestic business executives, had been established in March 1992 by a Yeltsin decree. Its purpose was to provide a business perspective for governmental decision making. Soon members were urgently voicing dissatisfaction with the government's neglect of private business, arguing that the government had created "a climate adverse to business development where the interests of production and entrepreneurship are infringed."[39]

This was not what Yeltsin had wanted to hear, and he did not soon meet with his Council. "The Gaidar team is open to dialogue," one member of the Council indicated, "but while listening, it does not hear much."[40] Yeltsin and Gaidar did speak positively about private ownership and entrepreneurship repeatedly during 1992, and Yeltsin promised that state support would soon stand behind the words. The private business community waited with anticipation for a Yeltsin decree that would afford them opportunities that would match some of the advantages being bestowed on state and privatizing enterprises. A decree intended to address the imbalance appeared on November 30. "The President's administration has finally issued its long-awaited document on private business, and it is not helpful at all," a *Delovoi mir* business editor concluded after examining the decree. "They probably don't understand that *real* measures to support small business were needed, as we say, yesterday."[41]

The 1993 privatization program did address the issue of stimulating the development of new private business. The government created a special fund under the State Property Management Committee to assist specific entrepreneurial ventures. With money provided by the Russian government, Western countries, and the European Bank for Reconstruction and Development, low-interest loans would be provided for private enterprises in the production sector that showed promise of increasing competitiveness in Russian business. Further, the program specified that tax rates would be lowered for small and medium-sized enterprises in the production, service, and construction spheres to stimulate business activity.[42]

Foreign Investment

The first legislation explicitly permitting joint ventures in the Soviet Union since the 1920s had been adopted in May 1983, under Yurii Andropov. According to that decree, joint ventures would be permitted with Council for Mutual Economic Assistance (CMEA) countries; in 1985, contracts were finalized for two Soviet-Bulgarian joint ventures.[43] On January 13, 1987, the USSR Council of Ministers adopted two more significant decrees on the creation of joint ventures with Western, as well as CMEA, nations. The first joint venture company formed as a result of the 1987 decrees was registered on May 12, and by the end of 1987, 23 joint ventures had been registered. In 1988, 168 more joint ventures were registered. Most were in Moscow and nearly all were in Russia.[44]

The provisions of the 1987 legislation, however, were not favorable to outside partners. For example, the Soviet share of an enterprise had to be at least 51 percent, and the president of the board and the managing director had to be Soviet citizens; further, joint ventures had to be isolated from the domestic market (being required to both buy from, and sell to, state enterprises); and they were placed under ordinary Soviet jurisdiction, which meant that they were obligated to follow thousands of unpublished legal acts which the foreign partner was not permitted to see. The USSR was clearly not an inviting environment for joint ventures.

This began changing in December 1988 with a decree of the USSR Council of Ministers (effective April 1, 1989) that was designed to make foreign investment, including joint ventures, more attractive to Western investors.[45] The provisions Western investors had found most objectionable in the earlier 1987 policy were eliminated. Now, up to 99 percent of a joint venture could be under foreign ownership, and the directors were not required to be Soviet citizens.

The Abalkin plan that was sponsored by Prime Minister Ryzhkov in 1990 had proposed a law on direct foreign investment, as had the Shatalin "500-Days" program—which had emphasized the need to move to a convertible currency within the 500-day period. Although these proposals were rejected, Gorbachev began implementing some of their key recommendations on foreign investment. As a result, before the end of 1990 the Soviet Union was opened to foreign investment more completely than in any period since NEP. Now foreign investors could become joint owners of almost any enterprise, and they could also establish their own businesses. The registration of joint ventures increased rapidly in Russia after that time, reaching 2,500 by the end of 1990[46] and 7,500 late in 1992.[47]

Many Soviet economists had viewed the idea of investment in the USSR economy by foreign firms as a form of colonialism,[48] and it was thus a surprise to many analysts when the USSR Supreme Soviet, following Gorbachev's lead, finally approved a new law encouraging foreign investment on July 5, 1991.[49]

Prime Minister Valentin Pavlov had set the tone for this event in a speech to the USSR Supreme Soviet on April 22 when he urged the adoption of "a comprehensive specific-purpose program" to "attract foreign capital. . . . The country needs the latest technologies, up-to-date equipment, ecologically clean production facilities, knowledge and expertise," Pavlov said. He added, "This is where the experience of the developed countries is irreplaceable."[50]

The new legislation expanded the range of foreign investors to include juridical persons, stateless persons, foreign states, and international organizations. For the first time since the 1920s, enterprises could be created with 100 percent foreign capital, and the law further specified that the legal conditions for foreign investors were to be as favorable as those for Soviet enterprises. The RSFSR Supreme Soviet passed a similar law that summer.

One of Yeltsin's first decrees after being granted special powers in early November 1991 was a measure to stimulate foreign investment. The decree[51] broadened the scope of economic activities permitted for foreign enterprises and joint ventures involving foreign partners, and it liberalized the operating procedures required of these firms. This decree underscored the importance of foreign investment for the Yeltsin government's economic reform plans, as did the text of the Economic Strategy of the Russian Government that was presented to IMF in February 1992, which also highlighted the government's desire to attract foreign capital.[52]

Yeltsin's decree of December 29, 1991, approved the Basic Provisions of the State Program for Privatization for 1992.[53] This document was sensitive to the fear of many Russians that, when property became available for privatization, foreigners would buy the best of it. They had more money to invest than Russians, it was argued, and the exchange rate of the ruble was unfavorable to Russians. Thus, it was widely believed, to allow property to be auctioned without restriction would result in "the selling off of Russia." To prevent this from happening, the decree specified that foreigners could take part in the first stage of privatization, without restrictions, only through investment competitions in which different proposals for using privatized property would be compared with one another. Foreign investors would be allowed to participate in direct auctions only with the permission of the State Property Management Committee. It was the intention of the Committee to limit foreign investment in these situations to unprofitable enterprises, firms that needed foreign supplies, and enterprises whose facilities were still under construction. Only in such cases would foreigners be able to buy the controlling share of an enterprise that was being auctioned.

Yeltsin's position about foreign investment was not universally applauded in Russia, however. To many entrepreneurs and state enterprise managers, the restrictions on foreign investment did not provide Russians enough protection. These interest groups still believed that they would be at a competitive disadvantage relative to foreigners as privatization accelerated. At a February 1992 conference of the Federation of Independent Trade Unions, the government was blamed for opening the door too widely to foreign investors. Chubais and Filippov attempted to assuage these concerns by emphasizing that, before foreigners could buy state property, they would be required to have invested capital in a different enterprise that yielded a profit, such as a joint venture. This was because *only money from the profits* of enterprises in Russia could be used to purchase state property that was being privatized; money from abroad could not be used in the privatization process.[54]

Chubais and other government planners were worried about the other side of that coin. The restrictions that the government had agreed to for foreign investors would almost certainly reduce the level of investment from abroad, and government officials knew that foreign capital was vital to Russia's economic improvement. At the conference, Chubais summarized a government proposal that was intended to address this problem—a "special investment exchange rate" that would, if adopted, permit the elimination of restrictions on foreign investment and at the same time ensure that foreigners would not benefit inordinately from the ruble's low value. The special rate would apply only to the purchase of state property with foreign currency. In these situations, the ruble would be assigned a higher-than-market value.[55]

Such discussions underscored the government's dilemma about how to balance the political necessity for the privatization program to be structured in a way that satisfied a large proportion of Russian people against the economic necessity of attracting foreign capital. Government officials who advocated legislation that would encourage foreign investment consistently emphasized the benefits that this strategy would produce at home. As Pavlov had put it in his 1991 speech in support of the USSR Law on Foreign Investment, "Who among us will be worse off if hundreds of foreign hotels and thousands of auto service centers, restaurants, and cafes are built in a year or two? Don't we have an interest in creating a strong food or medical industry?"[56]

In the summer after Pavlov's strong plea for liberalizing the government's foreign investment policy, however, we found that these arguments had not fully taken root. Overall, only 30 percent of our state-sector respondents said they had a positive attitude "about foreigners becoming stockholders or owners of Russian enterprises," and 57 percent stated that foreigners benefited more than Russians from foreign investment.[57]

The State Program for Privatization, which was approved by the Supreme Soviet in June 1992, created new investment opportunities for foreigners. It specified that foreign investors could now participate in all auctions and competitions for municipal property, with only the approval of local soviets. Contrary to the fears, and the hopes, of the two opposing sides in this dispute, there was no immediate rush from abroad to buy Russia's assets at auction.[58]

By early 1993 the value of foreign investments in Russia totaled $4 billion,[59] and further progress was being made to make investments more attractive to foreign businesspeople. The State Investment Corporation was established in February through a Yeltsin decree with the purpose of ensuring foreign investments against political instability. The government furnished gold, real estate, and other assets worth $1 billion to get the corporation under way.[60] In addition, a bill reminiscent of the NEP period was being considered in the Supreme Soviet to facilitate the creation of concessions in extractive industries.[61]

The government's foreign investment initiatives after June 1992 were an important correction of its earlier indecisiveness about how to reconcile two seemingly ill-fitting ideas: giving property to the people of Russia on the one hand, and attracting both outside capital and Western production technology on the other. One of the most positive results of the economic reform struggle in Russia from mid-1992 onward was the now clearly articulated policy of loosening restrictions on foreign participation in Russia's economy.

7

The Anatomy of Privatization:
Structure, Pace, and Scope

Introduction

The Yeltsin government's economic reform program had implications for citizens that cannot be fully explored through interviews with officials or the writings of specialists. In this and the next chapter, we utilize our interview and questionnaire data extensively to explore privatization and other dimensions of economic reform. Our 1992 four-city study was carried out at about the midpoint of the 18-month period of particular interest in this book. In the summer of 1992, there was still a widespread sense in Russia that the Yeltsin–Gaidar reforms just *might* work; relations between the Yeltsin government and the legislature had not yet soured to the point of mutual hostility. It was a good time to explore questions about economic reform with people who were familiar enough with the subject to have formed opinions, and who at that time had not been exposed to the polarizing political conflict that intensified after the summer.

The privatization decision-making process described below was still taking place when this book was completed at the end of April 1993.

The Privatization Decision-Making
Structure of the Government

According to the July 1991 Law on Privatization of State and Municipal Enterprises, the *State Property Management Commit-*

tee was charged with directing and coordinating the privatization program throughout the country.[1] Anatolii Chubais is its chairman. By law, the person filling this position should be a vice prime minister of the Russian Federation. The committee was charged with formulating and revising the State Program for Privatization, which requires approval by the Russian Supreme Soviet. Further, it was broadly mandated to organize and control the realization of the state program following its approval. The committee is responsible for preparing the proposal for dividing property among different administrative levels, from federal down to municipal.

The state committee is required to create additional *property management committees* in subsidiary governmental structures such as autonomous republics, oblasts, and larger cities (more than one million population). These lower-level committees are to make decisions about the privatization of enterprises at their level,[2] and their chairmen are vice heads of the government at that level. In addition to making privatization decisions, these lower-level property management committees propose privatization programs for property at their level. The state program specifies the types of enterprise that will be privatized during the year and the percentage in each economic sector to be privatized in every oblast. Subordinate privatization programs identify specific enterprises for privatization at each level.

A plan for privatization is developed by each enterprise slated for privatization, in collaboration with a working group appointed by the committee that is charged with preparing all necessary documents related to privatization. Enterprises of other types may also initiate privatization proceedings, whether or not they have been selected for privatization by the property management committee. In such cases, assuming that an enterprise is not prohibited from privatizing because of its type (e.g., enterprises that produced military goods were explicitly forbidden to privatize), the working group of a committee is required to begin creating a privatization plan, which will be considered by the privatization commission. A unit within an enterprise may also apply for privatization of only that unit, in which case it is separated from the larger state-sector enterprise. According to the July 1991 Law on Privatization of State and Municipal Enterprises (amended June 1992), various other legal entities may also initiate privatization actions, including vendors that supply materials to an enterprise, banks, creditors, and government agencies. In all cases in which privatization is initiated from outside a property management committee, the action must be endorsed by at least half of the affected workers in an enterprise.

The plan for privatizing an enterprise is required to be finalized within three months after the date of application (in Moscow, one month after August 1992). The property management committee's working group is legally mandated to assist in preparing the plan and in completing all necessary documents. Enterprise representatives and the working group may employ a consulting firm to help in assessing property values, determining capital requirements, and working out other details of privatization.

The privatization plan for an enterprise is submitted for approval to a *privatization commission.* These commissions are created by property management committees at each level of government to review plans for privatizing enterprises at that level. The chairman of each privatization commission is on the staff of the related property management committee. Other commissioners include members of the committee's working groups and may also be specialists with particular expertise on the subject, such as bankers, auditors, or people's deputies. Commissions are generally made up of ten to fifteen members. Their work is voluntary and unpaid, except for privatization committee members who carry out commission work as part of their regular employment.

Privatization commissions have three tasks: to determine the market value of the enterprise; to work out the privatization plan, including deciding whether or not it will be a joint-stock company; and to determine the method by which assets will be sold (at auction, through competition, or to lessors).[3] Restrictions apply to enterprises sold through competition, in order to ensure that the enterprise has a stable financial basis, that it will not quickly change the kinds of output it produces, and that it will not substantially reduce its work force.[4]

Commission decisions are usually made at a single meeting in which the privatization plan is presented and discussed, although sometimes decisions are postponed until revisions are made in plans that commissions have reviewed. Commissions do not have the option of deciding that an enterprise cannot be privatized. The only question at this point is how privatization should be carried out. Often, two or three enterprises are considered for privatization at one meeting. Depending on a commission's work load, it may meet once a month or more often. According to the July 1991 law, the plan is then submitted for approval to the appropriate soviet and to the employees of the enterprise. If the enterprise employees or the members of the soviet do not agree with a plan, it is returned to the commission for revision. Finally, the plan is reviewed by the supervising property management committee which, upon approval of the plan, authorizes the enterprise to begin reorganization under its supervision. After reorganization is completed, a certificate of ownership is awarded. The certificate is passed to the appropriate *property fund,* which is the sole authorized seller of the property being privatized.

Property funds have been created at every level of property ownership, from federal to municipal. Each soviet creates the property fund for its level, and each fund is staffed by full-time government employees. Technically, the property fund which holds the ownership certificate for an enterprise is the owner until the enterprise is sold. Depending on the privatization plan, the enterprise may be sold at auction or through competition (in which an enterprise is advertised for sale, after which potential buyers submit their proposals to buy and develop it). Any investors, including foreigners, may participate in many auctions; but in auctions for municipal property, the local soviet decides on a case-by-case basis whether foreigners can be buyers. Similarly, federal property can be sold to foreigners only with the permission of the Russian Supreme Soviet. At some auctions, only vouchers are accepted as payment for shares; some auctions deal only with cash; and others accept either cash or vouchers.

In the overall scheme of privatization decision making, property funds represent the interests of the legislature, and property management committees represent the interests of the executive branch of government, at each level. This system has built within it the potential for chronic conflict. On the one hand, these two branches of the privatization system must cooperate; but on the other, they heed different masters. There have been repeated eruptions over these conflicting interests at all levels of government.

According to the State Program for Privatization in 1992, details were elaborated which had been outlined in the July 3, 1991, legislation, On Privatization of State and Municipal Enterprises (with additions and changes approved by the Supreme Soviet on June 5, 1992). Small enterprises of fewer than 200 workers and with a value of less than one million rubles (based on the ruble value of January 1, 1992) are to be sold in their entirety, without the formation of joint-stock companies. They are to be sold at auction or through competition. Enterprises with more than 1,000 workers or valued at more than 50 million rubles are to be privatized through transformation into open joint-stock companies. Other enterprises may be privatized according to either of these two methods.

With the State Program for Privatization in 1992 approved on June 11, it also became possible for workers in an enterprise to choose from among three different ways to divide shares in the event that a joint-stock company was to be created. Only the first of these options was available before that time. This increased flexibility was a response by the government to dissatisfaction with the original provision, which had prevented an enterprise's employees from having a controlling interest in their firm. Beginning in June, enterprise employees (managers and nonmanagerial workers) could receive a total of 25 percent of an enterprise's statutory capital without charge, but these were nonvoting shares (nominal preference shares). Additionally, according to this variant, employees could buy 10 percent more of the enterprise's statutory capital with a 30 percent reduction in the face value of the shares;[5] management could purchase an additional 5 percent, at face value. Shares not distributed to employees in an enterprise were to be sold at auction by the property fund. The property fund could also be a buyer at the auction, using part of the proceeds from the sale of other government property.

Besides buying property with its receipts from privatization, the property fund was mandated to distribute dividends from the sale of enterprises in accordance with the State Program for Privatization, creating special funds for social welfare, environmental protection, support and development of urban infrastructures, and several other purposes. The soviet that oversees each fund determines how its receipts will be distributed.

If the property fund became a shareholder in an enterprise, it was mandated to represent the government at shareholder meetings; it carried responsibility and risk in proportion to its percentage of ownership. The property fund could control no more than 20 percent of the voting rights in any enterprise, although it could buy more than 20 percent of a company's shares as long as these additional shares did not include voting rights. Guidelines of the July 1991 law specified that property fund purchases should include enterprises that could advance desired national or local objectives, such as improving the environment or preventing the bankruptcy of a large enterprise that has particular significance for a city's economy.

A second option made possible with the June 1992 program was for employees to buy 51 percent of stocks at 1.7 times the face value of shares, with voting privileges. Half of the value of these shares could be paid for with privatization vouchers. Thus, unlike the first variant, here employees control their enterprises. They would not receive any stocks at a discount, however; and they were not permitted to pay for their shares in installments. The remaining shares were to be auctioned by the property fund.

For enterprises valued at between 1 million and 50 million

rubles (as of December 1991) and employing more than 200 workers, a third choice was available. For middle-sized enterprises in financial difficulty, this third alternative might be especially attractive. If a particular group within such an enterprise—the management, or the engineers, for example—agreed to assume responsibility for managing the enterprise and preventing bankruptcy, they could acquire the right to buy 20 percent of its statutory capital at face value if at least two-thirds of the employees agreed. These were voting shares. To gain the right to buy these shares, they had to agree to take the responsibilities specified for one year. If this third option were chosen, enterprise personnel could buy an additional 20 percent of the enterprise with a 30 percent reduction in face value (voting shares). They could pay for them through installments over a three-year period.

Among enterprises that had chosen one of the three privatization options by April 1993, only 5 percent had opted for the third variant. Enterprises were nearly equally split in choosing between the first two options (45 and 50 percent, respectively).[6] Among the largest enterprises, however, privatization with 51 percent ownership by enterprise personnel was nearly twice as popular as the other options by December 1992.[7]

Privatization Decision-Makers and Enterprise Personnel on the Pace and Objectives of Privatization

Our four-city research suggests that, superficially, the 1992 privatization program was supported more decisively by government decision-makers (DMs) than by enterprise personnel, as might be expected; but in probing for additional details, we found that DMs typically were more reluctant than work-force respondents to favor an *accelerated* transition to nonstate enterprise. The "letter" of the privatization program was thus more strongly favored by DMs as a group than the larger objective, articulated by the program's architects, of moving forward with privatization as rapidly as possible. Enterprise personnel, on the other hand, supported the concept of privatization more completely than they supported the specific privatization plan developed by the government.

Eighty-five percent of DMs told us that they agreed "completely" or "for the most part" with the government's 1992 program. Only 9 percent said that they did not support the program. Interestingly, however, DMs were much more likely than enterprise personnel to favor the present pace (21 percent of DMs) or to wish that privatization would proceed more slowly (24 percent of DMs; see Table B–7.1 for additional detail). Why did nearly half of DMs not want privatization to proceed more quickly? Suggestive answers can be found in the responses of DMs to our question about the negative effects of privatization. Their most prevalent concerns were unemployment, an undesirable increase in social inequality, the transfer of property "into the wrong hands" (especially the mafia), and possible social instability growing out of these changes. These were the main negative effects mentioned by DMs in all four cities and were more salient to them than other negative effects such as price increases, heightened crime, or reorganization of privatized enterprises to produce different kinds of goods (a frequently mentioned objection in the mass media).

Do these perspectives reflect a tacit disapproval of privatization among a substantial proportion of DMs, or are their assessments simply a reflection of the difficulties presented by privatization procedures? Many analysts have argued that economic reform in Russia is being hampered by government workers determined to thwart the Yeltsin program—which privatization decision-makers were in a very good position to do in 1992. Their jobs made them gatekeepers of privatization, and it was within their authority to erect a wide variety of barriers to the timely privatization of an enterprise. Further, in Moscow, although not in the other three cities we studied, a slight majority of DMs were professional bureaucrats and former party functionaries (52 percent).[8] Analysts have often suggested that these Communist Party carryovers may have both ideological and career-related reasons to stand in the way of privatization.

Our findings gave us no basis, however, for questioning the commitment of most DMs in 1992 to carrying out the privatization procedures in their charge. The most compelling evidence we have on this subject comes from responses to a series of questions about the likely social effects of privatization. DMs were even more likely than enterprise personnel to expect positive consequences of privatization (Table B–7.2). Although they were somewhat more prone than others to anticipate crime to increase and relationships to be depersonalized with the shift to a market economy, it does not follow that these assessments reflect a negative bias about privatization. They are, in fact, consistent with the second alternative offered above as a possible reason why DMs were less likely than others to favor an accelerated pace in the privatization program. Greater experience with the issues produces more thoughtful conclusions about both the timetables for privatization and the social outcomes of the process. It is notable that, although almost all DMs expected income inequality to increase with a shift to a market economy, only three out of ten saw that change as negative (Table B–7.2).

Many DMs also gave pragmatic reasons for opposing accelerated privatization—reasons that were tied to their day-to-day work. Conflicts among the personnel of privatizing enterprises were commonplace, they told us. For example, individual units of an enterprise sometimes wanted to privatize independently of the larger firm—a legal but administratively awkward procedure, especially if it was also being proposed that the entire enterprise privatize as a whole. Changing procedures also created problems for DMs. During one of our interviews with a member of the Moscow Property Management Committee, a representative of a gasoline station came to complain that his coworkers had petitioned to buy their leased enterprise—an action that was permitted by the government program. Before the purchase was initiated, however, the Moscow Property Management Committee had decided to auction all gasoline stations, whether they were leased or not. The workers in this particular station were upset about losing an opportunity they believed to be rightfully theirs, and an already overworked committee staff had to intervene.

Often the conflicts DMs had to resolve resulted from ambiguous or inconsistent regulations. The Moscow program was different in key respects from the state program, and power struggles involving different interpretations of these sets of regulations were frequent. "Our legislation is so imperfect," one commissioner of transport burst out at a meeting to consider privatizing a taxi enterprise, "that regulations can be interpreted in diametrically opposed ways! And every month, new bylaws and instructions are issued."

Many DMs wanted to slow the pace of privatization so that they would have more time to address the issues they encountered daily in privatization cases. As a member of the Moscow Committee put it, "everything is too complicated, and the process of privatization is not under control. . . . Sometimes when we are in the process of preparing privatization papers we receive a new instruction, and all the papers become invalid! Now that Popov [the former mayor of Moscow] has resigned, I'm sure that new decrees and instructions will be issued for Moscow; and they are certain to contradict the old ones."

The Problem of Corruption

To argue that DMs were committed to privatization is not to say that they were immune to corruption. As privatization proceeded in 1992 and 1993, the DMs' authority placed them in a unique position to control scarce and often desirable resources. Under the old system, Viktor Mironov points out, the administrative apparatus controlled everything and apparatchiks could get as much as they wanted for their own use. Mironov, as head of the independent Moscow Inspection Committee, which is responsible for auditing government decisions, has extensive experience with patterns of power in bureaucracies. "The main task of our committee," Mironov explained in a published interview, "is to monitor privatization decision making in Moscow to help prevent obstacles to economic reform." With the creation of the privatization program, Mironov stated, a new field was created for administrative profit-taking. Everything in this new field depends on the decisions of committees and commissions.

In his interview, Mironov provided details to illustrate his general point. In one case the Committee identified thirteen counts of illegal activity by the head of a single property management committee in one Moscow district. A member of a privatization committee in another district, who was also a deputy of the Moscow Soviet, was arrested for accepting bribes from commercial firms that wanted to purchase highly profitable state enterprises. The committee member was in charge of those privatization cases. The bribe payments had the intended effect. In a third district, Mironov explained, a privatization committee was found to have repeatedly delayed the privatization of profitable enterprises until commercial buyers, who presumably would pay bribes, could be found—although the employees had applied to purchase these enterprises themselves, as they were entitled to under the law. "Cases like these create the basis for public charges that corruption is flourishing in the structures that deal with privatization. Sometimes the rumors exaggerate the reality," he concluded, "but we have discovered a chain of officials at all levels of city power who are benefiting themselves and each other through privatization."[9]

Our primary and secondary data paint a consistent overall picture of government decision-makers' roles in the privatization process from its inception until early 1993. Most of them did not seem to be trying to obstruct privatization or to impede it because of ideological opposition. Many carried out their task of supervising the privatization process with integrity and dedication. Even most of those who acted differently were not working *against privatization,* but rather working *for themselves.*

A concern of many analysts is the phenomenon widely known as *nomenklaturnaia privatizatsiia,* or privatization benefiting primarily people well placed in the former bureaucratic structure of the Soviet Union. These members of the *nomenklatura*, well trained in strategies to extract maximum personal benefit from the old command system, had advantages of both position and knowledge over most other Russian citizens. With the advent of economic reform, the *nomenklatura* quickly moved to capitalize on the new opportunities created by the very reforms that were intended to undo the traditional system of privileges. Having monopolized power in the command structures, now they were seen as threatening to control a vastly disproportionate share of the nation's economic wealth and productive capacity. Andrei Grachev put this concern graphically: "The *nomenklatura* virus has demonstrated amazing vitality. It is neutral to ideology. The *nomenklatura* can be communist, anticommunist, and even 'democratic' with equal success."[10]

Leaders of the reform effort were also concerned about this problem. Gaidar, for example, warned in a speech to the Supreme Soviet in October 1992 that uncontrolled *nomenklatura* privatization, which he labeled "*nomenklatura* piratization" (*prikhvatizatsiia*), was rampant in Russia and threatened to intensify.[11]

The issue for critics was that the structure of the reform program, as they saw it, actually facilitated *nomenklatura* privatization and corruption of various types. This happened, they said, because positions of authority in the new system, as well as the old, offered tempting opportunities to turn superior knowledge and extensive personal connections into ownership of the very best enterprises that were being privatized—the most productive and most profitable.

Obviously, neither authoritarian nor democratic governments have solved the problem of corruption among government officials. Charges of power abuse can be used either to delegitimate or to improve a government. Valerii Zorkin, the chief justice of the Russian Constitutional Court, seemed to be no friend of the government's privatization program during the March 1993 special session of the Congress, when his public support of the old Soviet constitution dealt a stunning blow to Yeltsin's drive to revise his reform program. "We are moving at a very high speed toward a mafia state," Zorkin had objected a few months earlier, "and the privatization procedures being carried out until now constitute a legal form of *nomenklatura* privatization."[12] Petr Filippov, on the other hand, is a committed reformer who chairs the Privatization Committee of the Russian Supreme Soviet. In our interview with him during the summer of 1992, he repeatedly demonstrated his strong support of the government's reform program. Filippov also knows the dark side of administrative power. Writing in *Izvestiia* the week after we interviewed him, he discussed a variety of flaws in established privatization procedures, focusing especially on the prevalence of large bribes and the potential for abuse in the centralized structure of privatization planning. Yet the theme of Filippov's critique was how to refine the privatization program, not how to discredit it. "But we need to carry out the reform!" he concluded.[13]

General and Specific Support for Privatization

An overwhelming majority of our respondents in every category supported *the idea* of privatization, although substantially fewer agreed with the government's 1992 program. In addition to alternative types of privatization, respondents were presented with the choice, "There is no need for privatization." No DMs selected this answer, and only 12 percent of enterprise employees chose it—most of these, by far, in the state sector and among the less skilled workers (Table B–7.3). Most enterprise personnel, rather than questioning privatization, wanted it to proceed more quickly.

If enterprise owners and directors were less supportive than DMs of the government's 1992 privatization program, an overwhelming majority supported it at least "to some extent." Support dropped sharply, however, in lower occupational categories (Table B–7.4). Our findings suggest that the diminishing capacity of the state to support unprofitable enterprises was a development not lost on state sector directors. Thus, nearly nine out of ten state directors supported the government's privatization program at least to some extent, and more than six out of ten believed that privatization should be speeded up (Table B–7.1).

This support produced positive effects in the market. A panel study of 120 middle-sized enterprises found that, whereas in February, 63 percent of these enterprises reported a growing stock of unsold output, by December, that percentage had dropped to 25. A significant factor in this change, according to economist Vladislav Belianov, was the "adaptation of some enterprises to the conditions of market relations." Many of these enterprises had been privatized during the year. Belianov's research team found that an increasing number of directors had developed markets for their output themselves—thus becoming less dependent on the state distribution system.[14]

By September 1992, according to a nationwide study by the Center for Public Opinion and Market Research (CPO), enterprise directors were markedly more supportive of economic reform than the general population was. When asked, "Is it necessary to continue the economic reforms," 79 percent of directors answered affirmatively, while overall, only 53 percent said yes.[15]

Why were state directors so positive about privatization? The Yeltsin government's program "will transform directors of state property into real owners," economist Efrem Maiminas insisted. "It would be naive to expect them to oppose such a possibility."[16]

The Special Problems of Military Production Enterprises

Maiminas was not speaking of military directors. Military production enterprises had posed a thorny problem for the Soviet Union since the late 1980s; and with the collapse of the USSR, most of that problem became Russia's, since more than 70 percent of the Soviet Union's defense industries were located there.

It was obvious at the end of the 1980s that the halcyon days of the military production establishment, which housed the Soviet Union's most technologically advanced production facilities and employed many of its best-trained specialists, were over. Never before had there been huge cuts in weapons procurement, and the widespread cancellation of orders for a broad array of military equipment produced panic in the economic sector that had long been the most secure. In 1989 the Military Industrial Commission (VPK) developed a plan for the conversion of many military production facilities to civilian purposes. "Dual-use" technologies were emphasized in this proposal. Priority was to be given to electronics equipment, civilian communications and transport, and other nonmilitary items whose production could take advantage of the technology already highly developed in defense industries. Had there been no coup, Gorbachev might well have adopted the proposal. Had the coup succeeded, the VPK plan might have become the keystone of Soviet economic reform. For the military establishment, the course of events in August 1991 produced the worst-case outcome. Coordination in this complex and highly sophisticated industrial machine was completely disrupted.

With the disappearance of the principal coordinating mechanisms for the military production enterprises—the VPK, the State Planning Committee (Gosplan), the State Supply Committee (Gossnab), and the Communist Party of the Soviet Union—military production industries were thrown into confusion with no obvious means for rejuvenation. With orders slashed, many talented personnel left for other positions; and with coordinating structures no longer in existence, vital supplies and components often became unavailable almost overnight. Thus, according to military analyst Stephen Meyer at the Massachusetts Institute of Technology, "Since the beginning of 1992 every defense industrial facility has teetered on the brink of collapse."[17]

To have any hope of effectively utilizing a substantial portion of its productive and technical capabilities, what the military production sphere needed was painstakingly focused, centralized oversight. What it got, Meyer notes, was "organizational inertia."[18] Realizing that they could not survive for long in such a climate of inattention, many defense-related industries developed their own coping strategies. These were suboptimal at best and added to the dislocations that were commonplace in Russia's economy in 1993.

Meyer provides several examples. The Irkutsk Aircraft Production Association, which had been a production and repair facility for jet planes, began producing aluminum dishes, children's toys, and camping equipment. The Leningrad Optical Association, which formerly employed 25,000 workers, became part of a joint venture that kept fewer than 900 employees.[19] A Nizhnii Novgorod facility that formerly produced advanced insulation materials for space exploration was retooled to turn out ash trays.

Since all military production enterprises were excluded from the privatization programs for both 1992 and 1993, they could not reasonably hope for a quick bailout through privatization. For many of these directors, the only solution, at least in the short run, was state credits, to make it possible to continue production as they searched with little outside help for conversion possibilities. The Sokol aircraft plant in Nizhnii Novgorod, whose principal product had been MiG–29 and MiG–31 jet planes, began making amphibious aircraft for civilian uses in February 1993. Many other production facilities for military aircraft were simultaneously undergoing similar conversions.[20] These enterprises, long accustomed to assured demand from the state for their output, were now on their own, without benefit of market studies to guide their conversion decisions. Thus one of the world's most technologically advanced production systems tried to adapt to a rapidly changing environment.

When Gaidar began moving to decrease state subsidies in early 1992, he did not systematically account for the different economic situations of military and nonmilitary production enterprises. Early in the year, he implemented across-the-board cuts. Large military production enterprises could not have survived long under this approach. The most striking decline in production during 1992 was in the military sphere, which experienced a 23 percent slide from its 1991 level.[21] It is not surprising, then, that the strongest supporters of this interest group in the parliament, the "directors' lobby" and the Civic Union, urged credits from the Central Bank to these large enterprises.

In the spring of 1993, military-industrial directors proposed that the state provide them the ruble equivalent of $150 billion (R60 trillion) to facilitate conversion of their enterprises for civilian purposes. Other analysts were arguing that an infusion of the same amount of money into the nonmilitary sector would result in greater benefits for the country, including a broader array of consumer goods. Economist Nikolai Shmelev proposed that most military production enterprises be closed and that their former employees be paid until they could be retrained and secure private-sector jobs. Shmelev contended that his proposal would cost less than the policy of continuing to provide subsidies to huge and unprofitable enterprises, and that it would stimulate the incipient post–Cold War economy.[22]

Privatization Decision Making at the Enterprise Level

One problem with the privatization effort in 1992 was that privatization was well under way before details of the program were concretely fixed and the program approved. Yeltsin's December 1991 decree had only sketched out the principal features of the 1992 program. Many details could not be specified at that time because they had not been worked out; and debate about how privatization should be implemented continued right up to the time that the Supreme Soviet approved the 1992 program on June 11.

Even when the program was published, its complexity and ambiguity of several details made it difficult for many to understand the program's implications for their own enterprises. The result was that, a full year after general procedures for privatization had been specified by the Russian Supreme Soviet and six months after Yeltsin's decree outlining a privatization program for the year, half or more in each nonmanagerial occupational category told us that, although they had heard about the program, they did not know much about it. Among skilled workers, for example, only 8 percent said they were "very familiar" with the main regulations of the 1992 privatization program. The percentages were even lower among clerks, technicians, and unskilled workers. Clearly, then, privatization decisions were being made without full understanding of the program by a large percentage of the people who were supposed to be key participants in the process—the workers. As occupational level declined, uncertainty about the optimal pace of privatization increased substantially (Table B–7.1).

Many enterprise personnel who were familiar with the government's initiative had specific reasons for dissatisfaction with it. A large proportion of workers had a sense of being largely excluded from privatization decision making. According to the RSFSR Law on the Privatization of State and Municipal Enterprises (in effect since 1991), although privatization proceedings could be initiated from any of several sources, the actual privatization application could legally be considered by the appropriate property management committee *only* if it had been signed by at least half of an enterprise's employees. Once the privatization commission approved an enterprise's plan, it had to be endorsed by both the local soviet and the enterprise employees.

That was the law, but in practice, enterprises were being privatized without a clear mandate from workers. If a state enterprise director decided on a method of privatization for the firm, workers, fearing reprisals or loss of their jobs, were often afraid to oppose the ideas of the director, which made open discussion about alternatives practically impossible. A privatization method that would be in the interest of workers could therefore be ignored in favor of one that better fit the interests of administrators.[23]

This practice was sometimes justified by the widespread belief among elites that workers lack knowledge of pertinent issues related to privatization. Several administrators of the privatization program explained to us that the management of enterprises often had to make the important decisions about privatization because workers were poorly informed and thus were incapable of making critical privatization decisions. "They aren't ready for independent market activity," a Moscow property management committee member stated. Another responded, "Workers are buying their enterprises in formal terms, but actually the directors are the buyers." It may not be surprising, then, that in the privatized enterprises we studied, less than one-fourth of directors believed that workers had been the primary privatization decision-makers, and notably fewer nonmanagerial workers thought they had been (Table B-7.5). A substantial proportion—more than half in the less skilled occupational categories—believed that workers had little influence in the privatization process.

Privatization of Agricultural Land

"Plots of land used by citizens for a period of ten years become the citizens' property." So read the Shakhrai amendment to a resolution of the RSFSR Congress of People's Deputies. It signaled the reversal of more than six decades of Soviet agrarian policy. By a vote of 602 to 369, the deputies established private ownership of land as the legal equivalent of state, collective, and cooperative ownership. December 3, 1990, was a historic day for Russia. "Never before in all their history, not counting some very brief periods, have those who till the land received such rights," said an *Izvestiia* article reporting the event.[24]

"The main principle of the agrarian reform is voluntariness, with no coercion or compulsion," Boris Yeltsin had said when, as chairman of the RSFSR Supreme Soviet, he introduced the proposed legislation.[25] The voluntary acquisition of farmland for private use was to be a two-stage process. First, the legal status of state and collective farms would be changed, which would permit individuals to then apply, in the second stage, for private ownership of these large holdings. Originally, the Congress specified that state and collective farm personnel should decide within two years whether they would prefer that their agricultural units be cooperatives, joint-stock companies, or collective associations.[26] The term for re-registration was later prolonged by the Supreme Soviet to February 1, 1993.[27]

Agricultural land, then, became Russia's first object of massive reallocation of property from state into private hands. After December 1990, when a collective or state farm re-registered with a different organizational structure, all members of the agricultural enterprise, including pensioners, social workers, and teachers associated with the enterprise, became shareholders. They were entitled to receive, for their personal use, a portion of the enterprise property—with the stipulation that they would use the property for farm purposes. There was no charge for their share of property. If a shareholder should decide to move or did not want to engage in farm work, the property could be sold or leased to another member of the enterprise. It could *not* be sold to an outsider, however.[28]

In keeping with the 1990 legislation, special committees were created in each oblast for the purpose of facilitating the establishment of private farms in their region. The land for private farms was to be taken from state and collective farm holdings. When a person who was not already a farm worker wanted to become a farmer, the law specified that application should be made to a local soviet. It would be decided at the local level whether or not to approve each application and, if one were approved, where the land should come from to create the new private farm. Farm workers could apply to own land through the administrative office of their farm if it had been changed to a joint-stock company, a collective association, or a cooperative. (Ownership according to the 1990 legislation did not entail the right to sell farmland to other individuals.) On state and collective farms, however, workers were generally not allowed to own land, but they could lease it.

In early 1992, however, directors of state and collective farms objected so strongly to the re-registration and reorganization program that a government decree issued on April 6 added another variant to the alternatives specified earlier. Now, state and collective farm personnel could also choose to retain their existing legal status.[29]

At the end of 1992, of the 32,000 state farms, collective farms, and other agricultural enterprises in Russia, 50.4 percent had been converted into another form of ownership under provisions of the December 1990 legislation.[30] There were about 184,000 private farms (owned and leased),[31] which comprised more than 3 percent of formerly state and collective farmland.[32] Seventy-three percent of these new farms were created during 1992. The average private farm had three workers (usually in the same family). About 500,000 people worked on private farms at the end of 1992.[33]

The reluctance of many agricultural directors to proceed quickly with privatization was reflected in the attitudes of agricultural workers at the time the December 1990 legislation was approved. An Institute of Sociology survey in four republics that was completed early in 1991 found that only 18 percent of collective and state farm personnel planned to leave their enterprises, and a mere 12 percent believed that private farming should be the principal form of agriculture.[34] In another study of farm workers in the RSFSR, 40 percent said they opposed the private ownership of land.[35] Some of the hesitation among rural people to pursue private farming must be attributed to their uncertainty about the permanence of this new possibility. The Institute of Sociology study found that only 17 percent were confident that the December 1990 legislation would not be repealed.

There were probably other reasons for this reluctance. In a January 1993 interview, Prime Minister Chernomyrdin noted, "Peasants are not rushing to take land, because they know how difficult the work is. But I have to ask all others who *would* like to take land, 'Do you know anything about it?'"[36] Economist Leonid Abalkin pointed out that private farming has no deep cultural roots in Russia. The land reform initiated by Prime Minister Petr Stolypin under Nicholas II, "with very active government support," persuaded only 9 percent of peasants to acquire private farm land in a ten-year period. The accustomed pattern of communal agriculture remained largely intact.[37]

In the early 1990s, urban Russians were more supportive of private farming than farm workers were. A national survey conducted throughout the USSR by CPO at the end of 1990 found that 70 percent believed that agricultural land should be available for private ownership, and in October 1991 this idea was supported by 91 percent of respondents. In a CPO study of only Russia in February 1992, 48 percent thought that the privatization of land would help solve the problem of food shortages.[38] A study in Moscow and St. Petersburg that same month found that 73 percent believed private ownership of land would help lead Russia out of its economic crisis.[39]

Yet even among urban dwellers, there was no consensus about the desirability of large-scale farm privatization. We found in the summer of 1992 that even younger respondents, who generally expressed the most liberal views about privatization, tended to be reluctant about a wholesale transfer of farmland into private hands. Although younger respondents were more than twice as likely as older ones to favor massive transfer of farmland to individuals, even among people 18 to 25 years old, fewer than half thought that farmland should be owned primarily by private individuals. Forty-six percent favored a mix of state and private ownership of farmland (Table B–7.6).

In December 1992 the Constitution was amended to permit privately held land plots, including the structures on them, to be sold by their owners to other individuals as long as their use was not changed. These plots of land were usually the sites of dachas and village houses, sales of which had actually been common since the Brezhnev era; the amendment simply made this practice legal. *Farmland*, however, was another matter. When the Supreme Soviet enacted the new law, the legislators emphasized that agricultural land was *not* included in the liberalization.[40] There were advantages to the new law. Land plots could now become collateral for loans, for example. But the long-standing Soviet idea that farmland should not be bought and sold at will was still intact.

We find it fascinating that in early 1993 the principal proponents of more rapid privatization in the agricultural sphere were urban dwellers, not farmers. In a March 1993 national survey conducted in small towns and villages throughout Russia, as well as in larger cities, only 25 percent of village people said that they would *not* want to return to the conditions before 1991—that is, to the period before the beginning of radical reforms and the opportunity to privatize land. Only 42 percent of the village respondents said that they believed that it was "necessary to continue economic reform."[41]

For many radical democrats, the issue of land ownership was paramount in 1992 and 1993. They had long criticized the inefficiency they thought was characteristic of collective farming, and their sensitivity to the injustices and injuries wrought by Stalin's forced collectivization motivated them to want those wrongs to be rectified. After the watershed December 1990 legislation, they objected that private farmers had to work their land for ten years before they actually owned it, and that if they later wanted to sell it, there were severe restrictions on who the buyer could be. (The land could be inherited, however, by relatives.) Even Mikhail Gorbachev believed in early 1993 that his most serious mistake was in not beginning the reform process with agriculture;[42] and he maintained that the most important priority in Russia should be to expand private ownership of farmland.[43] Further, radical democrats often insisted, if the centralized agricultural system could be dismantled, the legacy of communist control could finally be transcended.

Having land, however, is only one of the conditions necessary for successful private farming. A late 1992 study by the State Statistical Committee of 78,000 Russian private farmers found that, for 80 percent of the respondents, the most critical problem in working their farms was "the extremely high price of equipment and building materials." The average price agricultural workers and enterprises received for their farm products increased by 8 times in 1992 over 1991, but the average price of industrial products increased 18 times during the same period. Some price increases were even greater. Gasoline cost 35 times more at the end of 1992 than it had a year earlier. Consequently, two-thirds of the farmers reported that they could not afford to buy equipment, fertilizers, gasoline, and even grain they needed to plant.[44] Obtaining loans was another major problem, and farmers complained that interest rates were too high.

One in five private farmers stated that they had also encountered external obstacles to privatizing farmland—problems with directors of agricultural enterprises and local officials, as well as negative attitudes among the local population. The literature on this subject includes a significant amount of material suggesting that local opposition to private farming has been a major impediment in some places.[45] An *Izvestiia* report underscores the larger significance of the legislation that established a new legal basis for private farming, even though resistance to this development lingers among some of the populace: "In some places this possession of one's own share of land and production equipment is actual while in others it is hypothetical, *but the division has taken place.* . . . Thus, a huge amount of land now no longer belongs to the state."[46]

Housing

On July 4, 1991, the RSFSR Supreme Soviet approved the Law on Privatization of the Housing Stock.[47] The aim of this law was to make it possible for citizens to own their dwellings, and to buy and sell them freely. The law mainly affected state and municipal urban housing, since private ownership of houses in rural areas was already widespread. Housing not owned by the state or municipalities, such as apartments for personnel of collective farms and production enterprises, was not covered by the legislation.

According to the law, the apartments where people lived could be privatized for no charge if the apartment size did not exceed stated restrictions based on the number of members in a family. The per-person allocation was 18 square meters, with an additional 9 square meters for a family. These allocations could be increased by local soviets. If an apartment was larger than the allocated size, a charge would usually be assessed to cover the overage.

At the end of 1992 there were 32.5 million housing units eligible for privatization in Russia, 8 percent of which had already been privatized according to the July 1991 legislation. The number privatized in 1992 was 21 times the number privatized during the last six months of 1991; but although this rate of increase was impressive, the total number of privatized units was not.[48] There clearly was no rush toward home ownership.

Two months after the housing law was approved, CPO found in a study conducted throughout Russia (not the USSR) that housing privatization was supported by 48 percent of respondents. Only 15 percent had a negative reaction. The other 37 percent did not have a firm opinion about the question. When asked whether they intended to privatize their own apartments, only 28 percent answered affirmatively. CPO concluded that a fear of high taxation was one reason for the general reluctance to privatize. Many people worried that the government might some day reverse its position and reclaim the apartments that had been privatized. Respondents also often wondered if they would be able to arrange for necessary apartment repairs on their own.[49]

The idea of private home ownership was not becoming noticeably more attractive over time. Only 22 percent of the respondents in our summer 1992 study believed that most urban housing should be owned by individuals; a substantial majority believed that a preferable pattern would be a mix of state and individual ownership. Significantly, although age has a strong effect on the distribution of responses, even among younger respondents, only about one-fourth favored primarily individual ownership (Table B–7.6).

To increase the appeal of privatizing dwellings, the Russian Supreme Soviet on December 23, 1992, approved a law eliminating several restrictions that had been written into the July 1991 law; and it specified that, no matter how large the dwelling, people could privatize the place where they lived without charge. Now, property owned by state farms[50] and urban enterprises could be privatized, as well as apartments that had been registered as historical monuments. Some kinds of dwellings remained excluded from potential privatization, for example, dormitories, housing in closed military towns, and housing in need of major renovation.

Early in 1993, privatization of housing was proceeding at a brisk pace at least in Moscow and St. Petersburg. In mid-February 1993 the 500,000th apartment was privatized in Moscow, and officials were predicting that a majority of Moscow's three million apartments would be privately owned by the end of the year.[51] For the state and for municipalities, privatization of housing had the distinct advantage of transferring responsibility for the cost of routine maintenance and repair into private hands. While allowing authorities to save money, privatization also provided them a means to continue collecting at least as much revenue through taxation as they had previously received from rents. Apartment rents had always been very low, although they began increasing significantly in 1992; and to convince people to privatize, officials promised that taxes on privatized dwellings would not be higher than rental costs. The only obstacle to more rapid acceleration of this process was most people's reluctance to embrace the idea of home ownership.

The 1993 Privatization Program

The government's privatization program for 1993 was approved by Yeltsin's ministers on November 30, 1992, and presented to the Congress of People's Deputies in December. The priority of the 1993 program was "people's privatization" (*narodnaia privatizatsiia*)—the distribution of state property for vouchers. Of all the property to be privatized in 1993, about 23 percent would be sold for money at auctions; the other 77 percent would be redeemed with vouchers.

According to the State Property Management Committee, 1993 would be the most critical year for "building a fair people's capitalism." As many people as possible would be involved in voucher auctions for state property.[52]

In an *Izvestiia* interview, Chubais noted that the previous stage of privatization involving primarily small enterprises (*malaia privatizatsiia*) had been simple compared to the second stage just getting under way. The first stage went so smoothly, and so many people were interested in buying these enterprises, Chubais said, that "privatization was faster than it should have been." Because most privatized small enterprises had been municipal property and had been sold for money, local governments had received part of the profit from their sale, and that made local authorities eager to facilitate the privatization process. "Now," Chubais warned, "they won't get anything but problems [as large enterprises are auctioned for vouchers]. They will even lose money to organize the auctions. . . . Our opponents," he continued, "have already spotted this problem. . . ."[53]

The 1993 program included a provision permitting enterprises to buy the land on which their firms were situated in exchange for vouchers. Also, workers could now convert their nonvoting shares into voting shares, after all shares of an enterprise were distributed. This change was a significant concession to enterprise employees who had complained that, if they chose the privatization option of receiving shares free of charge, the free shares would not carry voting rights. The government hoped this modification would encourage enterprises to privatize more quickly.

The Congress did not approve the 1993 program, demanding substantial modification of the proposal. But Yeltsin's government was not willing to bargain. "There won't be any basic changes in our approach to privatization," Chubais emphasized. "We are absolutely against it. Now, it isn't just a theoretical disagreement between Associate Professor Chubais and full professors with a different point of view. The course of privatization has already been approved, and it is unfolding fairly well. To change today's procedure would be to cheat millions of people who believe in it, and who are playing according to rules which were approved by the government and the same parliament which we have now."[54]

When asked whether Chernomyrdin agreed with the proposal for the 1993 program, Chubais responded (in January), "The state program for 1993 will be presented to the parliament by Chernomyrdin's government. . . . We discussed the program point-by-point with Viktor Stepanovich [Chernomyrdin], and— I'm being very honest—we did not find any important points of disagreement.

"I know what the opposition will be like," Chubais continued. "Today, no one in his right mind would admit to opposing privatization, even if he is a Communist Party member three times over. That strain has entirely disappeared. Opponents will insist that they are definitely in favor of privatization 'with all their hearts,' but the only questions they will raise will concern what to privatize and according to what terms. Most of the opposition are people whose slogan is, 'Priority to workers!' In reality, however, their political aim is not to defend workers at all. Workers don't need such a defense, and they aren't asking for it. The aim behind this position is to stop the privatization process."[55]

On the eve of the April referendum, however, the government modified its 1993 privatization program proposal. Two objectives guided the revision. First, the government wanted to protect the program in the event of an unfavorable referendum vote. They thus hoped to preserve the privatization program even if the executive branch lost in its confrontation with the legislature. Second, privatization planners were worried about escalating regional resistance to the program. An increasing number of regional officials had halted voucher auctions in their jurisdictions. Often, these officials were not stopping privatization; rather, they were reformulating privatization procedures according to their own interests. With its modifications, the government believed that this trend toward decentralized privatization decision making could be reversed.

In order to make privatization a more attractive source of income for localities, the revised program included an increased emphasis on "small privatization." According to the revised plan, the privatization of retail enterprises, services, and public catering would be completed in 1993. All revenue from this privatization would be turned over to local authorities. None would be shared with federal authorities—a deviation from the procedure in 1992. It was hoped that, with this financial incentive for "small privatization," the privatization of large production enterprises would also be viewed more favorably.[56] Of the 6,500 large enterprises slated for privatization in 1993, about 4,000 had been transformed into joint-stock companies by the end of April—the first step toward "people's privatization" through voucher auctions. At this pace, the government believed, additional incentives might be necessary to keep the process moving—to prevent it from being stopped before it could be completed. Local authorities in several oblasts had already postponed voucher auctions by April, and the government wanted to discourage this development.[57]

Opposition Mounts to the Program

By the end of April 1993, about 68,000 small enterprises had been privatized in retail, public catering, and consumer services, and the privatization of large enterprises was well under way. Voucher auctions were being held throughout Russia, and shares in about a thousand enterprises had been sold before May 1. Overall, about one-fourth of all state enterprises either had completed the privatization process or were in the process of being privatized. Yet the voucher program, which was the heart of the privatization effort, continued to draw fire from many opponents. An important opposition bloc was composed of labor groups and organizations of industrial directors, in concert with like-minded political groups. Their continuing objective was to secure more privileges for workers in privatization. Another source of emerging opposition could be found among local authorities. We had found in mid-1992 that administrative decision-makers seemed generally to support privatization; the growing list of localities where officials were refusing to conduct voucher auctions was alarming to privatization planners in early 1993.

To Chubais, the loss of support for privatization at the local level could be explained as a reaction to the program's *successes.* Local authorities "are losing their control," Chubais suggested.[58] "The obvious success of privatization helped to intensify the political struggle";[59] and, "Today they are stopping voucher auctions, and tomorrow they will try to get property back in the hands of oblast soviets."[60]

From the inception of the privatization effort, the State Property Management Committee had enjoyed virtual autonomy in establishing privatization procedures, deciding what types of property would be privatized, setting the schedule for privatization, and creating procedures for privatization decision making at all administrative levels. Chubais's committee thus controlled most of the property in Russia—from production enterprises to retail establishments to apartment buildings and land. They had created the privatization proposals which, after approval by the parliament, served as the blueprint for Russia's privatization program. Then they exercised day-to-day authority in determining how privatization of the country's vast property holdings would be carried out.

Early in 1993, resistance from other government officials to the extensive power of Chubais's committee became more pronounced. The parliament had frequently complained that the State Property Management Committee was keeping too much power to itself. Moreover, government agencies that were affected by the privatization process wanted more control at the level of decision making. In mid-April, the vice premier in charge of industrial management, Georgii Khizha, proposed that government ministries most directly concerned with specific production enterprises be empowered to negotiate privatization plans instead of Chubais's committee. According to the proposal, the ministries would not only be involved in privatization decision making, but they would also retain a measure of control over enterprise activity even after privatization was completed.

On April 20, Chubais stated in a press conference that "several governmental departments want to take charge of state property. If they manage to have their way, it will be the end of the privatization process."[61]

By making this point, Chubais was struggling to keep the established privatization procedures intact as opponents closed in from all sides. And now Chernomyrdin, who had earlier seemed positive about the program, began articulating a different position about both privatization and the broader plan for economic reform that the government had earlier presented. Chernomyrdin had decided that fewer enterprises should be privatized in 1993 than had been originally planned. Insisting that he favored privatization, he explained that he was "against foolishness in privatization."[62] He now wanted to maintain a strong state presence in several broad areas—especially in the spheres of energy, food, science, and social services.[63] These spheres include a substantial proportion of the entire economy; and although Chernomyrdin argued that he was proposing only temporary retrenchment, critics maintained that these changes would halt privatization in the targeted fields.[64]

By April, then, support among top government officials for the government's privatization program had been seriously compromised. Chubais's committee was scheduled to make a formal presentation of its revised privatization proposal in early May, but the storm clouds gathering both within government and among outspoken critics did not bode well for this, the only clearly successful component of Gaidar's 1992 economic reform program. Even Yeltsin's most optimistic supporters were forced to concede that the near-term prospects for the privatization initiative were not good.

Not all of the heavy fire that the privatization program was drawing could be accounted for, as Chubais wanted to believe, by the program's successes. Many critics wanted to modify it significantly or abandon it altogether because of alleged *failures.*

A proposal called the "fourth variant" was developed in the Russian Federation's State Property Fund by one of its vice chairs, Vitalii Kliuchnikov. Not satisfied with the mid-1992 concession allowing enterprise employees to become majority shareholders of joint-stock companies, proponents of this idea were advocating a different kind of enterprise structure. Their plan called for the creation of "collective people's enterprises." This formulation shared ground with Larisa Piiasheva's 1990 proposal, in that it was based on the idea that enterprise personnel should own and control their firms. Unlike Piiasheva's idea, Kliuchnikov's proposal would require personnel to pay for their enterprises over a period of several years, although the price would be low relative to the enterprise's assessed value. Vouchers would *not* be accepted as payment.

When the "fourth variant" was made public on January 14, 1993, the market value of vouchers plummeted immediately. Voucher prices continued to drop until January 19, when the Committee on Economic Reform rejected the proposal.[65] After that, however, Kliuchnikov's proposal was discussed several times in the Supreme Soviet and was gaining support by the spring.

In April 1993, political analyst Boris Kagarlitskii summarized another proposal that was attracting attention among some Russian economists—the "zero variant."[66] This proposal called for the cessation of privatization and the return of privatized enterprises to the state. Some of them would again be privatized, but only after the development of new rules and laws for privatization which would create a different basis for acquiring property.

"Zero variant" proponents maintained that under the State Program for Privatization, the legal rights and obligations of buyers, owners, and sellers were not clear. Rather than guaranteeing rights for property, which is necessary for public confidence, the state was simply distributing property rights, argued People's Deputy Vitalii Tambovtsev. And much of the distribution was going to the old party *nomenklatura*. This amounted to legitimation of the *nomenklatura*'s power, he said.[67]

Kagarlitskii objected to the idea of a wholesale property distribution, which had been a central feature of the Yeltsin government's economic reform program until then. Gaidar's path toward a market economy had destroyed necessary network connections between suppliers and producers, producers and distributors, and distributors and consumers. Because procedures had been established for privatizing "everybody at one time"[68] within specified enterprise-size parameters, there were inevitable disruptions of interorganizational connections. Those relationships had been vital to effective business activity, and they could not quickly be reestablished. Now, the "zero variant" advocates argued, the broken egg should be put back together. Next time, privatization should be initiated with more attention to organizational needs and less concern with abstract economic principles. They also insisted that it was more important to privatize property according to rules that would facilitate good management and work-force effectiveness than to adhere single-mindedly to the radical egalitarian principle of distributing a small share of state property to everyone.

Voucher privatization should be abandoned, "zero variant" advocates believed. It had not helped enterprises because it did not furnish them with needed capital. Further, citizens who invested their vouchers were likely to end up with a share of a bankrupt business; many specialists believed that most privatized enterprises would not survive being cut off from the state system. As Kliuchnikov stated it, the voucher privatization program "is an attempt to get rid of Russian plants and factories that are on the edge of bankruptcy—worn out and unprofitable. The State Property Management Committee is trying to make millions of people the co-owners of these failing enterprises. It's time to say clearly and openly that the 'people's privatization' program announced by the State Property Management Committee is deliberate deception."[69]

Whether the ferment surrounding privatization in the early months of 1993 was due more to the government program's successes, as Chubais maintained, or to failures in economic reform, as critics insisted, it was obvious that the privatization program was not a settled matter—even though privatization was continuing largely according to plan.

8

Perspectives from the Work Force

Vasilii Tsvetkov

When I met Vasilii Tsvetkov in the summer of 1991,[1] he was the low-key but energetic owner of a new private record company, Arin Records—the first recording enterprise to compete with state-owned Melodiia. Melodiia had enjoyed a total monopoly of recording and album sales throughout the fifteen republics of the Soviet Union before Tsvetkov started his business. Sensing that I was wondering how this David could hope to take on the Melodiia Goliath, Tsvetkov remarked, "We pay musicians much more than the state does. That's why they are eager to record for us." He continued, "We own one store where we sell our records, and they are also distributed through Melodiia stores. Melodiia doesn't have a future in recording. Increasingly, it needs companies like ours in order to have good records to sell."

"My biggest problem," Tsvetkov reflected, "is that I don't know how to manage. I need more management skills." As he spoke, several nearby employees smiled affectionately. I could see that, whatever he lacked in "management skills," he made up in personal warmth and enthusiasm for his work. "Before starting Arin, I was a musician. Now I understand the problems of the music industry from both sides—as a performer *and* as an executive. Being a manager isn't easy, and it's a job I don't have training for."

Our interview, which lasted about two hours, was punctuated by the usual afternoon tea and by several brief chats with musicians and technicians who stopped in to ask a quick question. Arin records, I thought, is an energetic place. People like their work here, and there is an unusual freshness and sense of purpose. At one point, the conversation turned sober. "I'm uncertain about the future of my company," Tsvetkov said quietly, "because of political instability and the frequent changes in laws regulating private enterprises. I'm also very optimistic, though," he added with conviction, "because there's high demand for our work, and artists are enthusiastic about our company."

I left Vasilii Tsvetkov's office with a sense that entrepreneurs with his qualities offered tangible hope for the transition to a market economy which, in July 1991, was more an idea than a reality in Russia. He has all the right traits to be a successful entrepreneur, I thought while riding the metro back to my apartment. My mind was so occupied with the interview that at first I didn't hear a passenger across from me asking, "What do you have there?" Such questions to strangers are uncharacteristic metro behavior in Moscow, and I looked up with some surprise. The young man of 22 or 24 was staring at a record Tsvetkov had given me—one of Arin's first.

"Oh," I answered, "this is a recording by Arin. Do you know the company?"

"No," he said, "but I'd like to see the album cover. May I?" Tsvetkov is onto a good thing, I said to myself.

Six months later I was in Moscow again, and I telephoned Tsvetkov to say hello and to ask how his company was doing. He had told me on the first of July that he planned to release about fifteen records in 1991. It was now the end of the year, and I wondered if he had met his goal.

Tsvetkov seemed happy to hear my voice again; but, after we exchanged greetings, rather than answering my question about Arin's recording accomplishments, he suggested that I come to his office the next day for tea. I did, with Irina Kuzes, and the three of us exchanged pleasant conversation while sipping tea and eating pastries. I noticed, though, that the easy manner Vasilii had shown during our first meeting now had a harder edge. "There is a deficit of individuality in this country," he said impatiently. "And the situation won't change soon. The totalitarian system we have all known here created children's minds. That is the legacy of communism."

When I introduced the subject of Arin Records, Tsvetkov's face clouded. "I don't make records any more," he said matter-of-factly. "Now I'm a trader. I export timber, and in France and several other countries I buy chocolates and perfumes—whatever I think will sell in Moscow. This is the only kind of business that can succeed here now." My mind flashed back to our conversation the summer before—to the excitement Tsvetkov had obviously felt about taking on Melodiia, and the artistic integrity he had spoken of then. Now he was more restrained. There were no reflective pauses, no open smiles.

"My case is very typical," he continued. "There is only one form of business that makes money now in Russia: speculation, not production."

I couldn't help responding, "But what about your music? I thought you were a musician above everything else."

Tsvetkov's eyes focused hard on the empty desk top in front of him as he answered, "Some day . . . after I've made more money, I'll return to music. But not for awhile. Arin was in a very difficult financial situation. . . . It took me only two hours, when I started thinking about it, to decide everything. The only successful entrepreneurs today are speculators."

Evgenii Vostrikov

Evgenii Vostrikov's small square living room not only is where he visits with guests, but also serves as his television studio and the nerve center of his cable TV business. Broadcasting equipment is packed tightly into the high bookcases that line one wall, and behind his sofa is a huge mural of birch trees—a fitting backdrop for the television camera that stands only a few feet away across the room. As Irina and I settled into the ample cushions of the sofa, we noticed that on the television monitor a Cable News Network announcer was dutifully reporting on the aftermath of the San Francisco earthquake. "CNN," I said aloud, mostly to myself. "I haven't seen it for months."

"Our subscribers can watch it every day," Evgenii quickly answered, smiling softly. "I also show two new films daily, plus another one that was shown earlier; broadcast interviews with experts about many different subjects; furnish information about problems in this district; and carry advertisements. This is the only Moscow station that broadcasts 24 hours every day."

As this friendly, slight man talked, I began to realize that his self-effacing demeanor masked a dynamo of strength and initiative. Evgenii told us how he had begun his business on August 1, 1990—the first day enterprises such as his were permitted. Now his twenty workers were adding 10,000 new subscribers every month to his already extensive cable system, and he hoped to begin expanding the service beyond his district to all of Central Moscow by September.

It was July 1991. In a month and a half Evgenii's ambitious plans would be all but forgotten as he videotaped the action at the Russian White House where Boris Yeltsin and thousands of other coup resisters were staring down Soviet tanks and gunners—and as he persisted in broadcasting news and announcements to his viewers at real personal risk.

Even in July Evgenii was worried. The state couldn't stop private enterprise now, he said, finishing with an implied question: But the old legislation that made private business a crime was still in effect—who knows what might happen? The resistance to change is still strong. "Our past isn't distant enough," he said forcefully. "It could return if nobody helps us."

We met again in December. During the interim, the past had returned but was defeated—without help from the outside. Evgenii was optimistic about the future. He told me: "A friend called early that morning to tell me about the coup, and I left home quickly for the White House, where the resisters were gathering. I learned there that a demonstration was planned for Manezh Square at noon. The problem was, how to inform people about it. I returned to announce the demonstration on my station, but two KGB people had turned off my electricity. I was off the air. I threw the power switch just before they handcuffed me, and my channel was back in service. The handcuffs didn't prevent me from typing an announcement onto the screen: 'NO FASCISM HERE. COME TO MANEZH SQUARE AT 12.' The people in my district were depending on me to keep them informed."

"Why did they let you do it?"

The bashful grin returned. "I'm not sure. I told them that I'm a deputy in my district, and that it was illegal for them to arrest me. They didn't know what to do. I typed. The handcuffs didn't slow me down very much." The many other obstacles to starting and operating a television station in the Russia of 1990 and 1991 did not slow him down, either.

Evgenii Vostrikov, the engineer-turned-entrepreneur, has yet to make a profit. But now he is less worried. He expects to.

Tatiana Antonova

"Working for the state doesn't have any advantages at all over working for yourself," Tatiana Antonova said with conviction. "It is true that I can't get credit easily for my [newly privatized] business. It is true that the market is limited for the kind of knitwear we manufacture at Rossiianka, and that some of our workers [the company employs 1,600] need better training and motivation. But," she emphasized, "I would never return to state employment—not for higher income, not for security, not for anything. It's a big problem to get supplies now, because the distribution system has been destroyed. Formerly, we got material from Ukraine, and now we can't. We have had to find other suppliers. But privatization has brought a huge advantage that more than offsets the problems. Our workers now have a sense of ownership. Also, we now have hope that our company will grow and that we will receive the benefits.

We now sell in Italy and hope to expand our market. We have gotten financial backing when we needed it from private investors."

"You seem confident about the future," I said.

"Yes, I am. I could find another job any time I want to. That's partly because I worked for a cooperative for several years, and I know how to identify opportunities. I could be more satisfied with my pay. I wish it weren't so difficult to find good workers. But interesting work is more important to me than money, and I believe privatization will make people's lives better. There are more opportunities here now than ever before. Why shouldn't I be confident?"

Aleksandr Goldberg

The offices of Magnet Enterprises, located on a small side street fifteen minutes by trolley bus from the Paveletskii train station, are spartan in every detail. There isn't even a sign in front of the firm's modest brick building (perhaps more to avoid attracting the attention of would-be burglars than out of concern for fixed expenses). "We use our money to develop software," Aleksandr Goldberg, the deputy director of the company, explained affably.

In 1991 Magnet Enterprises was a subsidiary of the Nantucket Corporation. It employed 30 people and turned a high profit, according to Goldberg. "Almost all of our *supplies* are from the Soviet Union," he explained. "But we sell our *products* for hard currency."

Having spent many unsuccessful hours searching from one kiosk to another for blank three-and-a-half-inch disks, I wondered to myself how he was able to obtain a consistent supply of even the bare necessities for his enterprise. As if he had read my mind, Goldberg added, "We have a special supplies department to locate what we need. Those people work very hard. The most important thing is that they know where to look. It's a real challenge."

Supplies were only one of Magnet's hurdles. Locating good

workers is more difficult in Moscow than in Silicon Valley. "Our employees make twice as much as state workers with the same qualifications," Goldberg told me. "But it's still difficult to find qualified people. We don't usually hire people with experience in computer software. We have found that the result is better if we hire bright, motivated people and teach them."

Goldberg and his foreign investors also had to confront the potentially negative economic consequences of an unstable political environment. As he pointed out, "Nantucket is willing to risk only so much. We have to keep overhead costs low and show a high profit to justify their investment. They aren't confident in the government, and the Supreme Soviet is continually approving unfavorable laws. We never know what to expect. Our profits are impressive, but we still don't get much from Nantucket."

These are challenges software executives in the United States could not imagine, I thought. And there are others. Just a few minutes before my meeting with Goldberg, a fire had been extinguished in a nearby building—but not before the power lines to Magnet Enterprises had been destroyed. Fortunately, Goldberg's office had a small window which provided enough light for us to examine his company's products, from data-base software to a trade publication called *Nantucket News* which they printed and distributed to advertise their software.

The halls, however, had no alternative light source. We navigated the corridors and several sets of stairs with the aid of a small flashlight. "This kind of thing isn't so unusual," Goldberg remarked as I stumbled on the landing at the bottom of a stairwell, "and sometimes, there isn't even a fire to account for it. Of course, we pay the officials."

IBM management knew all of these problems well. "We don't pay bribes," Brian Robins told me. Robins was IBM's director of administration in Moscow. "When you pay one person, there are five others to pay. Maybe," he mused, "that's why we don't have an international telephone." Robins had met me in the tastefully decorated foyer of IBM's newly refurbished building not long after I arrived at IBM's offices near the Dobryninskaia metro station for our interview, and he apologized in typical British fashion as a cheerful Russian receptionist was about to direct me, unescorted, to his second-floor office. "We have to teach them," he said, with a touch of weariness in his voice.

IBM has been in Moscow since 1972, but, Robins told me, "The company has never made a profit here. IBM *hopes* there will be money to be made in Moscow.... We broke even last year and *would have* this year if people had any money."

IBM's Russian agenda is duplicated by many foreign firms with branches in Moscow. Caterpillar's Waldemar Staniak phrased Robins's concerns slightly differently. "We can't afford *not* to be here," the company's Moscow director told me. "This is potentially a very large market." Glen Steeves, the area supervisor of McDonald's in Moscow, sounded even more upbeat. "This is potentially our largest market anywhere in the world."

Steeves was echoing the established McDonald's philosophy. When I asked how his company viewed the political uncertainty in the country, and whether McDonald's was concerned that, in a worst-case scenario, their fifty-million-dollar plant in Moscow might have to be closed, he was quick to respond. "We don't think that way. We find solutions to challenges; we don't see problems as insurmountable."

Since my interview with Aleksandr Goldberg at Magnet Enterprises, the parent company in Los Angeles has been bought by Computer Associates in Ilandia, New York, and the name of the subsidiary has been changed to CA-Russia. Goldberg is now director of the operation. In January 1993 I spoke with John Zakarin, the international sales manager for Computer Associates, about the Moscow business.

"Has it met your expectations?" I wondered.

"Well," Zakarin replied crisply, "it's new."

Yakov Vartanian

My initial impression of Yakov Vartanian, the managing director of Bracen Ventures, was that his mind was somewhere else. I soon learned why. My head began to spin as he enumerated the different kinds of work carried out by this British-Soviet joint venture which was created in 1989. "Medical equipment sales, hotel management, radio and television repair, metal castings production, investment consulting. . . . I think those are about all of our activities," Vartanian told me as he handed me papers that gave short descriptions of each business venture. "No . . . we also make furniture."

This is horizontal integration with a vengeance, I thought, scanning the printed descriptions of these diverse enterprises. "And how many people work at your company headquarters in Moscow?"

"Twelve."

A few minutes later Vartanian acknowledged, "Accounting is a problem. If we used our British accountant, we'd go bankrupt. Russia requires its own accounting system. Accounting is a minor frustration, though, compared to managing the work force in our production facilities. Our workers can't make decisions on their own. It's the result of more than seven decades of 'Don't do this . . . .' Recently, a hospital that had bought one of our heart monitors returned it. It was malfunctioning. We removed the lid and found a cigarette butt inside. Imagine . . . a *cigarette butt* lying on a circuit board full of transistors and intricate wiring!"

"What can you do about this kind of thing?" was the obvious next question.

"It's simple," Vartanian quickly responded. "We contract out all of the actual production that we can to other companies."

"How does that solve the problem?" I wondered.

"It doesn't," Vartanian answered with a shrug. "But then, it's not *our* problem. It's *theirs.*"

The Russian Labor Force

"We pretend to work, and the government pretends to pay us." Thus many Russian workers have long characterized one of Russia's most intractable economic problems. Viktor Chernomyrdin posed the problem only a little differently shortly after he was named prime minister. "We cannot live as they live in the West and work as we work in Russia," he said.[2]

This perspective is consistent with the way most work-force respondents in our four-city study viewed the productivity of Russian workers in comparison to their Western counterparts. Two-thirds of the enterprise personnel in our study believed that most people work harder in the West than in Russia, and of those, two-thirds believed the difference to be large (Table B–8.1). There was not much variation in the responses by enterprise type; but it may be significant that, among non-managerial workers, those in the private sector tend to have less negative assessments of the Russian work force than do workers in the state and privatized sectors. Department heads and specialists in the state sector, for example, are 50 percent more likely than their private-sector counterparts to believe that there is a large difference in how hard Western and Russian employees work.

We think that the less negative assessments of many private-sector workers are due to the high degree of selectivity that characterizes many private firms. The manager of Dow Chemical Company in Moscow, Slobodan Kostoc, described a recruitment procedure that we found to be common among many private businesses—both Russian and foreign. "We pick our own workers from among people we meet in the field," Kostoc noted. "We have very good workers." Speaking about foreign firms explicitly, Barbara Duvoisin of Price Waterhouse said, "Foreign companies can't just walk into Moscow and find good workers. They need to search."

Private enterprises offer incentives that should allow them to skim the cream off the supply of workers. A major one is salary. Most directors and owners we interviewed in the private sector said that they paid at least two or three times the state average for comparable work. Many, such as Pizza Hut, paid a great deal more. With a Ph.D. in chemistry, Olga Milanova might seem an unlikely candidate to wait tables. Until she took her new job at

Pizza Hut, she worked at Russia's most prestigious research institute in chemistry. Milanova is self-confident, poised, and energetic. "Why do you work here?" I asked bluntly. A one-sentence reply told the entire story. "I make *forty times* as much money here," she said with a faint shrug.

"Do you like the change?"

"I don't like to be poor."

Even with higher salary incentives, many businesses have persistent difficulty locating the kinds of employees they want. Karina Mikaelian, the executive manager of Alpha Graphics, repeated the conclusion of many managers: "It has been difficult to find workers with work habits and attitudes which the company finds acceptable." Yakov Vartanian of Bracen Ventures told me, with some urgency, "Our biggest problem is finding good employees. The Soviet system had a huge effect. It taught workers not to decide things for themselves." Both Russian and Western managers stated that view frequently and emphatically. "Workers here can't make decisions for themselves," Waldemar Staniak of Caterpillar stated. "They come to me with every little question." And Boris Komulainev, the director of Finnpap, observed, "It's difficult to delegate authority to Russian employees. They aren't comfortable using it." Vladimir Sevastanov, the general manager of Computer Technologies, had the same complaint: "Workers are not trained, and often they aren't motivated. We pay high salaries, but they don't know how to sell." Sevastanov, himself a Russian, offered one solution: "The managers of foreign firms should be from the West," he stated, "to get the most from their employees." And Aleksandr Kostiia, director of a Russian-Austrian machine-tool company, insisted that foreign businesses have a better chance at making a profit in Russia than indigenous firms do because "only they can provide qualified management."

To many managers we met, capital and technology were not the only transfers badly needed in the Russian marketplace. A recurring theme in our interviews was the idea that a culture of entrepreneurship should be better developed. Vladimir Rokitianskii, the director of an artistic cooperative, argued, "We have to revive the traditions of Russian merchants." In the words of Sergei Ivanov, the youthful director of a scientific research enterprise, "The main problem in Russia is the absence of an enterprising culture."

Glen Steeves of McDonald's was confident, however, that his company had found the solution to worker productivity. "We have no difficulty finding good workers," he said. "There is no absentee problem here." Frank Klare, vice president and general manager of the Radisson Slavyanskaya Hotel, agreed. "There are plenty of good Russian workers," he told me. "It's simply necessary to train them in our work methods. Many are eager to do a good job."

The manager of Salamander's six factories in Russia for processing leather and making shoes also refused to accept the commonplace negative characterization of Russian workers. George Tchkheidze, a personable man in his fifties who seems excited about his work and Salamander's prospects for profit in Russia, emphasized, "There are no worker problems here. The secret is to create the right environment. We try to make our workplaces comfortable—like German or Italian factories. Their salaries are high, and we provide good incentives. The difference between efficient and inefficient factories in this country is organization. Workers here are just like workers anywhere else. They need to work in a place where they are rewarded for good performance and where they feel good about their working conditions." When I interviewed Tchkheidze again, the following December, the only change in his assessment of the Russian market was that he had become even more optimistic. "We're about to begin exporting shoes," he told me animatedly. "And they're as good as any in Germany or Italy."

Steeves and Tchkheidze were hardly alone in contradicting the negative stereotype about the quality of the Russian work force. Evgenii Vostrikov of Khamovniki Television told us unequivocally that he had no problem finding qualified workers, as did Tomatsu Nishida of Kanematsu Corporation and many others.

Our four-city data suggest that workers in such private-sector enterprises have good reason to be more productive. They are markedly more satisfied with their incomes, and they are distinctly more likely than workers in state or even privatized firms to believe their good work will be recognized and rewarded (Table B–8.1). This divergence of private-sector personnel from those in state and privatized enterprises is a pattern we found repeatedly in our analysis. Clearly, legal privatization is only the first stage in a more complex process of reorientation to the expectations and rewards of a changed organizational structure.

Both our quantitative findings and data from our personal interviews with directors and owners suggest that carefully focused personnel selection and skillful management are probably even more critical in Russia than in most Western countries. Workers who are new to private businesses have the burden of adjusting to a new work environment, and in this situation effective management styles and training programs are of vital importance.

Almost all managers we interviewed agreed that teaching new skills is easier than breaking old habits. "We don't hire people who have experience in Russian hotels," Frank Klare told me. "At the Slavyanskaya we don't want our employees to have learned bad work practices." Alisdar Munro of DHL applied the same general rule in a different way. "We have found that it's best to hire young workers," Munro said. "They haven't acquired as many bad habits as older workers, and we can train them."

Age was frequently mentioned in our interviews as a critical determinant for private-sector employment. Rajan Pilenskij, the general director of the Russian-Canadian joint venture clothing chain Elegant put it bluntly: "We hire only people who have never worked for the state. And they *must* be under forty. Everyone else has learned bad work habits which are almost impossible to correct." Anatolii Koldashev, director of a Russian-German joint venture, identified the same age ceiling: "The generation of people over forty is lost for enterprise." Underscoring this conclusion, Barbara Duvoisin of Price Waterhouse remarked, "We get support staff who haven't learned bad habits from other work settings. We take them new, while they are eager to learn. They are wonderful workers." We were to hear variations on this refrain again and again at a diverse array of businesses. It is worth the extra investment required to train novice workers, many managers in Russia seem to have found—to start fresh. And the younger the better.

Thus, the job characteristics most in demand among employers in Russia are the opposite of those often sought in the West. Young, inexperienced workers are preferred over more mature, experienced applicants. It is not surprising, then, that older workers are far more concerned than younger ones about their employment prospects if they should lose their jobs, even though, as they saw it, they put as much effort as young people did into their work (Table B–8.2). It is probably to be expected, then, that younger workers would want privatization to proceed at a faster pace, although people of all ages expected privatization to cause an increase in unemployment. Since these factors are also associated with several other variables, and we wanted to examine the "pure" effects of age in this part of the analysis, we controlled for several possible sources of spuriousness in the relationships between age and the dependent variables of interest. The relationships described above, and several others discussed in the narrative below, present our results with controls included in the regression equations (see Appendix A).

The Private-Sector Advantage

When we interviewed Vladimir Ispravnikov, a people's deputy in the Supreme Soviet, one of his principal concerns was the fear that the government's reform program would produce massive unemployment. "The government doesn't have a plan to create new jobs that would take the place of those that will be eliminated as state subsidies are withdrawn from unprofitable enterprises," Ispravnikov said. "It's no wonder that many young people are going into crime. It's a substitute for jobs that don't exist."

Ispravnikov's concern about the effects of privatization is mirrored in the opinions of enterprise personnel we studied. Eight out of ten respondents believed that privatization would increase unemployment, and nearly half of the people who worked in state and privatized enterprises believed that they might lose their job during the next twelve months (Table B–8.3). A large majority of those workers thought that it would be difficult to find another job with about the same income. Nearly three out of ten state workers believed that a significant number of the employees in their enterprises would lose their jobs during the coming year.

Unemployment was not the only social problem that concerned our respondents. Most enterprise personnel in almost every employment category thought that crime rates would increase with the transition to a market economy, and a large percentage expected personal relations among people to become less close (Table B–8.4). Most respondents suspected that moral values might decline. Four out of five expected income inequality to increase, and respondents were almost equally split on the question of whether such an outcome might be desirable. (A substantial percentage were uncertain.)

Although people tend to expect some key consequences of the shift to a market economy to be adverse at the societal level, the overwhelming majority of our respondents said that they would prefer nonstate over state employment if they were to change jobs (Table B–8.5). People who worked in the state sector were more likely than others to prefer state employment, as were less skilled workers. Even among state workers, however, only about one-fourth would choose state-sector work over other alternatives. The most frequently selected choice was work in a joint venture, with private businesses and foreign firms also drawing substantial interest. Joint-stock companies were less appealing to respondents, and only an overall average of about 5 percent would choose cooperative employment.

The characteristics of a job that make it desirable are generally very different for private- and state-sector workers (Table B–8.6). In choosing among "high income," "job security," and "work that is important and interesting," private-sector workers were considerably more likely than state employees to rank "high income" as the most important characteristic. This difference held across all job levels. Job security was the most important feature for state workers. Privatized-enterprise personnel chose preferences that fairly closely matched those of state workers. Consistent with these stated preferences, when we asked private-sector personnel why they had left their previous job, 40 percent responded that they wanted higher incomes. Another 32 percent indicated that their principal reason was a desire for fuller self-realization.[3]

In our interviews, private-sector owners and directors tended to be emphatic about the distinct advantages they were finding in nonstate employment. "I realized in my state job that nothing could be changed," publisher Vladimir Rokitianskii noted. "Not a single idea that I had would be acted upon. I needed freedom to *initiate* and a right to make my own mistakes." Journalist Svetlana Gurnakova underscored the point: "It is impossible to work normally in the state sector. I helped establish our information bureau because I needed freedom for creative self-expression. Money isn't my principal motive, but when people work properly they will earn enough money."

" . . . And of course, I needed money," Konstantin Avelichev admitted, defending a motivation that had long been suppressed in the Soviet system. "I left state work because I wasn't satisfied with the money I made," shop owner Olga Konorova said with businesslike finality. "It was that simple."

Filmmaker Aleksandr Diagterev nicely summarized the importance of both motivations: "I don't know which comes first— the desire for creative work or dissatisfaction with low pay in the state sector." And oceanographer Boris Talochkin mused, "A year and a half ago, as we were starting our consulting company, I would have said I was going into business for 'big money.' But the reason I stay is for independence and the self-realization I've gained by being here."

Were these entrepreneurs worried about job security? "If I

don't succeed in business I'll go back to the state sector," Rokitianskii said with a shrug. Many of our respondents were not so flexible, however. Most did not expect to fail, but if they did, they were prepared to begin anew—on their own. Again and again, we heard what Nikolai Kapustin, the manager of a trade cooperative, stated resolutely: "Never in my life would I go back to the state sector!" And clothing manufacturer Vadim Iziumov added, "After four years in my own business, I've grown out of the restrictiveness and idleness of state work. On my own, everything is possible."

In light of most workers' clear preference for private-sector employment, and the unwillingness of a large proportion of our respondents to consider the notion of returning to state-sector work, it was surprising that job satisfaction was only marginally higher among private-sector workers than among others (Table B–8.7). Although sector of employment is not strongly related to *job* satisfaction, its correlation with other aspects of life satisfaction is substantial. Private-enterprise personnel were markedly happier, overall, than workers in either state or privatized firms; their happiness had increased more during the past year; they derived more satisfaction from their family lives; and their family satisfaction had shown more improvement (Table B–8.7).

From the more detailed questions we asked enterprise directors and owners about their work experiences and preferences, we found more evidence that the effects of private-sector work for *individuals* tend to be positive, in spite of expected negative *social* effects. In both privatized and private enterprises, directors and owners tended to find little to recommend state employment. Thirty-nine percent found no advantages at all in state-sector work. Although 33 percent mentioned job security as an advantage, a solid 59 percent stated that there were no circumstances under which they would return to state work.[4]

Most nonstate directors and owners experienced more difficulty securing necessary materials and supplies now than when they worked for the state, but the problem had seldom proved to be insurmountable. Having heard many complaints about supply problems, we were surprised to find that financing was more often a serious problem for respondents than either supplies or personnel. Obtaining materials became a more serious problem after a business was established than at the beginning,[5] but working with local authorities became easier. Directors of privatized enterprises and owners of private firms tended to have very similar management problems (Table B–8.8).

"The government creates problems for business," Rajan Pilenskij told me as we chatted in the lobby of the Hotel Moskva. Pilenskij's upscale clothing store, which carried Benetton products, was tiny but swarming with customers and staffed by several smiling salespeople. "The government bites the hand that feeds them," he complained. "We pay taxes in hard currency, which they need; but they impose regulations which make it difficult for us to operate. We never know when there will be a new regulation."

We heard about a broad spectrum of barriers to nonstate enterprise from directors and owners. "Not everything is all right with our entrepreneurship," said Sergei Anisenko. A manufacturer, Anisenko resented nonproductive speculation. "Ninety percent of Russian engineers are simply engaged in profiteering," he lamented. Aleksandr Kostiia, the machine-tool executive, seemed to be unconcerned about speculators. "I have great difficulty getting raw materials and equipment," he complained, "and I don't think we will ever get out from under the state bureaucracy." The chairman of a growing Russian-German sales company had a different concern. "Our *laws* are raw," he exclaimed. "Statements are uncertain, and general policies are unstable. Additionally, I have difficulty securing capital for my company's expansion, and it is nearly impossible to find more space."

Most owners and directors we met were aware of business failures among their acquaintances, and they typically knew some of the details. We asked what they thought had gone wrong. The most prevalent answer by far centered around lack of experience and knowledge about the basics of a market system— poor management, inadequate sales skills, inability to understand market forces. In spite of the very real *external* impediments to success posed by unfavorable and unpredictable regulations, and the difficulty of securing capital, these reasons were a distant second and third place to personal competence. Only one percent of our respondents cited lack of raw materials as a reason for business failure. Two percent mentioned corruption and racketeering. Seven percent said lack of credits. Fifteen percent highlighted unfavorable legislation and regulations. But 32 percent said that the business failures they knew about were caused primarily by *internal* management problems and inexperience.

In 1993, however, most nonstate enterprises in Russia were still in business. Many of the successful owners and managers in these firms were enthusiastic about their newfound opportunities when we interviewed them, and a substantial number were preoccupied with the demands and benefits afforded by nonstate work. There was also a reflective and thoughtful strain in many of our conversations. The threat of widespread unemployment as economic reform continues, and the government's inability to provide adequate social guarantees to people displaced by the inevitable bankruptcies and reorganizations, were cause for real anxiety. Although several respondents agreed with a 25-year-old broker's facile observation, "The more rich people there are, the wealthier the country will be," many other executives were worried, for different reasons. Anatolii Koldashev observed that "hungry people are capable of staging riots." Tatiana Borovina, the owner of a commercial shop, was more sensitive to the widening gulf between the poor and the affluent, and the implications of this change for her personal values. "I hope charity will grow," she said, "along with the development of private entrepreneurship. Everyone needs a stable income." As if to respond, Egor Polskii remarked: "The idea of equality . . . we have been brainwashed with it for seventy years, and it is still alive." A 48-year-old commodities broker summarized a sentiment we heard often and with feeling: "The number of rich people has rapidly grown, but most of them never think about those without enough money for the necessities of life. Under such conditions, there can be no real prosperity."

The path to a market economy is largely unmarked, and the obstacles are formidable. Yet an optimistic director of a Moscow currency exchange summarized concisely an overarching perspective that was common to most entrepreneurs we interviewed: "The state sector belongs to yesterday!"

9

Politics and the Promise of Economic Reform

Reform from Above?

Shortly after the October Revolution, Lenin expressed a longing for a time when "socialism in reality," rather than by government mandate, would be the driving force for a new kind of property relations. In reflecting upon the economic policy struggles of that time, Academician Sergei Fateev describes a Lenin who "grieved" that the new property arrangements were not quickly reflected in the people's mentality.[1] More recently, the experiment Lenin began has shown that collectivization of property did not produce the permanent reorientation of thinking that the Bolsheviks had expected. But it did have an effect. Students of Russian history are familiar with the long-standing collectivist strain in Russian culture, and communist ideology intensified that characteristic. By the end of the Soviet period, then, although a socialist mentality had not been firmly established, authoritarian rule had left a distinctive mark on Russian culture. Andrei Siniavskii, a severe critic of communism's cultural effects, states the point emphatically: "The way of life seems cursed for its having been built on a wasteland where there is neither individual nor society, only the State."[2]

The state banished the utopian dreams that had nourished Marx and Lenin but failed to shed the tendency toward instanta-

175

neous policy reversals which can only be carried out in a highly centralized system. The Lenin who had proclaimed in 1917, "We shall now proceed to construct the socialist order,"[3] approved the legalization of private trade in 1921 and launched NEP, which, to many revolutionaries, signaled an abandonment of the fundamental tenets of Bolshevism.[4] But Stalin reversed Lenin's initiative before the end of the decade. From the October Revolution through the time of *perestroika,* government policy often changed unexpectedly and swiftly on questions of family relations, nationalities, education, religion, alcohol use, and many other aspects of economic, political, and social life. In that sense, the Yeltsin government's radical approach to economic reform was a familiar theme replayed.

In the Gaidar–Chubais privatization program, as in Stalin's collectivization, which privatization was intended to correct, the plan from the beginning was top–down transformation. "We are ready to unveil Big Privatization," Anatolii Chubais declared with the beginning of price liberalization in January 1992. "We have worked out the required tasks for privatization in regions, oblasts, Moscow and St. Petersburg."[5] According to Chubais's estimate, more than 50,000 government personnel would be required to implement the privatization program. In January 1992 he said that the government had applied to the Central Bank for five hundred million rubles (R500,000,000) just to purchase office equipment and supplies for work related to privatization. Most of the employees Chubais was seeking to fill the new jobs for privatization would, in his words, come from "branches where massive staff reductions are now in progress." That is, he was hiring seasoned veterans of the state system to staff yet another bureaucratic machine.

"It sounds too familiar," observed Vladimir Orlov, an editor of *Moscow News.* "It sounds like the old 'planning system.'"[6]

Anders Åslund, Gaidar's chief foreign economic adviser in 1992, considered private ownership "necessary for the creative destruction, entrepreneurship and innovation that Joseph Schumpeter cherished,"[7] but nether Åslund nor his Russian colleagues in Gaidar's planning team ever suggested how this innovative and creative energy could be mandated through administrative order. The price liberalization scheme that Åslund advocated and Gaidar partially implemented did not make people economically free—an essential feature of market relations in a democratic context. Because "Gaidar's strategy was reform from above," Democratic Russia leader Yurii Afanasev stated, "sooner or later the strategy was bound to fail."[8]

Political Agendas That Transcend Economics

Monetarist and Conservative Positions

In trying to dismantle the centralized Soviet system with quick and strategic action to usher in a market economy, the Yeltsin reforms from late 1991 through early 1993 created enormous hardship and few tangible successes except for impressive progress in privatizing state enterprises. The debate in Russia about "where to go from here" involved, at its extremes, a dispute between monetarists, who agreed with the government's early financial stabilization initiatives, and conservatives, who wanted to restore significant elements of the state planning system. Many centrists, of course, held positions somewhere between these two points.

Before the end of 1992, monetarists were insisting that the government's financial stabilization plan had been seriously compromised, while conservatives were claiming that the Western approach to reform was a formula for Russia's economic ruin. Monetarists argued that economic vigor in Russia depended on swiftly cutting the "umbilical cord" that joined enterprises to the state, while conservatives said that the symbiotic relationships that had been built up over decades in the command system should not be destroyed overnight—that the transition should be evolutionary, to facilitate better adaptation of enterprises and less social dislocation. Monetarists were warning of economic decline and a feared return of the communist system if their prescription was not followed, and conservatives worried about the negative social and economic consequences of such bitter medicine. They also had doubts that the monetarists' strategy would produce the promised results. Trying to avoid the dangers of both extremes, Gaidar's team ultimately pleased few; and perhaps more critically, the economy was in far worse condition by December 1992 than Yeltsin and Gaidar had predicted.

Pure Theory

"Russians have shown little interest in the experiences of other countries that had changed their economic systems," Åslund argued at a June 1992 conference on the Russian economy.[9] Dismissing economist Nikolai Petrakov's suggestion that the Russian economic situation "cannot be described by general rules," and disdaining the reservations several Russian specialists had expressed about Åslund's attempt to formulate economic policies for Russia on the basis of the Polish experience, Åslund concluded, "The ignorance here was palpable."[10]

Our analysis indicates, however, that the narrow theoretical vision of radical reform advocates, both in Russia and abroad, contributed significantly to the failures of Russia's reforms in 1992, and they were probably one of the principal causes of the widening rift between the Yeltsin government and the legislature, which by April 1993 presented a serious threat to political stability and democratization. Inconsistent application of monetarist principles, which undoubtedly *did* contribute substantially to the inflation spiral toward the end of 1992, was another negative result of trying to fit a country's economy too closely with a general theoretical idea. Western theoreticians were not willing to acknowledge that financial stabilization considerations sometimes must give way to other priorities. What followed from this single-minded focus was a series of difficult concessions by the government as the noose tightened around the necks of the directors of large enterprises. These actions promoted both political realignment and a sense that the government was not in control of the economic situation. The government clearly was *not* in control, but the unrealistic demands placed on the reformers from the outside, especially from international financial institutions, were partly responsible for the problem. We agree with analyst Grigorii Tsitriniak, that "the scheme of the reform should have been different—not so abrupt and striking," but more applicable to the real economic situation.[11]

Perhaps Åslund, Sachs, and other like-minded Western advisers *were* as blindly committed to controversial macroeconomic ideas as their pattern of reasoning in the Russian case would suggest. Another plausible explanation, however, is that their economic advice was partly driven by a political agenda in which human hardship and industrial decline were only secondary considerations. Indeed, rather than fully acknowledging the severity of radical reform's effects on everyday life, Yeltsin's advisers tended to downplay the obvious problems. "In our view, these costs are exaggerated," Lipton and Sachs stated in September 1992.[12] Michael Mandelbaum argued in early 1993 that declining productivity in Russia was not necessarily bad, because "Russia makes too much of the wrong things. . . . It is good for the world," Mandelbaum continued, "for Russia to make fewer tanks and missiles."[13]

Mandelbaum failed to discuss Russia's declining production of milk and shoes in this context, or the worsening overall quality of people's diets. And Sachs, while noting that Yeltsin's "support is being sapped" by the negative effects of reform, added encouragingly that "every country in Eastern Europe has experienced a decline in industrial production of more than 30 percent since the end of 1989, but the fastest reformer, Poland, has had the smallest decline."[14]

Clearly, the goals of Western experts and of Russian decisionmakers were not all the same when Russia undertook its unprecedented economic experiment. Mandelbaum articulated a common Western perspective in discussing the goal of Western participation in the effort to overcome Russia's crisis. After observing that

"Western economic assistance cannot make Russia rich," he added, "But the goal is not to raise Russians' standard of living. The goal is stabilization."[15]

Russian decision-makers could not afford to be so detached from the real-world effects of macroeconomic stabilization policies. Vladimir Ispravnikov, chair of the Supreme Economic Council of the Russian Supreme Soviet, underscored this point when we interviewed him in May 1992. "Something very obvious needs to be emphasized," he said. "The 'transition to the market' is not the aim. It is only a vehicle to develop the normal 'human' economy. Market mechanisms are necessary only to help a person live better. . . . In accordance with the *real* aim of economic reform, the government must guarantee a minimum level of subsistence for all citizens, without which economic reform loses its meaning."[16]

The Course of Economic Reform in Early 1993

It was widely believed in Russia that Gaidar's replacement by Viktor Chernomyrdin meant a shift in the course of economic reform.[17] That, indeed, was what the Congress had called for and also what a substantial proportion of the people seemed to want.

The Supreme Soviet was happy with Chernomyrdin, and Yeltsin's foes believed that they had won a significant victory. At first, Chernomyrdin seemed to be following the expected script developed by the legislature's more conservative deputies. On January 5, he outlined his economic proposals for 1993 to a group of industrial directors and entrepreneurs who had assembled in Moscow. The most important task, he emphasized, was to stop the decline in production. To achieve that objective, he said, it would be necessary to provide subsidies for state enterprises. Further, he stressed, state property should be protected from thoughtless privatization, and a variety of managerial functions that had been removed from state authority should be restored. "I am myself a former director," Chernomyrdin declared. Pointedly distancing himself from "unproductive" entrepreneurs, he added, "There are some businessmen who have never in their life made a nail or a brick."[18]

Responding swiftly to Chernomyrdin's retreat from Gaidar's course, Sachs and Lipton cautioned that the new prime minister had quickly shown himself to be a threat to the reforms.[19] Over the course of the month, however, Chernomyrdin's position changed. In his first major policy address to the Russian parliament, he described an unavoidable impending choice between two undesirable alternatives: "industrial decline or unrestrained price growth and inflation. The former is bad," he noted, "and the latter is very bad."[20] He repeated this perspective on January 30, at a conference in Davos. "We are not just for reform, but we are for its deepening and broadening," he said, "and there is no way back."[21] He also affirmed the necessity for financial stabilization and Russia's need for foreign investments.

Sachs and Åslund were also at the Davos conference. When asked, shortly after Chernomyrdin's presentation, whether the Russian government would be able to continue market reform, Sachs responded, "Yes, I'm confident that they are."[22] And Åslund added that the new prime minister "is off to a very good start and will be able to take the reforms further than Gaidar."[23]

That the Yeltsin government's reform program was not quickly reevaluated after Gaidar's departure was due, at least in part, to Yeltsin's selection of Chernomyrdin as the new prime minister. The Congress clearly had seen the ousting of Gaidar as a major step toward changing the course of economic reform; but while Yeltsin agreed to appoint the deputies' third choice for prime minister, he secured Chernomyrdin's agreement to keep the most important proponents of economic reform in the government—at least through early 1993.[24] Anatolii Chubais, for example, who was the principal designer of the privatization program, stayed as vice premier and chairman of the State Property Management Committee. The choice of Chernomyrdin over the Congress's more favored candidates, Georgii Khizha and Yurii

Skokov, suggests that Yeltsin believed he could prevail upon Chernomyrdin to hold to his reform course better than the others.

But in early 1993, both Yeltsin and Chernomyrdin were trying to please both democrats and conservatives, as well as the International Monetary Fund and Western governments. In the resulting barrage of contradictory signals, a new course for the government's economic policy seemed to be taking shape.

The most conspicuous sign of this trend could be found in a new tone articulated by both Yeltsin and Chernomyrdin. Speaking to a group of directors of large state enterprises a week before the April referendum, Yeltsin promised "a correction in the strategy and tactics of reform."[25] And Chernomyrdin, speaking to directors of large industries the same week, declared, "We survived the period of 'reform romanticism.' Now, it's time not to change strategy but to change procedures."[26]

Clues to what Yeltsin and Chernomyrdin meant are provided by the record of administrative appointments under Chernomyrdin. "As far as the makeup of the cabinet is concerned, the basic team will be preserved," Yeltsin's spokesperson Viacheslav Kostikov had said shortly after Gaidar was replaced by Chernomyrdin in December 1992.[27] Before year's end, however, Petr Aven, the government's representative to Western financial institutions, had been dismissed. In March, Andrei Nechaev, the minister of the economy, and Vasilii Barchuk, the minister of finance, were replaced. Taking Nechaev's place was Oleg Lobov, whose conservative economic position was well known. The only clear reformer added to the government was Boris Fedorov, who had been a director at the European Bank for Reconstruction and Development. At the time Lobov and Fedorov were appointed, however, the job descriptions for their positions were changed: Fedorov would have lower status than Lobov. Anatolii Chubais, who had conceptualized and directed the government's privatization program from the beginning, was under heavy pressure from the legislature to resign. By the end of April, many analysts in Moscow believed that Chubais would soon lose his key reform post.[28] The position of Andrei Kozyrev, the foreign minister, was also far from secure.

With these personnel changes, Nechaev said, "the government's support of industry was officially declared by the Prime Minister." He predicted that massive subsidies and credits would soon be forthcoming, along with a restoration of vertical administrative structures.[29]

The core of the government's proposed financial policy for 1993 was developed under Vice Premier Boris Fedorov's direction in mid-January. "The Russian economy is in a very deep crisis," the report on the program began, "and is now threatened with self-destruction." After highlighting the slide in productivity, the reduction of capital investments, the destruction of the state financial system, uncontrolled inflation, and the sharp decline in living standards, the report stated that it was "now imperative that strict and systematic procedures" be implemented to turn the economy around.[30]

The principal goals of the program for 1993 looked a great deal like the principal goals of the 1992 program: to reduce the pace of inflation to 5 percent per month by year's end, to reduce the state budget deficit to 5 percent of the gross national product, to stabilize the ruble, to slow the production decline, to improve the provision of social services, and to keep unemployment under control. A strong emphasis in the program was the need to reduce state subsidies, with the objectives of curbing inflation and making headway in decreasing the budget deficit. Gaidar had said the same thing a year before.

There was one notable difference, however, between Chernomyrdin's 1993 stance and Gaidar's a year earlier. Now, the prime minister was arguing not only that authority for economic reform needed to be consolidated in the executive branch, but also that government control should extend to nonstate enterprises. "Private enterprises should not be outside the state sphere of influence," he stated at a February meeting with the heads of republics in the Russian Federation. It is necessary to create a special "governing mechanism for all forms of property: state property, private property, leased and others."[31]

Gaidar had never suggested anything like that. Rather, he had hoped to eliminate most state control in all spheres—so much so that EBRD president Jacques Attali criticized the Gaidar team for too much idealism in believing that an economic system could operate without state oversight.[32] By contrast, in April 1993 Chernomyrdin took issue with the government's earlier decision to dismantle the old central planning and distribution structures. "In a somewhat different form," he said, Russia still needs Gosplan (the State Planning Committee) and Gossnab (the State Supply Committee). Russia needs reforms, Chernomyrdin insisted, but the economic transformation now under way requires sharp correction. And he concluded, "The government is going to put in order many things in Russia now."[33]

Yeltsin and the Russian Legislature: 1990–1993

Yeltsin and the Congress had enjoyed generally amicable relations before April 1992. In 1990, when Yeltsin headed the Supreme Soviet of the RSFSR, they worked together to initiate radical economic reform. They approved the Shatalin economic plan almost unanimously, and they created legislation that made private ownership the legal equivalent of state ownership. Growing even bolder in 1991, the RSFSR Supreme Soviet decided that any person could now open a private business—an unimaginable possibility just a short time earlier. At mid-year they suggested for the first time in law that privatization accounts could be established which would enable all citizens to acquire property that had been owned by the state. The Russian Congress of People's Deputies nominated Yeltsin to be Russia's first president, and during the election campaign the majority of deputies worked for his election in their home regions.

During the August coup, many deputies of the Supreme Soviet stood with Yeltsin in a White House threatened by tanks and soldiers. When, on October 30, he asked for unprecedented power to pursue his economic reforms—a level of authority and autonomy unknown to presidents in the West—the Congress granted it. On November 6, when he issued a decree banning the Communist Party of the Soviet Union in the Russian Republic, the Supreme Soviet applauded him, and when he announced the demise of the Soviet Union, the deputies supported his initiative. At that time, he commanded the clear support of more than two-thirds of the deputies.

By the time the Sixth Congress convened in April 1992, Yeltsin's support in the Congress had dropped considerably, but more than half of the deputies continued to back most of his economic initiatives. Yet many deputies were increasingly doubtful about of the government's economic reform program, and even more troubling to legislators was Yeltsin's drive for additional presidential power. At that session, the Congress approved the idea of a new constitution, with power shared between the legislature and the president. Yeltsin surprised the deputies, however, by proposing his own draft for a new constitution, which was based on the idea of a "strong presidential republic." According to Yeltsin's variant, presidential power would be enhanced. This action, analyst Anatolii Kostiukov states, started the spiral of suspicion, accusation, and conflict that led to the April 1993 referendum.[34]

When the Seventh Congress completed its December 1992 session, less than one-third of the deputies could be counted on to support Yeltsin's economic reforms. People's Deputy Viktor Sheinis pinpointed December 3 as the day when "a drastic change in the Congress's mood occurred. . . . The center had swung toward the opposition." Sheinis explained this development as a negative response by many deputies to Yeltsin's proposal at the beginning of the Congress that he be granted additional special powers. (The special powers he had requested a year earlier expired the day the Seventh Congress convened.) This move "was assessed," Sheinis observed, "as an attempt by the executive branch to encroach on the prerogatives of the legislative branch."[35] The Congress refused to acquiesce, and from then on, relations between Yeltsin and the legislative majority rapidly worsened.

Analyst Liudmila Telen concluded that the decisive shift had occurred even before the Congress convened on December 1. In November, the political bloc that supported Yeltsin most strongly, Democratic Russia, had started a campaign to dissolve the Congress. Foreign Minister Andrei Kozyrev and privatization director Anatolii Chubais, among others, urged at a press conference for foreign journalists that the session of the Congress that was scheduled to begin December 1 should be canceled. Yeltsin, too, hinted in several public statements that he would rather that the Congress not meet in December.[36] The result of these actions, Telen said, was that "the political centre read the signs as the President's renouncing the tactic of compromise just before the Congress."[37]

It is not surprising, then, that the Congress was decidedly unhappy with Kozyrev in December, and also with the Gaidar team—for reasons other than issues of economic policy. The Congress was unable to remove Kozyrev, but Gaidar was more vulnerable. The day after Gaidar was rejected as prime minister, Yeltsin angrily called for a national referendum to let the voters choose between him and a legislature he now attacked unmercifully. "What they failed to do in August 1991, they have decided to repeat now by means of a creeping coup," Yeltsin charged in a televised address.[38] These were fighting words—especially since many members of the Congress, including the chair Ruslan Khasbulatov, had fought as courageously as Yeltsin *against* the coup. *Washington Post* correspondent Michael Dobbs reported that Yeltsin's challenge "was greeted by gasps and shouts of protest from the hall."[39] Yeltsin then "stalked out of the Grand Kremlin Palace" and asked his supporters in the Congress to join him. No more than 20 percent did.[40] Thus the rift between Yeltsin and the Congress was dramatized for the world to see.

The question Yeltsin wanted to put to voters was whether they supported him or the Congress. Between December and March, when a list of four questions was finally decided upon, the proposed referendum was a subject of heated controversy. Along the way, Yeltsin's attempt to characterize the Congress as moving in the direction of a "pro-communist dictatorship" intensified.[41]

The coordinated effort to discredit a legislature that had become unhappy with Yeltsin's economic policies was aimed at the West as much as at Russian voters. Foreign Minister Kozyrev was a major actor in this offensive. Four days after Yeltsin's unexpected referendum announcement, Kozyrev shocked a Stockholm audience of foreign ministers and diplomats by delivering a lengthy speech in which he pretended that Russia was now taking an aggressive stance toward the West. In a second address, nearly a hour later, he clarified the intent of his dramatization. The statement he had read earlier, Kozyrev explained, would have been far too mild to satisfy "the demands of the most radical members of the opposition."[42] He was particularly referring to opponents of Yeltsin's economic reform program.

The maneuver worked handily. Most of the major U.S. media were effectively netted by the stratagem, and their news reports began to reflect the stereotype crafted by Yeltsin's team. Opposition to Yeltsin's economic initiatives was now characteristically interpreted as opposition to *any* economic reform and also to democracy. Serge Schmemann wrote in *The New York Times* of "a legislature packed with neo-Bolsheviks, nationalists and old apparatchiks," while Fred Hiatt of *The Washington Post* described the Russian legislature as an assembly of "holdover Communists and nationalists" who threatened to "derail his [Yeltsin's] privatization program, unseat his reformist ministers and slow the demilitarization of Russia's economy."[43] Predictably, several popular analysts painted even more vivid descriptions in this dispute, which was increasingly being viewed in the West as a good-versus-evil confrontation, an image that was fostered by several academics who dutifully warned, in the mode of Sachs, against the "unrepentant apparatchiks of the Russian congress."[44] Cautions by thoughtful analysts were largely drowned out in the West by a crescendo of support for Yeltsin.[45]

As early as April 1992, Yeltsin strategist Gennadii Burbulis had begun to label Russia's established legislative bodies as "historically the last link with the totalitarian system," hinting at a possible conflict between the Yeltsin forces and the deputies at the session of the Congress where Yeltsin would first propose a "presidential republic." Burbulis's approach was not that of a government official seeking to work cooperatively with the legislature.[46] "We realized that the legislative branch would be a brake [on reforms], and I thought that the idea of a presidential vertical [system] would be best—and the idea of a parallel power structure," Burbulis recalled early in 1993.[47]

Before the Seventh Congress convened on December 1, Kozyrev noted that the Western mass media had already effectively created a negative image of the Russian legislature. As a result, he argued at a press conference, if Yeltsin were to dissolve the Congress, the West would support it.[48]

Kozyrev's interpretation was correct. Following his setbacks at the Eighth Congress in March, Yeltsin had sounded out Western leaders about his idea of declaring "special rule," and apparently no heads of Western governments voiced major objections. Through Kozyrev, he notified the ambassadors of the G–7 nations of his plan on the same day he announced this decision to the Russian people; and again, there seem to have been no strong reservations about Yeltsin's political course.

It would be nearly unthinkable that a Western president and his aides might do what Yeltsin accomplished in the months before his referendum victory—successfully orchestrating a movement to discredit the country's legislators *en masse* with the support of an international cadre comprised of the heads of other powerful nations. It could happen in Russia in 1992 and 1993 because Yeltsin was playing simultaneously to Russians' urgency to shake off what remained of their communist past and to the West's lingering suspicion of anyone branded as a holdover from the communist period, even when the accuser himself is a former high party official.

With increasing signs that the conflict between the legislative and executive branches was escalating, many Russian liberals felt that they had to make a choice of loyalties. The old Soviet constitution, which specified the division of authority among state power structures, precluded a real balance of power between the legislative and executive branches; and Yeltsin, rather than himself advocating a balance, instead made every effort to get more power for himself. His strategy not only sowed further discord between his government and the Congress, but it also created a dilemma for democrats. For those who saw Yeltsin as Russia's best hope—and there were many with this view—it was difficult to avoid consenting to Yeltsin's appeals for "presidential power" over a legislature with whom he found it increasingly difficult to work.

Thus former Moscow mayor Gavriil Popov argued that "temporary presidential rule" was the best solution, but with "guarantees for democracy" and only until 1995.[49] Commenting on Yeltsin's March 20 declaration of "special rule," Yurii Lotman, an eminent philosopher and humanist, argued that "Russia needs a strong individual leader—temporarily. And, I repeat, this need for such a leader is temporary. . . . I remain Yeltsin's supporter and believe that now is the time to take decisive steps. I can't say that I am completely satisfied with all of his actions, but I think that now he is doing the right thing."[50] Business leader and political activist Konstantin Borovoi agreed, arguing that Yeltsin's only possibility to carry out his economic agenda was to consolidate power in the executive branch and dismiss the Congress.[51] And *Moscow News*'s chief editor Len Karpinskii argued that while Yeltsin's opponents were decrying the threat of "authoritarian rule by the President," Russia had "already slid into authoritarian power of the Congress."[52] This line of reasoning was predominant in the thinking of democrats prior to the April referendum. But even Yeltsin supporters were often hesitant, if not entirely unwilling, to grant his demand for additional power. The editor-in-chief of *Nezavisimaia gazeta*, Vitalii Tretiakov, sounded a familiar caution in an open letter to Yeltsin: "I will vote for you in the referendum on April 25th, if it is held (but actually, I am not sure that it will be the right thing to do), and I will also vote for you in the presidential elections (if they are held this year and if I don't see among young politicians another one who could continue the way of Russian democracy). But why did you call the referendum? Who needed it? The legislature can be dismissed only if there is a dictatorship."[53]

On the one hand, the Russian Congress was vulnerable to a series of serious criticisms. But on the other, most deputies were not as extreme as Yeltsin persistently charged, and many of their complaints against his policies were appropriate. Further, even if the Congress *had been* as uncooperative as Yeltsin said it was, his tactics to circumvent its authority were indefensible within a democratic framework. Underscoring this point, Tretiakov minced no words in judging the Congress after its late March session: "The Congress is terrible, and deputies are saying ridiculous things." He quickly added, "But it should not be broken up, even if the West should express support for President Yeltsin's strict measures 25 times more."[54]

It is true that relations between Yeltsin and the legislature during this period deteriorated to the point that fruitful negotiations of differences became increasingly difficult; and people on both sides of the political battles often took extreme positions. Yet, during the period when the Congress was, according to Yeltsin, moving toward a "pro-communist dictatorship," *most* political realignment in the legislature was, instead, toward the center—away from both the right and left extremes.

By the beginning of 1993, there were fourteen factions in the Congress representing a broad political spectrum. Of the 1,033 deputies (reduced by eight from the 1,041 elected in 1990), 834 belonged to one of these factions. The Institute for Complex Social Studies began tracking the political positions of deputies in the Congress in 1990. The most populous faction then was Communists of Russia, which could claim the support of 355 deputies. According to the research of the Information Analysis Group (IAG), which rated congressional factions in the Seventh Congress in December 1992 on a scale distinguishing between, at the extremes, "firm support for the course of radical political and economic reforms" (+100) and "sharp opposition to them" (-100), the Communists of Russia averaged -89.[55] This faction was "the most consistent and disciplined" in the Congress, the researchers stated, "which not once in three years has allowed itself to wobble at all or make any compromises." Membership in this most conservative faction in the Congress consistently declined after the deputies were elected in 1990. In the Ninth Congress in April 1993, membership in the Communists of Russia had dropped to 67, or 19 percent of its strength three years earlier (Table B–9.1).[56]

At the other political extreme were Radical Democrats and Democratic Russia, with IAG ratings of +89 and +82, respectively. The Radical Democrats faction had not existed in 1990 but claimed 50 members at the Ninth Congress. Democratic Russia had 205 members in the summer of 1991, and its membership declined to 48 in April 1993.

In April 1993, Kostiukov estimated that between 240 and 250 deputies, or no more than 25 percent of the Congress, held a procommunist orientation (which included most members of the last four factions listed in Table B–9.1).[57] At the other end of the continuum, he characterized about 100 deputies as "radical liberals," who wanted to eliminate the remaining vestiges of Russia's command economy as quickly as possible.[58] "Liberal democrats" consisted of 230 to 250 legislators,[59] who comprised a self-identified "democratic center"; and the generally more conservative "social democrats" included 280 to 320 deputies.[60]

The makeup of the Congress before the April referendum was hardly a democratic reformer's ideal, but Yeltsin's increasingly shrill attacks seem to be best explained as his way of acquiring unchallenged power. The U.S. Congress at that time was hardly a rubber stamp for President Clinton's economic proposals, either; but to disband the legislature rather than continue to search for common ground was not a democratic option in the United States.

At the time Western heads of state were supporting Yeltsin's belligerent moves against Russia's legislature, there was already persuasive evidence from other former Soviet republics of the dangers presented by strong presidents with weak legislatures. Georgia was such a case. Zviad Gamsakhurdia had promised to bring democracy and a market economy to a republic long deprived of autonomy, and in October 1990 his Round Table won a landslide victory.[61] Fourteen months later, with the newly independent country's parliament building in ruins and the capital in a state of near anarchy, the democratic promise of a popular leader had turned into an unimagined nightmare.

Conclusion: A New Mandate and a Familiar Danger

Our analysis indicates that the Yeltsin–Gaidar economic program of 1992 was based on inadequate attention to reform solutions that could have helped creatively to transform Russia's production system on the way to a market economy. The radical reformers were too willing to see the established system wrecked, rather than changing it in ways that would effectively utilize its resources and potential. In pursuing their objective of achieving momentous change as rapidly and decisively as possible, the reformers largely ignored the negative social consequences that were certain to follow. Western-backed economic policy initiatives in smaller East European countries were themselves based on questionable logic that is vigorously debated in the economics literature. Attempts to shape Russia to the East European mold introduced additional distortions. It is true that the Yeltsin–Gaidar plans were never fully implemented in the way that foreign advisers and officials of Western financial institutions had wanted them to be; but we find little empirical basis for the contention that these proposals could have been any more efficacious under other circumstances. The East European examples, although often offered in evidence, do not provide an affirmative answer to this now-theoretical question.

Thus, while Yeltsin's strong referendum showing says a great deal about Russians' fervent rejection of the old command system, we suspect that if the referendum results were to be interpreted as a mandate for deepening monetarist reform policies, even the legitimacy of the reform process itself might be jeopardized.

That outcome, however, seemed unlikely in late April 1993. There were many signs that, rather than deepening reforms along monetarist-inspired lines, the government was intensifying its effort to please more conservative constituencies at home while also trying to ensure continued IMF and G–7 participation in Russia's economic reform effort.

How long Yeltsin and Chernomyrdin could credibly appear to be following these two divergent paths simultaneously was uncertain. In the spring, Western powers had committed themselves to Yeltsin more pointedly than ever before, however, and it would be difficult to backtrack from their promise of support again, as they had in 1992. Western leaders were hoping to prop up Yeltsin's charismatic authority at the expense of less personal and more stable forms of institutionally anchored power. Economic reform was certainly one of their concerns, as was an obvious determination to help prevent a resurgence of communism in Russia. But these two agendas were not entirely compatible, and therein was the source of serious difficulties for the government and for the economy.

The political crisis Yeltsin had helped to create beginning in late 1992, with his aggressive stance toward the legislature, restored much of his diminishing symbolic capital, both in Russia and in the West. By increasing his political leverage through confrontation, however, he had severely restricted his options at home. It was not the first time he had played this same card to buy more time, but it would probably have to be the last—if, as he claimed, he planned to continue securing his legitimacy from the people. Now, his government would have to fashion a more realistic economic program than the one hammered out by the Gaidar team—one less sensitive to the monetarist emphasis on financial stabilization. We find the argument persuasive that, if Yeltsin had chosen a more gradual economic reform approach in late 1991—as many reform-minded Russian economists had urged without success—some of the economically and politically costly developments of 1992 and 1993 might well have been avoided. Our analysis further suggests that, in trying to eliminate the threat of a communist resurgence through rapid economic reorganization, the reformers inadvertently heightened the risk that authoritarian forces in Russia might gain increasing support.

As the midpoint of 1993 approached, the resoluteness of Russia's movement toward both a market economy and a democratic power structure with checks and balances was uncertain. A clearer trend was the growing influence of the nation's traditional elites. Emboldened by Yeltsin's economic policy failures, their voices had grown stronger, and responding to their pressure, the Yeltsin government had revised its economic priorities toward a decidedly more conservative emphasis. Once again, the latent strength of state officialdom was being shown—but this time, with an unintended boost from the government's reform planners.

Yeltsin's failure to capitalize on his political advantage after the August 1991 coup was fresh in the minds of his supporters after the April 1993 referendum. "We urge the president to fully use the results of the victory *and not indulge in inexplicable inaction, as was the case in the post-August 1991 days*," said Sergei Yushenkov, a radical democratic adviser to Yeltsin.[62]

Yeltsin was not slow to take advantage of his new opportunity. Four days after the referendum vote, he brought together regional leaders and presented them with a new draft constitution, which would diminish the legislative branch's power and enhance the authority of the president.

The constitution Yeltsin proposed would firmly establish the president as the highest official in the land, with authority to disband the legislature and call new elections in certain situations. Impeachment of the president would be a complex process involving the country's highest court (according to the draft constitution, the Supreme Judiciary). There would be no vice president. Advantages to the president of the proposed structure were obvious. According to the constitution in effect at the time Yeltsin presented his draft, the president could be impeached by the legislature; he could not disband the legislature; and the vice president—in this case Yeltsin's rival, Aleksandr Rutskoi—would succeed the president if the office should be vacated for any reason.[63]

"It must be brought home to everyone that the president and the policy of reform are all under the protection of the people from now on," he declared. "Decisions that run counter to the popular will, whoever makes them, will not be implemented and are to be abolished."[64] Yeltsin continued the same theme in an April 29 meeting with his cabinet: "We cannot tolerate resistance from inside. We need to get rid of those who are not on the same path as us."[65]

Thus the stage was prepared, either for further confrontation with possible destabilization of the country, or for a highly centralized administrative system headed by a president with a demonstrated preference for unquestioned authority and an unsettling pattern of treating his rivals harshly. As the summer of 1993 began, a critical juncture had been reached in Russia's struggle for economic and political transformation. Unmistakable warning signs attesting to the hazards of unchecked political ambition had been ignored. Yeltsin had successfully discredited those who feared his drive for power and convinced both constituents at home and leaders in the West that a radiant Russian future now depended on him.

Appendix A

Technical and Supplementary Material

Features of the Four-City 1992 Study

Research Sites

Our research in 1992 was carried out in Moscow, Smolensk, Voronezh, and Ekaterinburg. We chose Moscow because of its political importance as a large capital city and center of intellectual and cultural activity, and because it was the locus of many early privatization efforts. Ekaterinburg (population 1,372,000)[1] is the largest city in the Urals region and a major manufacturing center. Chemical equipment, electric turbines, and heavy machinery account for half of the city's industrial production; but there are also a large number of other enterprises there as well. Ekaterinburg was a closed city until recently; it has long been a major military production center. Voronezh (population 895,000) is in south-central Russia near the Don River. Heavy machinery, electronics equipment, chemicals, construction materials, processed food, and clothing are among Voronezh's principal products. Smolensk is one of Russia's oldest cities, and with a population of 346,000 was the smallest city in our study. Located on the Dnieper River in western Russia, its industries include automation equipment, electronics equipment, clothing, aircraft, and household appliances.

Data Collection Procedures

I visited each target city in early May, before data collection began.[2] One objective of these visits was to determine who the key privatization decision-makers (DMs) were for each city and to secure the cooperation of city and oblast officials. We interviewed all the decision-makers in Voronezh and Smolensk and samples in Ekaterinburg and Moscow based on our judgments of who were key decision-makers in those cities. (In Ekaterinburg we did not have access to all privatization decision-makers because of serious political tensions there between city and oblast officials.)

We obtained lists from city and oblast officials of state, privatized, and private enterprises in each city. Outside Moscow, we carried out our research in all the privatized enterprises where we were able to secure permission; and in Moscow, we sampled from a large number of already privatized enterprises—selecting all industrial enterprises that had been privatized and sampling randomly from others. We constructed our state- and private-enterprise samples to match as closely as possible the distribution of spheres of enterprise activity characterizing our privatized-enterprise subsample.

Themes of Interviews and Questionnaires

In the interviews with DMs we examined the process through which privatization was being carried out; and we explored both the formal regulations and the informal procedures of commissions and committees. Our interviews with other government officials and specialists broadened our understanding of issues surrounding economic reform and alternative reform proposals that had been widely discussed.

The interviews with directors and owners focused, at different points, on the opportunities and problems presented by the ferment surrounding the shift under way in Russia from a centrally planned economy to one driven more by the market. We explored the perspectives of directors and owners on larger issues surrounding economic reform, and we inquired about the implications of reform for the enterprises they headed. Our interviews outside the state sector focused on the problems owners and directors encountered in satisfying administrative regulations that were applicable to their businesses; in securing licenses and permits and surmounting other political obstacles; in obtaining supplies, work space, and equipment; and over staffing issues. We wanted to learn what opportunities and obstacles were especially salient to these businesspeople, and what factors had contributed most prominently to success and growth of their enterprises. We also inquired into the causes of business failure in other nonstate businesses they were familiar with. We asked directors of privatized firms about advantages and disadvantages of changes in the organizational structure of their enterprises, and effects of restructuring on productivity. In state enterprises, we inquired into management's and workers' plans for privatization.

Our research among nonmanagerial workers concentrated on their opinions about the government's economic reform program, details about supervisory and reward structures in their enterprises, and their job satisfaction and motivation. In state and privatized enterprises we also asked about privatization procedures that were planned, or had been used, in their enterprises, and judgments about the likely effects of privatization on opportunities for advancement where they worked. Nonmanagerial personnel were randomly selected by our field-workers, when possible, from personnel lists. These respondents completed questionnaires in the presence of a field-worker, who was available to answer questions about the study or about specific questionnaire items.

The interview schedule for privatization decision-makers was the shortest, but these were the longest interviews. Many of the questions were open-ended, and interviewers probed for additional information based on the initial responses of the interviewees. Interviews with decision-makers and enterprise directors and owners were tape-recorded.

Translation and Backtranslation

Problematic questionnaire and interview items that were taken from English-language sources were discussed in a working group of five people, who deliberated over alternative phrasings in an effort to preserve the original meaning of the questions. Backtranslation was carried out by a translator who had not been involved in the working group.

Unusual Fieldwork Problems and Frequency Distribution of Respondents

Our work in the Sverdlovsk Oblast was seriously delayed because of a decision by the Ekaterinburg City Council and Sverdlovsk Oblast officials to restrict access to the lists we needed of private and privatized enterprises. I had spent two days early in the summer talking with a large number of these people, and I left Ekaterinburg assured of their full cooperation as our research proceeded. Our discussions had been cordial, and I had no indication at all that a political storm was on the horizon—a conflict unrelated to our research but which, because of the kinds of information we needed, affected our work directly. Both city and oblast officials adopted a policy early in the summer of taking issue with privatization procedures being implemented there. There were also conspicuous and troubling criminal activities directed against some new private enterprises. One of the effects of the power struggle over procedures and the concern about crime against entrepreneurs was that city and oblast officials decided to withhold information about privatization and entrepreneurship from all nongovernmental personnel, including our research group, reporters, businesspeople, and other individuals interested in the privatization process in the region. (The crime problem also created other complications for the study. We found that many owners of private businesses recorded false addresses for their firms on official documents to forestall threats, thefts, and murders.)

It took us nearly two months to overcome the secrecy policy that had been established as a result of this turn of events, but ultimately we were largely successful. Oblast and city officials remained split on the larger question of privatization procedures and on the issue of making official records available to nongovernmental personnel, however, and thus our refusal rate among privatization decision-makers was markedly higher in Ekaterinburg and Sverdlovsk Oblast (60 percent) than at any of our other research sites.

We also had some difficulty securing information we needed in a few Moscow districts, because several officials either were initially uncooperative or wanted money to furnish the information we requested. These were localized problems, however, not citywide. We were able to resolve them satisfactorily on a case-by-case basis (without paying any money). It was because of the delay created by these temporary obstacles that our data collection in Moscow proceeded more slowly than in Voronezh and Smolensk. In those two cities, our work went smoothly, with the full cooperation of all officials with whom we needed to work.

Respondents were distributed by job work type and city as follows:

	Moscow	Ekaterinburg	Voronezh	Smolensk
Decision-makers	68	17	50	36
Directors/owners				
State	106	63	136	100
Privatized	116	7	26	14
Private	99	102	142	55
Nonmanagerial workers				
State	422	614	498	699
Privatized	452	219	352	122
Private	400	280	398	189

Our response rates for decision-makers, managers and owners, and workers were, respectively, 66 percent, 74 percent, and 81 percent.

The 1991 Moscow Interviews

Our work in Moscow during 1991 was exploratory. We formally interviewed 101 enterprise managers/directors/owners to gain a better understanding of the course of entrepreneurship up to that time and to identify critical issues for further study. The 1991 study provided valuable insights for developing our more extensive project the following year, and the interviews also yielded useful qualitative information regarding several themes in this study. No data from the 1991 study were included in the quantitative analysis.

Quantitative Data Analysis

Part of what makes the study of human behavior so interesting is that nearly everything seems to be related to almost everything else. Personnel in state enterprises in our sample, for example, were significantly different in the aggregate from private-enterprise personnel on sociodemographic dimensions; and these other factors could, if not controlled, influence the causal importance a researcher might be inclined to attribute to an enterprise type. Are people in the private sector *really* more likely than state employees to favor wholesale privatization of farmland, or are bivariate differences due to the different age and education distributions among workers in these different types of enterprise?

Depending on the question being asked, it may or may not be desirable to introduce control variables in such cases. If a researcher wonders whether the type of enterprise in which people work either causes or results from some other factor, separate from the influence of sociodemographic factors, then controls may be needed. On the other hand, if a researcher wants to compare *aggregates of people expressly as aggregates,* then systematic sociodemographic variation among these aggregates should not be filtered out. Controls in such cases could muddle rather than clarify a question of interest.

In part of our analysis, we were interested in the "pure" effects of several potential predictors, especially city of residence, age, education, sex, and enterprise type. Typically, tables presenting our results with these variables when controls had been introduced utilize the typological regression standardization (TRS) procedure, which is briefly summarized below and discussed in more detail elsewhere.[3]

Regression standardization is a form of test factor standardization[4] and is commonly used in simplified form by demographers. Comparisons of fertility and mortality rates among nations, for example, are more meaningful if differences in the age structure of the countries can be taken into account. The "direct method" of standardization[5] permits a researcher to eliminate the effects of age differences in such cases by comparing the age-specific fertility and mortality rates in one country—the country on which rates are being standardized—to those of each other country in the analysis. If, for example, one wanted to compare fertility and mortality rates in the United States and Mexico—taking into account the fact that Mexico's population is disproportionately young—one could standardize on the United States and determine through regression analysis how Mexico's fertility and mortality rates would be affected if that country's age structure were adjusted to that of the United States.

If one thinks of regression standardization as a mathematical translation of constructed typologies, the versatility of the TRS technique becomes obvious—provided, of course, that appropriate assumptions are reasonably well met. TRS combines the analytical power of ordinary multiple regression with the clarity of typological conceptualization. The following is a straightforward interpretation of the percentages we derived through regression standardization: *The percentages signify the values each cell would take if respondents in every category had the same characteristics as the "standard"—characteristics defined by the specified control variables.* The tables are readily interpretable, even though several control variables have been taken into account.

We carried out significance testing throughout our analysis, with both regressions and cross-tabulations, using t-tests with regressions and chi-square tests with tables. With tables, whether they were simple cross-tabulations or standardized proportions, we were usually interested in comparing specific cells (which limited the utility of chi-square)—and often in so many cells (across both rows and columns) that presenting significance test results for tests of pairs would have been cumbersome. Further, since our overall sample is quite large, statistical significance was often not a good indicator of substantive significance. Therefore, we do not present significance test results in this book. With most of our comparisons, percentages differences of 4 to 6 points (depending on the ns) are statistically significant. In our analysis, we consistently required differences of a substantially greater magnitude than this before making much of them.

Significance of the Control Variables for Privatization Attitudes

Moscow residents were more likely than respondents in the other three cities to want privatization to be speeded up, and they were more positive about large-scale privatization of farmland and urban residences (Table B–A.1). If Muscovites were no more satisfied with their jobs and incomes than other respondents, they found the prospects of unemployment due to privatization less threatening—probably because Muscovites were distinctly less likely than residents of the other cities to fear that it would be difficult to find a satisfactory job if they became unemployed (Table B–A.2).

In general, younger people were more favorable about privatization than older respondents, and males supported privatization more than females did (Table B–A.3). The age differences were not strong, however; and age had no effect on responses to some questions. Male-female differences in privatization attitudes held, for the most part, in each of the four cities (Table B–A.4). Men were more worried about job reductions in their enterprises than women were, but women were more likely than men to think it would be difficult to find another suitable job if they became unemployed (Table B–A.5).

Both enterprise type and education had modest effects on privatization attitudes in the controlled condition. Responses from state- and privatized-enterprise personnel were almost indistinguishable on the question of the optimal pace of privatization, but private-sector respondents were more likely to want the privatization process to accelerate (Table B–A.6). Support for privatization tends to be highest among respondents with higher education experience (Table B–A.7). Support for farmland privatization is especially sensitive to educational background.

Appendix B

Tables

Table B–6.1

Number of Rubles to the Dollar at the Moscow Currency Exchange, January 1992–January 1993 (monthly highs)

Month	Rubles
January 1992	230
February	139
March	161
April	137
May	147
June	130
July	161
August	210
September	448
October	403
November	398
December	417
January 1993	568
February	593
March	686
April 27	812

Source: Adapted from *Izvestiia,* no. 15 (27 January 1993), 1; *Delovoi mir,* no. 38 (27 February 1993), 1; and unpublished material.

Table B–7.1

"Do You Think That Privatization in Russia Should Proceed More Quickly Than Now, More Slowly, or at the Present Pace?" (row percentages)

Type of respondent	More quickly	At present pace or more slowly	Don't know
Administrative decision-makers (DMs)	52	45	3
Enterprise personnel			
State enterprises			
Directors	62	21	17
Dept. heads/specialists	51	16	34
Skilled workers	52	18	30
Clerks/technicians	39	15	46
Unskilled workers	44	14	42
Privatized enterprises			
Directors	78	11	11
Dept. heads/specialists	57	13	30
Skilled workers	51	16	33
Clerks/technicians	44	12	43
Unskilled workers	42	12	47
Private enterprises			
Owners/directors	70	20	10
Dept. heads/specialists	67	11	22
Skilled workers	57	21	22
Clerks/technicians	50	16	34
Unskilled workers	49	19	32

Table B–7.2

Perceived Social Consequences of Privatization Among Administrative Decision-Makers, Enterprise Directors and Owners, and Nonmanagerial Enterprise Personnel (percentages)

Response choice	Decision-makers	Directors and owners	Nonmanagerial personnel
Privatization will make people's lives better	67	60	43
If Russia achieves a market economy, the living standards of a majority of the people will improve	44	35	20
Income inequality will increase with the shift to a market economy	95	89	80
Increased income inequality will be a negative effect of the shift to a market economy	30	28	32
Unemployment will increase with privatization	82	81	82
Crime rates will increase with the shift to a market economy	75	69	68
Moral values will decline with the shift to a market economy	44	42	41
Friendships and personal relations among people will become less close with the shift to a market economy	64	57	57

Table B–7.3

Extent of Support Among Enterprise Personnel for the View That "There Is No Need for Privatization" (percentages by occupational and enterprise type)

Enterprise type	Owners/ directors/ managers	Dept. heads/ specialists	Skilled workers	Clerks/ technicians	Unskilled workers
State	10	13	15	21	24
Privatized	1	7	12	9	16

Table B–7.4

Extent of Support Among Enterprise Personnel for the Government's 1992 Privatization Program (percentages by occupational and enterprise type)

Response choice Type of enterprise	Occupational type				
	Directors/ owners	Dept. heads/ specialists	Skilled workers	Clerks/ technicians	Unskilled workers
Support "completely" or "to a considerable extent"					
State	43	26	23	19	18
Privatized	48	25	23	16	15
Private	52	33	29	16	18
Support "to some extent"					
State	46	34	28	24	20
Privatized	42	34	25	23	18
Private	40	37	23	34	20
Do not support the program					
State	10	10	10	10	11
Privatized	10	6	11	8	11
Private	6	6	12	6	6
Don't know					
State	1	30	39	48	51
Privatized	0	35	41	53	57
Private	2	24	37	44	55

Table B–7.5

Responses of Personnel in Privatized Enterprises to the Question "Are Workers Today Able to Participate in Decision Making About the Privatization of Their Enterprise?" (row percentages)

Type of respondent	"Workers are the primary decision-makers"	"Workers have a great deal of influence"	"Workers have only a little influence" or "Almost no influence"	"Don't Know"
Administrative decision-makers (DMs)	43	32	24	1
Enterprise personnel				
Directors	23	38	38	1
Dept. heads/ specialists	10	22	57	12
Skilled workers	10	38	24	21
Clerks/technicians	7	24	55	13
Unskilled workers	8	21	51	21

Table B–7.6

Preferred Forms of Ownership for Farmland and Urban Residences, by Age of Respondent (row percentages)

	Farmland			
Age category	Private individuals	Individuals/ state	State/collective farms	Don't know
18–25	48	46	4	2
26–33	43	46	7	3
34–41	33	54	10	3
42–49	30	54	13	3
50+	21	63	14	3

	Urban residences			
Age category	Private individuals	Individuals/ state	State	Don't know
18–25	26	60	11	3
26–33	24	59	15	3
34–41	21	59	17	4
42–49	18	61	17	5
50+	18	56	22	4

Table B–8.1

Attitudes About Work Habits and Work Recognition (percentages by occupational and enterprise type)

Response choice Type of enterprise	Overall	Directors/ owners	Dept. heads/ specialists	Skilled workers	Clerks/ technicians	Unskilled workers
			Occupational type			
Most people work harder in the West than in Russia						
State	68	72	70	61	73	63
Privatized	69	77	74	65	70	63
Private	66	72	69	50	71	59
Of respondents who believed that Western personnel work harder, percent who believe that the difference is large						
State	68	72	68	66	70	65
Privatized	68	80	73	62	72	57
Private	65	68	42	67	55	52
"Very satisfied" or "somewhat satisfied" with my income						
State	20	25	24	16	17	17
Privatized	21	29	28	20	18	15
Private	36	42	35	32	34	32

There is at least a 50
percent chance that I will be
recognized for good work

State	33	—	29	39	35	34
Privatized	36	—	40	37	37	32
Private	45	—	50	43	46	39

There is at least a 50
percent chance that I will be
promoted to a higher
position in my enterprise

State	11	—	12	14	10	10
Privatized	12	—	17	11	10	10
Private	24	—	23	30	19	27

Table B–8.2

Attitudes About Work, Unemployment, and Privatization (percentages by age and sex; standardized on people aged 34–41, with city, enterprise type, occupational level, and education controlled)

Response choice Sex	Age				
	18–25	26–33	34–41	42–49	50+
It would be "not easy at all" to find another job with about the same income					
Males	39	47	47	46	57
Females	54	63	66	74	73
I put "a considerable amount" or "a great deal" of effort into my work					
Males	70	72	75	71	71
Females	59	69	77	73	73
Privatization should proceed more quickly					
Males	66	65	61	59	54
Females	59	56	51	47	42
Privatization will cause unemployment to increase					
Males	79	81	79	79	83
Females	77	75	76	78	79

Table B–8.3

Attitudes About Unemployment (percentages by occupational and enterprise type)

Response choice Type of enterprise	Overall	Occupational type				
		Directors/ owners	Dept. heads/ specialists	Skilled workers	Clerks/ technicians	Unskilled workers
It is "very likely" or "fairly likely" that I will lose my job in the coming 12 months (four-point scale)						
State	48	—	48	49	52	45
Privatized	49	—	44	39	50	57
Private	37	—	40	34	38	34
More than 10 percent of the work force in my enterprise will lose their jobs within the next 12 months						
State	29	17	43	29	28	20
Privatized	23	13	32	29	19	25
Private	10	11	10	5	10	10
It would be "not easy at all" to find another job with about the same income						
State	65	50	75	62	72	60
Privatized	65	35	67	62	73	74
Private	53	30	61	55	64	66

Table B–8.4

Expected Social Consequences of Privatization (percentages by occupational and enterprise type)

Response choice Type of enterprise	Overall	Directors/owners	Dept. heads/ specialists	Skilled workers	Clerks/ technicians	Unskilled workers
			Occupational type			
The shift to a market economy will cause crime to increase						
State	72	76	70	75	71	69
Privatized	73	78	72	73	76	69
Private	58	59	63	42	59	61
The shift to a market economy will cause friendships and personal relationships to become less close						
State	62	63	69	55	61	57
Privatized	59	57	64	63	61	53
Private	47	51	53	34	47	42

The shift to a market
economy will cause
moral values to
decline, or, Do not know
what to expect

State	66	58	67	60	70	69
Privatized	67	56	66	70	72	69
Private	57	56	60	38	62	63

The shift to a market
economy will cause an
increase in income
inequality

State	84	91	89	86	80	75
Privatized	81	94	91	86	77	70
Private	77	84	88	61	78	63

Increasing income
inequality will be a
positive change

State	34	51	35	35	25	27
Privatized	36	68	42	37	26	24
Private	48	63	54	42	39	30

Table B–8.5

"If You Should Change Your Job, What Kind of Job Opportunity Would You Prefer?" (percentages by occupational and enterprise type)

Response choice Type of enterprise	Overall	Occupational type				
		Directors/ owners	Dept. heads /specialists	Skilled workers	Clerks/ technicians	Unskilled workers
State enterprise						
State	27	22	24	22	28	36
Privatized	12	8	10	10	15	13
Private	8	5	5	11	9	14
Cooperative						
State	4	2	2	11	3	5
Privatized	4	1	2	6	3	7
Private	7	1	4	18	8	13
Joint-stock company (without foreign investors)						
State	9	12	11	7	9	6
Privatized	16	13	20	13	17	16
Private	11	16	15	3	11	9

Private business (not a joint-stock company)						
State	13	19	9	12	11	14
Privatized	19	32	20	17	16	16
Private	26	37	18	31	20	26
Joint venture						
State	23	24	24	22	23	18
Privatized	22	23	24	19	27	17
Private	21	19	27	16	24	16
Foreign firm						
State	13	9	13	17	12	13
Privatized	20	17	17	30	15	22
Private	19	17	24	13	24	16
Other						
State	13	12	17	7	14	8
Privatized	8	6	8	4	8	9
Private	7	6	7	7	8	5

Table B–8.6

"Which of These Job Characteristics Would Be the Most Important to You in Choosing a Job, If You Had Free Choice?" (percentages by occupational and enterprise type)

Response choice Type of enterprise	Overall	Occupational type				
		Directors/ owners	Dept. heads/ specialists	Skilled workers	Clerks/ technicians	Unskilled workers
High income						
State	29	17	26	39	29	37
Privatized	30	19	26	38	28	35
Private	40	29	37	45	47	50
Job security						
State	43	39	37	44	51	44
Privatized	40	27	34	40	49	44
Private	27	20	23	34	34	32
Work that is important and interesting and gives a feeling of accomplishment						
State	28	44	38	17	20	19
Privatized	30	54	40	22	23	21
Private	33	51	40	21	19	17

Table B–8.7

Job and Life Satisfaction (percentages by occupational and enterprise type; standardized on skilled workers in the state sector, with age, sex, education, and city of residence controlled)

Response choice Type of enterprise	Occupational type				
	Directors/ owners	Dept. heads/ specialists	Skilled workers	Clerks/ technicians	Unskilled workers
"Very satisfied" or "somewhat satisfied" with my job					
State	53	50	50	53	52
Privatized	51	45	53	53	45
Private	57	59	51	63	50
"Very happy" or "pretty happy"					
State	43	30	33	28	31
Privatized	39	28	25	23	21
Private	55	40	45	47	39
"A great deal" or "somewhat" happier now than a year earlier					
State	16	15	14	14	14
Privatized	26	21	10	17	12
Private	31	22	13	22	17

(continued)

224

Table B-8.7 *(continued)*

Derived "a great deal" or "a substantial amount" of satisfaction from family life (five choices)					
State	49	34	34	33	34
Privatized	48	31	30	34	33
Private	51	39	35	40	41
"A great deal" or "somewhat" more satisfied with family life now than a year earlier					
State	23	20	17	19	17
Privatized	25	22	15	22	16
Private	32	22	19	27	19

Table B–8.8

(1) "What Was the Most Serious Problem You Faced When You Started Your Business?" (2) "What Is the Most Serious Problem Now?" (column percentages)

Response choice	(1) Privatized enterprise	(1) Private enterprise	(2) Privatized enterprise	(2) Private enterprise
Obtaining/utilizing premises	9	20	10	8
Obtaining financing	38	34	37	38
Obtaining machinery	4	8	2	8
Obtaining materials	6	7	23	12
Locating good personnel	7	11	3	11
Working with local authorities	16	10	5	4
Attitudes in the population	1	1	2	3
Racketeers, mafia	4	1	3	3
Other	16	9	15	14

Table B–9.1

Factions in the Congress of People's Deputies: Membership and Political Orientations

Faction	Number of deputies (April 1993)	IAG rating* (December 1992)
Radical Democrats	50	+89
Democratic Russia	48	+82
Accord for Progress	54	+76
Left Center/Cooperation	61	+24
Free Russia	54	+5
Motherland	57	−10
Workers' Union	53	−19
Sovereignty and Equality	50	−40
Rising Generation/New Policy	53	−43
Industrial Union	51	−49
Fatherland	51	−67
Agrarian Union	130	−73
Russia	55	−76
Communists of Russia	67	−89

Source: Adapted from *Delovoi mir,* no. 63 (6 April 1993), 5; *Megapolis-Express,* no. 15 (21 April 1993), 23; and *CDPSP,* vol. 45 (24 March 1993), 1–3.

*A rating of +100 indicated "firm support for the course of radical political and economic reforms"; −100 indicated "sharp opposition to them." See pages 190–91, above.

Table B–A.1

Preferred Pace and Scope of Privatization by City (percentages standardized on Moscow with enterprise type, occupational level, education, age, and sex controlled)

Response choice	City			
	Moscow	Ekaterinburg	Voronezh	Smolensk
Privatization should proceed more quickly	63	55	47	47
Private individuals should be the principal owners of farmland in Russia	45	32	31	22
Private individuals should be the principal owners of urban residences	27	22	17	17
Owners of private businesses should own both the associated buildings and land	72	71	63	65

Table B–A.2

Attitudes About Unemployment and Job Satisfaction by City
(percentages standardized on Moscow with enterprise type, occupational
level, education, age, and sex controlled)

Response choice	City			
	Moscow	Ekaterinburg	Voronezh	Smolensk
Privatization will cause unemployment to increase	82	79	76	85
More than 10 percent of the work force in my enterprise will probably lose their jobs within the next 12 months	21	26	29	21
It would be "not easy at all" to find another job with about the same income	50	61	70	71

Table B–A.3

Privatization Attitudes by Age and Sex (percentages standardized by people aged 34–41, with city, enterprise type, occupational level, education, and sex controlled)

Response choice Sex	Age				
	18–25	26–33	34–41	42–49	50+
Privatization should proceed more quickly					
Males	66	65	61	59	54
Females	59	56	51	47	42
Private individuals should be the principal owners of farmland in Russia					
Males	46	41	37	36	32
Females	37	38	33	32	29
Private individuals should be the principal owners of urban residences					
Males	25	26	21	24	25
Females	18	18	21	17	21
Owners of private businesses should own both the associated buildings and the land					
Males	74	74	77	78	74
Females	65	67	69	66	67

Table B–A.4

Privatization Attitudes by Sex and City (percentages standardized on Moscow males, with enterprise type, occupational level, education, and age controlled)

Response choice Sex	City			
	Moscow	Ekaterinburg	Voronezh	Smolensk
Privatization should proceed more quickly				
Males	67	63	54	56
Females	62	50	43	42
Private individuals should be the principal owners of farmland in Russia				
Males	47	28	33	24
Females	41	32	26	18
Private individuals should be the principal owners of urban residences				
Males	31	23	19	21
Females	24	21	17	13
Owners of private businesses should own both the associated buildings and the land				
Males	78	75	72	76
Females	72	72	60	61

Table B–A.5

Attitudes About Unemployment and Job Satisfaction by Age and Sex
(percentages standardized on people aged 34–41, with city, enterprise type, occupational level, education, and sex controlled)

Response choice Sex	Age				
	18–25	26–33	34–41	42–49	50+
Privatization will cause unemployment to increase					
Males	79	81	79	79	83
Females	77	75	76	78	79
More than 10 percent of the work force in my enterprise will probably lose their jobs within the next 12 months					
Males	24	21	20	25	24
Females	18	20	23	20	16
It would be "not easy at all" to find another job with about the same income					
Males	39	47	47	46	57
Females	54	63	66	74	73
"Very satisfied" or "somewhat satisfied" with my job					
Males	59	59	51	54	52
Females	57	48	49	44	51
"Very satisfied" or "somewhat satisfied" with my income					
Males	32	28	28	26	29
Females	24	26	30	28	30
"Very satisfied" or "somewhat satisfied" with my career progress					
Males	62	61	57	59	60
Females	49	61	60	55	60

Table B–A.6

Privatization Attitudes by Enterprise Type (percentages standardized on state enterprises, with city, occupational level, age, education, and sex controlled)

Response choice	Enterprise type		
	State	Privatized	Private
Privatization should proceed more quickly	49	49	54
Private individuals should be the principal owners of farmland in Russia	29	30	34
Private individuals should be the principal owners of urban residences	18	20	20
Owners of private businesses should own both the associated buildings and the land	62	70	69

Table B–A.7

Privatization Attitudes by Education (percentages standardized on secondary and technical school graduates, with enterprise type, occupational level, city, age, and sex controlled)

Response choice	Education			
	Less than secondary	Secondary/ technical	At least some higher education	Graduate degree
Privatization should proceed more quickly	44	47	54	51
Private individuals should be the principal owners of farmland in Russia	27	34	34	41
Private individuals should be the principal owners of urban residences	20	22	26	25
Owners of private businesses should own both the associated buildings and the land	60	64	66	67

Notes

Chapter 1. Introduction

1. Charles Tilly, *Big Structures, Large Processes, Huge Comparisons* (New York: Russell Sage Foundation, 1984), 145.

2. Ibid., 33.

3. Theda Skocpol, "Bringing the State Back In: Strategies of Analysis in Current Research," in *Bringing the State Back In,* ed. Peter B. Evans, Dietrich Rueschemeyer, and Theda Skocpol (New York: Cambridge University Press, 1985), 27.

4. See, for example, A.R. Louch, *Explanation and Human Action* (Berkeley: University of California Press, 1969).

5. Barrington Moore, Jr., *Social Origins of Dictatorship and Democracy: Lord and Peasant in the Making of the Modern World* (Boston: Beacon Press, 1966), xvii.

6. Paul Feyerabend, *Against Method* (London: Humanities Press, 1975), 270.

7. Fernand Braudel, *The Perspective of the World,* vol. 3 of *Civilization and Capitalism, 15th–18th Century* (New York: Harper and Row, 1979), 17.

8. See Martin Carnoy, *The State and Political Theory* (Princeton: Princeton University Press, 1984); and Evans, Rueschemeyer, and Skocpol, eds., *Bringing the State Back In.*

9. Peter B. Evans et al., "On the Road Toward a More Adequate Understanding of the State," in Evans, Rueschemeyer, and Skocpol, eds., *Bringing the State Back In,* 350.

10. Alfred Stepan points out that the state "must be considered as more than the 'government.'" (See his *The State and Society: Peru in Comparative Perspective* (Princeton: Princeton University Press, 1978), 20.

11. Ibid., 9. See also Samuel Huntington, *Political Order in Changing Societies* (New Haven: Yale University Press, 1968).

12. *Current Digest of the Soviet Press,* vol. 42 (16 January 1990), 10; from *Izvestiia* (17 December 1989), 2.

13. Milovan Djilas, *The New Class: An Analysis of the Communist System* (New York: Praeger, 1959), 45.

14. See Niklas Luhmann, *The Differentiation of Society,* trans. Stephen Holmes and Charles Larmore (New York: Columbia University Press, 1982), 139.

15. Robert W. Campbell, *The Socialist Economies in Transition* (Bloomington: Indiana University Press, 1991), 4.

16. Ellen Kay Trimberger, *Revolution from Above: Military Bureaucrats and Development in Japan, Turkey, Egypt and Peru* (New Brunswick, NJ: Transaction Books, 1978), 2–3.

17. Reinhard Bendix, *Embattled Reason: Essays on Social Knowledge* (New Brunswick, NJ: Transaction Books, 1988), 170–72.

18. Max Weber, *Economy and Society,* vol. 2, trans. Ephraim Fischoff et al., ed. Guenther Roth and Claus Wittich (Berkeley: University of California Press, 1978), 1117. See also Bendix, *Embattled Reason,* 170–72. Weber points out that "'ideas' have essentially the same psychological roots whether they are religious, artistic, ethical, scientific or whatever else; this also applies to ideas about political and social organization" (1116).

19. "Comments and Discussion" following David Lipton and Jeffrey D. Sachs, "Prospects for Russia's Economic Reforms," in *Brookings Papers on Economic Activity,* no. 2 (1992): 267.

20. See Bendix, *Embattled Reason,* 174.

21. Weber, *Economy and Society,* vol. 2, 1133.

22. Ibid., 1121–22.

23. Skocpol, "Bringing the State Back In," 15.

24. Senior resercher, Moscow Institute of Sociology of the Russian Academy of Sciences.

25. See, for example, Kenneth D. Bailey, *Methods of Social Research* (New York: The Free Press, 1987), 290–300.

26. David W. Benn, "*Glasnost'* and the Media," in *Developments in Soviet and Post-Soviet Politics,* ed. Stephen White, Alex Pravda, and Zvi Gitelman (Durham, NC: Duke University Press, 1992), 189.

27. For a discussion of survey research issues during the Soviet period, see Vladimir Shlapentokh, *Soviet Public Opinion and Ideology: Mythology and Pragmatism in Interaction* (New York: Praeger, 1986).

Chapter 2. From NEP to Yeltsin

1. R.W. Davies, "Introduction: From Tsarism to NEP," in *From Tsarism to the New Economic Policy,* ed. R.W. Davies (Ithaca, NY: Cornell University Press, 1991), 13–16.

2. Ibid., 14.

3. Naum Jasny, *Soviet Industrialization 1928–1952* (Chicago: University of Chicago Press, 1961), 40–41.

4. V.I. Lenin, *Polnoe sobranie sochinenii* (Moscow, 1958–65; cited hereaf-

ter as Lenin, *PSS*), 43:159 (quoted in Alan M. Ball, *Russia's Last Capitalists: The Nepmen, 1921–1929* [Berkeley: University of California Press, 1987], 24).

5. Lenin, *PSS*, 44:159 (quoted in ibid., 10–11).

6. Peter Gatrell and R.W. Davies, "The Industrial Economy," in Davies, ed., *From Tsarism to the New Economic Policy*, 154–55.

7. Reasons for this drop are discussed in R.W. Davies, *The Socialist Offensive: The Collectivisation of Soviet Agriculture, 1929–1930* (London: Macmillan, 1980), 39, 42.

8. From Lazar' Kaganovich's speech at the July 1928 plenum of the Central Committee, quoted in Hiroaki Kuromiya, *Stalin's Industrial Revolution: Politics and Workers, 1928–1932* (New York: Cambridge University Press, 1988), 6.

9. Ball, *Russia's Last Capitalists*, 154.

10. Stalin, *Sochineniia*, 11:47 (quoted in Kuromiya, *Stalin's Industrial Revolution*, 11).

11. Quoted in Kuromiya, *Stalin's Industrial Revolution*, 10.

12. The poor grain harvest in 1928 was also probably a factor. See Davies, *The Socialist Offensive*, 41ff.

13. Stalin, *Sochineniia*, 11:231 (quoted in Ball, *Russia's Last Capitalists*, 64).

14. See Davies, *The Socialist Offensive*, 117.

15. Quoted in Davies, *The Socialist Offensive*, 167.

16. As Davies puts it, "The November plenum thus ... finally confirmed the change which was maturing in the previous few months. The completion of collectivisation was not a matter of decades but of a few years, and much could be undertaken immediately" (Davies, *The Socialist Offensive*, 174).

17. Akademiia Nauk SSSR, Institut istorii, *Materialy po istorii SSSR*, vol. 6: *Dokumenty po istorii monopolisticheskogo kapitalizma v Rossii* (Moscow, 1959), 173–95, quoted in Fred V. Carstensen, "Foreign Participation in Russian Economic Life: Notes on British Enterprise, 1865–1914," in *Entrepreneurship in Imperial Russia and the Soviet Union*, ed. Gregory Guroff and Fred V. Carstensen (Princeton: Princeton University Press, 1983), 141. Carstensen contends that government policy was less important in attracting foreign capital than the recognition among foreign investors that Russia's vast resources and mass markets offered appealing profit potential.

18. Alec Nove, *An Economic History of the USSR* (New York: Penguin Books, 1989), 9. Some other estimates are lower. See, for example, Paul R. Gregory and Robert C. Stuart, *Soviet Economic Structure and Performance* (New York: Harper and Row, 1986), 43.

19. Gregory and Stuart, *Soviet Economic Structure and Performance*, 43–44.

20. A useful review of concessions granted during this period is provided in Anthony C. Sutton, *Western Technology and Soviet Economic Development*, vol. 1: *1917 to 1930* (Stanford: Hoover Institution Press, 1968).

21. Manufacturing concessions were typically for several years. A few were for much longer, for instance, the Swedish General Electric concession,

which was started in 1927 and was contracted to run until 1962. The largest concession, Lena Goldfields, Ltd. (valued at more than $89 million after Soviet expropriation), was scheduled to be effective until 1975 (see Anthony C. Sutton, *Western Technology and Soviet Economic Development*, vol. 2: *1930 to 1945* [Stanford: Hoover Institution Press, 1971], 18). Trading concessions were for one year, and renewable.

22. Fifty–fifty at first, but later 51 percent Soviet-owned.

23. Armand Hammer, with Neil Lyndon, *Hammer* (New York: G.P. Putnam's Sons, 1987), 126.

24. Sutton, *Western Technology,* vol. 1, 237, 349.

25. Ibid., 287.

26. R.W. Davies, *The Soviet Economy in Turmoil, 1929–1930* (London: Macmillan, 1989), 33.

27. Quoted in ibid., *The Soviet Economy in Turmoil, 1929–1930,* 123.

28. Davies, "Introduction: From Tsarism to NEP," 10–11.

29. Sutton, *Western Technology,* vol. 2, 343.

30. The project is outlined by Sutton, *Western Technology,* vol. 2, 249–52.

31. Ibid., vol. 1, 246–47.

32. Ibid., vol. 2, 343.

33. Ibid., 11.

34. Davies, *Soviet Economy in Turmoil, 1929–1930,* 123.

35. Ibid., 392–94.

36. Naum Jasny, "The Great Industrialization Drive," in *Russian Economic Development from Peter the Great to Stalin,* ed. William L. Blackwell (New York: New Viewpoints, 1974), 300–301.

37. Vladimir Katkoff, *Soviet Economy 1940–1965* (Westport, CT: Greenwood Press, 1961), 433.

38. The reference here is to member nations of the Council for Mutual Economic Assistance (CMEA) at the end of the Soviet period plus China, Cuba, Vietnam, North Korea, and Yugoslavia.

39. Quoted in Harry Schwartz, *The Soviet Economy Since Stalin* (New York: J.B. Lippincott, 1965), 190.

40. Sutton argues that "Soviet technology was almost completely a transfer from Western countries" (*Western Technology,* vol. 2, 329). See also Gregory and Stuart, *Soviet Economic Structure and Performance,* 305.

41. Donald R. Hodgman, *Soviet Industrial Production 1928–1951* (Cambridge: Harvard University Press, 1954), 131.

42. These percentages are taken from Gregory and Stuart, *Soviet Economic Structure and Performance,* 300.

43. Trevor Buck and John Cole, *Modern Soviet Economic Performance* (New York: Basil Blackwell, 1987), 147.

44. John P. Hardt and Richard F. Kaufman, "Gorbachev's Economic Plans: Prospects and Risks," in *Gorbachev's Economic Plans: Study Papers Submitted to the Joint Economic Committee, Congress of the United States* (Washington, DC: U.S. Government Printing Office, 1987), vol. 1, ix.

45. Nove (*Economic History of the USSR,* 348) illustrates several problems

that can develop from using aggregated indicators of output to fulfill economic plans, including jokes by Khrushchev on the subject.

46. Ibid.

47. For a useful discussion of research and development in the Soviet Union, see Buck and Cole, *Modern Soviet Economic Performance*, 118–37.

48. Nikolai Shmelev and Vladimir Popov, *The Turning Point: Revitalizing the Soviet Economy*, trans. Michele A. Berdy (New York: Doubleday, 1989), 226.

49. Quoted in Hertha W. Heiss, "U.S.-Soviet Trade Trends," 448–73, in *Gorbachev's Economic Plans*, vol. 2, 465.

50. "O merakh po usileniiu bor'by s netrudovymi dokhodami," in *Resheniia partii i pravitel'stva po khoziaistvennym voprosam (1985–1986)* (Moscow: Izdanie politicheskoi literatury, 1988), 280–85.

51. See Joseph S. Berliner, "Organizational Restructuring of the Soviet Economy," in *Gorbachev's Economic Plans*, vol. 1, 79.

52. "Ob individual'noi trudovoi deiatel'nosti," in *Resheniia partii i pravitel'stva po khoziaistvennym voprosam*, 489–99.

53. International Monetary Fund, The World Bank, Organization for Economic Cooperation and Development, and European Bank for Reconstruction and Development, *A Study of the Soviet Economy* (Paris: OECD, 1991), vol. 1, 22.

54. "O sozdanii kooperativov po bytovomu obsluzhivaniiu naseleniia," in *Sobranie postanovlenii Pravitel'stva SSSR* (otdel pervyi), vol. 11, art. 43, 1987, 227–32.

55. "Zakon o kooperatsii v SSSR," *Vedomosti Verkhovnogo Soveta SSSR,* vol. 22, art. 355, 1988.

56. Gregory Guroff, "The Red–Expert Debate: Continuities in the State-Entrepreneur Tension," in Guroff and Carstensen, eds., *Entrepreneurship in Imperial Russia and the Soviet Union,* 205.

57. Teodor Shanin, *Russia as a "Developing Society"* (New Haven, CT: Yale University Press), 103.

58. Shanin, *Russia as a "Developing Society,"* 123.

59. Nove, *An Economic History of the USSR,* 8.

60. Guroff, "The Red–Expert Debate," 206.

61. Charles A. Ruud, *Russian Entrepreneur: Publisher Ivan Sytin of Moscow 1851–1934* (Montreal: McGill-Queen's University Press, 1990), 3.

62. "Ob ekonomicheskom polozhenii strany i kontseptsii perekhoda k reguliruemoi rynochnoi ekonomike," *Pravda,* no. 165 (25 May 1990), 1–4.

63. *Current Digest of the Soviet Press* (hereafter *CDSP*), vol. 42 (4 July 1990), 13; from *Izvestiia* (26 May 1990), 1–2.

64. Yurii Levada, "Social and Moral Aspects of the Crisis: Their Sources and Consequences," in *The Disintegration of the Soviet Economic System,* ed. Michael Ellman and Vladimir Kontorovich (New York: Routledge, 1992), 67.

65. *CDSP,* vol. 43 (19 June 1991), 1–2; from *Izvestiia* (20 May 1991), 3.

66. Quoted in Ellman and Kontorovich, "Overview," in Ellman and Kontorovich, eds., *The Disintegration of the Soviet Economic System,* 20.

67. Shatalin locates the date in July. *A Study of the Soviet Economy* (p. 61)

states that the Gorbachev–Yeltsin agreement was made in August.

68. Levada, "Social and Moral Aspects of the Crisis," 69.

69. Grigorii Iavlinskii, "Igra v otkrytuiu," *Moskovskie novosti,* no. 26 (30 June 1991), 8.

70. Ibid.

71. "Annotatsiia osnovnykh zakonodatel'nykh i normativnykh aktov, reguliruiushchikh otnosheniia sobstvennosti i privatizatsiiu gosudarstvennykh i munitsipal'nykh predpriiatii v Rossiiskoi Federatsii," *Delovoi mir,* no. 131 (10 July 1992), 7. This law was passed on December 24, 1990.

72. "O predpriiatiiakh i predprinimatel'skoi deiatel'nosti," *Ekonomika i zhizn',* no. 4 (January 1991), 16. This law was passed December 25, 1990.

73. "O predpriiatiiakh i predprinimatel'skoi deiatel'nosti," 15, 17.

74. "Ob obshchikh nachalakh predprinimatel'stva grazhdan v SSSR," *Izvestiia,* no 86 (10 April 1991), 2.

75. "Ob osnovnykh nachalakh razgosudarstvleniia i privatizatsii predpriiatii," *Izvestiia,* no. 188 (8 August 1991), 3.

76. See A. Stepovoi and S. Chugaev, "Konets monopolii gossobstvennosti," *Izvestiia,* no. 156 (2 July 1991), 1–2; and "Ob osnovnykh nachalakh razgosudarstvleniia i predpriiatii," *Izvestiia,* no. 188 (8 August 1991), 3.

77. "O privatizatsii gosudarstvennykh i munitsipal'nykh predpriiatii v RSFSR," *Zakony RSFSR o privatizatsii gosudarstvennykh i munitsipal'nykh predpriiatii, zhil'ia* (Moscow: Sovetskaia Rossiia, 1991), 3–36.

78. "Annotatsiia," *Delovoi mir,* no. 131 (10 July 1992), 5.

79. Georgia, Armenia, Moldova, and the Baltic republics did not participate.

80. Many more cooperatives than this were registered but not operating.

81. Lidiia Belokonnaia, "No Faith in the Future," *Business World Weekly,* no. 2 (27 January 1992), 3.

82. *CDSP,* vol. 43 (September 11, 1991), 23, from *Izvestiia* (7 August 1991), 3.

83. Vladimir Tikhonov, "Vlast' i rynok," *Vek (Delovoi mir* supplement), no. 11 (22–29 October 1992), 6.

84. "Debaty: sud'ba programmy, napisannoi v Garvarde, reshaetsia v Moskve . . . ," *Moskovskie novosti,* no. 26 (30 June 1991), 9.

85. As *Izvestiia* correspondents I. Karpenko and G. Shipitko described it, "the way in which the deputies, and sometimes even B.N. Yeltsin himself, treated the President of the USSR often grated on us. Why was it necessary [right after the coup attempt] to make M.S. Gorbachev, who had not yet recovered from the shock of events, read, like a naughty schoolboy, a text accusing members of his team of treason? Or to demand that every Communist be declared a criminal?" See *CDSP,* vol. 43 (25 September 1991), 10; from *Izvestiia* (24 August 1991), 2.

86. Russia, Belarus, Armenia, Kazakhstan, Uzbekistan, Turkmenistan, Kyrgyzstan, and Tajikistan.

87. *CDSP,* vol. 43 (20 November 1991), 10; from *Izvestiia* (16 October 1991), 1.

88. *CDSP*, vol. 43 (27 November 1991), 1; from *Izvestiia* (28 October 1991), 1–2.

89. *CDSP*, vol. 43 (18 December 1991), 1; from *Komsomol'skaia pravda* (19 November 1991), 1.

90. *CDSP*, vol. 43 (8 January 1992), 1; from *Komsomol'skaia pravda* (10 December 1991), 1.

91. Grigorii Tsitriniak, "Pogranichnaia situatsiia," *Literaturnaia gazeta*, no. 44 (28 October 1992), 11.

92. Irina Demchenko, "Epokha 'reformatorstva sverkhu' v Rossii zakonchilas'," *Nezavisimaia gazeta*, no. 20 (4 February 1993), 5.

93. Ibid.

Chapter 3. Russian and Western Voices on Radical Economic Reform

1. *The Current Digest of the Soviet Press* (hereafter *CDSP*), vol. 43 (27 November 1991), 3; from *Izvestiia* (28 October 1991), 1–2.

2. Anders Åslund, "A Critique of Soviet Reform Plans," in *The Post-Soviet Economy: Soviet and Western Perspectives*, ed. Anders Åslund (New York: St. Martin's Press, 1992), 172.

3. Ibid., 170 (emphasis added).

4. Ibid., 174–75.

5. Ibid., 169 (emphasis added).

6. Ibid., 172 (emphasis added).

7. Egor Gaidar, "Rossiia i reformy," *Izvestiia*, no. 187 (19 August 1992), 3.

8. "Ekonomicheskaia strategiia pravitel'stva Rossii," *Bizness, banki, birzha*, no. 12 (22 March 1992), 1.

9. Jeffrey Sachs, "The Grand Bargain," in Åslund, ed., *The Post-Soviet Economy*, 209.

10. Vladimir Popov, "Hyperinflation Is Setting In," *Business in the USSR*, no. 18 (December 1991), 19.

11. Aleksandr Zaichenko, "Short Sharp Shock?" *Business in the Ex-USSR*, no. 20 (February 1992), 16.

12. Aleksandr Zaichenko, "Pleasing No One," *Business in the Ex-USSR*, no. 21 (March 1992), 16.

13. *Megapolis-Express*, no. 7 (13 February 1992), 15. The survey included 1,960 respondents. CPO is known in Russia as VTsIOM.

14. Tat'iana Boikova, "Draka poka ne zakazana," *Megapolis-Express*, no. 7 (13 February 1992), 21.

15. Aleksandr Sidiachko, "Pravitel'stvo u nas khoroshee," *Megapolis-Express*, no. 25 (17 June 1992), 19.

16. Michael Ellman and Vladimir Kontorovich, "Overview," in *The Disintegration of the Soviet Economic System*, ed. Michael Ellman and Vladimir Kontorovich (New York: Routledge, 1992), 2.

17. Jeffrey Sachs, "The Road to the Market," *The Washington Post*, no. 113 (28 March 1993), C2.

18. Ibid.

19. Yakov Urinson, "The Main Thing Is . . . ," *Delovie lyudi*, no. 29 (December 1992), 36.

20. Sachs, "The Road to the Market."

21. Stephen F. Cohen, "Can We 'Convert' Russia?" *The Washington Post*, no. 113 (28 March 1993), C1–C2.

22. *CDSP*, vol. 43 (4 December 1991), 8–9; from *Rossiiskaia gazeta* (30 October 1991), 1, 6.

23. *Current Digest of the Post-Soviet Press* (hereafter *CDPSP*), vol. 44 (8 July 1992), 10; from *Moskovskie novosti* (24 May 1992), 9–16.

24. Ibid.

25. Vladimir Tikhonov, "Vlast' i rynok," *Vek* (supplement to *Delovoi mir*), no. 11 (22–29 October 1992); 6.

26. Grigorii Tsitriniak, "Pogranichnaia situatsiia," *Literaturnaia gazeta*, no. 45 (4 November 1992), 10.

27. Leonid Abalkin, "Mounting Misgivings," *Delovie lyudi*, no. 22 (April 1992), 21.

28. Nikolai Petrakov et al., "Russian Government Loses Control Over Economic Processes," *Business World Weekly*, no. 8 (24 March 1992), 4.

29. Tsitriniak, "Pogranichnaia situatsiia."

30. Nikolai Petrakov "Choice and Will," *Business in the USSR*, no. 3 (July–August 1990), 14.

31. "Ob uskorenii privatizatsii gosudarstvennykh i munitsipal'nykh predpriiatii," in *Vse o privatizatsii v torgovle* (Moscow: Torgovlia, 1992), 47–60.

32. Vladimir Orlov, "Gosudarstvo idet s molotka," *Moskovskie novosti*, no. 2 (12 January 1992), 14.

33. *Izvestiia*, no. 160 (13 June 1992), 32.

34. Gaidar, "Rossiia i reformy."

35. "O privatizatsii munitsipal'nykh i gorodskikh predpriiatii torgovli, bytovogo obsluzhivaniia i obshchestvennogo pitaniia v g. Moskve," in *Vse o privatizatsii v torgovle*, 155–57.

36. B. Iakovlev, "Budem zhit'!" *Vecherniaia Moskva*, no. 16 (24 January 1992), 2.

37. Viktoriia Kharnas, "Moskva vershit novye normativno-metodicheskie akty," *Kommersant*, no. 5 (27 January–3 February 1992), 7.

38. Leonid Lopatnikov, "Privatizatsiia: razgovor glukhikh?" *Delovoi mir*, no. 102 (29 May 1992), 1.

39. "Radovat'sia rano . . . ," *Delovoi mir*, no. 239 (11 December 1992), 2.

40. Galina Burmistrova, "A skazhite, ch'i vy, magaziny Moskvy," *Delovoi mir*, no. 224 (20 November 1992), 3.

41. Additional details and examples are provided in Anatolii Velednitskii, "Nam skazali—my progolosovali," *Delovoi mir*, no. 84 (30 April 1992), 2.

42. Later in the summer, the department store of which Osovtsev spoke, GUM, *was* privatized.

43. Lora Velikanova, "Larisa Piiasheva v roli komissara Kattani," *Literaturnaia gazeta*, no. 37 (9 September 1992), 10.
44. Ivan Rodin, "Beskontrol'noe samoupravstvo vlastei," *Nezavisimaia gazeta*, no. 151 (8 August 1992), 6.
45. "O privedenii raboty po privatizatsii gosudarstvennykh i munitsipal'nykh predpriiatii v g. Moskve v sootvetstvie s Gosudarstvennoi programmoi privatizatsii," *Kommersant*, no. 32 (3–10 August), 22.
46. Igor' Karpenko, "Chto my znaem o vauchere," *Izvestiia*, no. 265 (8 December 1992), 2.
47. Lopatnikov, "Privatizatsiia: razgovor glukhikh?"
48. Elena Kotel'nikova, "Goskomimushchestvo: predprinimateli i babushki budut dovol'ny," *Kommersant*, no. 31 (27 July–3 August), 14.
49. Anatolii Ershov, "G. Iavlinskii nachinaet v Nizhnem," *Izvestiia*, no. 133 (8 June 1992), 2.

Chapter 4. April–December 1992

1. Key legislative acts of both the USSR Supreme Soviet and the Russian legislature are summarized in Lynn D. Nelson, Lilia V. Babaeva, and Rufat O. Babaev, "Perspectives on Entrepreneurship and Privatization in Russia: Policy and Public Opinion," *Slavic Review* 51 (Summer 1992): esp. pp. 274–76.
2. Anatoly Chubais, "Privatization Goes Ahead." *Delovie lyudi*, no. 27 (October 1992), 46.
3. Igor' Karpenko, "A. Chubais: U nas net raznoglasii s V. Chernomyrdinym po programme privatizatsii," *Izvestiia*, no. 10 (20 January 1993), 5; and Valentina Ukhina, "Volgograd prinimaet estafetu u Nizhnego Novgoroda," *Delovoi mir*, no. 10 (20 January 1993), 9.
4. N. Marinich, quoting Anatolii Chubais in "Otkryta dver' v giperinfliatsiiu," *Vecherniaia Moskva*, no. 13 (21 January 1993), 1.
5. Karpenko, "A. Chubais: U nas net raznoglasii s V. Chernomyrdinym po programme privatizatsii."
6. "Gosudarstvennaia programma privatizatsii gosudarstvennykh i munitsipal'nykh predpriiatii Rossiiskoi Federatsii na 1992 god," *Delovoi mir*, no. 64 (2 April 1992), 12–13.
7. *The Current Digest of the Post-Soviet Press* (hereafter *CDPSP*), vol. 44 (29 July 1992); from *Moskovskie novosti* (24 May 1992), 20.
8. Ibid.
9. Aleksandr Orfenov, "Kogo podderzhivaiut Rossiiane," *Megapolis-Express*, no. 17 (25 April 1992), 13. The study included 1,300 respondents and was carried out by the Public Opinion Foundation in thirteen cities.
10. Vladimir Boikov, "Vlast' priznaiut, no uzhe ne doveriaiut," *Megapolis-Express*, no. 30 (29 July 1992), 7. The survey included 1,200 respondents in thirty regions of Russia and was conducted by the Institute for Complex Social Studies from June 1 to June 5.

11. *The Current Digest of the Soviet Press* (hereafter *CDSP*), vol. 43 (4 December 1991); from *Izvestiia* (30 October 1991), 7.

12. *CDSP,* vol. 43 (4 December 1991); from *Izvestiia* (2 November 1991), 7.

13. Ibid.

14. "Economic Index," *Delovie lyudi,* no. 31 (March 1993), 6.

15. *CDPSP,* vol. 44 (13 May 1992), 6; from *Izvestiia* (13 April 1992), 1.

16. *CDPSP,* vol. 44 (13 May 1992), 9; from *Megapolis-Express* (22 April 1992), 3.

17. T. Chalov, "Deputaty o reforme," *Vecherniaia Moskva,* no. 69 (8 April 1992), 1.

18. Larisa Piiasheva, *Mozhno li byt' nemnozhko beremennoi?* (Minsk: Polifakt, 1991), 29–47 (from an article published June 1990). See also H. Marinich, "Larisa Piiasheva: 'Mne nikogda ne bylo tak tiazhelo,'" *Vecherniaia Moskva,* no. 127 (3 July 1992), 1–2.

19. Sergei Alekseev, "Prokliatie nashego obshchestva," *Nezavisimaia gazeta,* no. 52 (17 March 1993).

20. Oleg Bogomolov, "Razdaetsia nicheinoe bogatstvo," *Nezavisimaia gazeta,* no. 13 (23 January 1993), 4.

21. See, for example, Mark Massarskii, "Davaite zhit' druzhno. Inache bit' budut oboikh," *Megapolis-Express,* no. 5 (30 January 1992), 10.

22. See Bogomolov, "Razdaetsia nicheinoe bogatstvo."

23. "Gosudarstvennaia programma privatizatsii gosudarstvennykh i munitsipal'nykh predpriiatii v Rossiiskoi Federatsii na 1992 god," *Ekonomicheskaia gazeta,* no. 29 (July 1992), 15–18.

24. Anatolii Velednitskii, "Priblizhaetsia delezhka. Gosimushchestva," *Delovoi mir,* no. 110 (10 June 1992), 1.

25. Dmitrii Vasil'ev, "1 oktiabria—nachalo privatizatsii v Rossii. Dlia kogo? Chto nuzhno sdelat' k etomu sroku?" *Izvestiia,* no. 214 (25 September 1992), 2.

26. Mikhail Berger, "Privatizatsii ugrozhaet diktatura proletariata," *Izvestiia,* no. 129 (3 June 1992), 2.

27. Vasilii Kononenko, "Pravitel'stvo RF obsuzhdaet programmy reform na zavtra," *Izvestiia,* no. 118 (21 May 1992), 2.

28. Ten percent for nonmanagerial workers and 5 percent for management.

29. A fourth person appointed to the position of vice premier at this time, Anatolii Chubais, was already chairman of the State Property Management Committee. Chubais's activity as vice premier continued without significant changes. He remained chairman of the Committee.

30. Mikhail Berger, "Novye naznacheniia El'tsina—veroiatnost' 'Abal-kanizatsii' pravitel'stva Gaidara," *Izvestiia,* no. 129 (30 June 1992), 2.

31. Nelli Marinich, "Gaidarom bol'she, Gaidarom men'she," *Vecherniaia Moskva,* no. 110 (9 June 1992), 1.

32. "Gosudarstvennaia programma," 15–18.

33. Boikov, "Vlast' priznaiut, no uzhe ne doveriaiut," 7.

34. Vladimir Boikov and Evgenii Levanov, "Pravitel'stvo no liubiat. No poka eshche uvazhaiut," *Megapolis-Express,* no. 24 (10 June 1992), 13.

35. Anders Åslund, "Shokovaia terapiia v Rossii—mif," *Finansovye izvestiia* (*Izvestiia* supplement), no. 251 (18 November 1992), 1.

36. "O vvedenii v deistvie sistemy privatizatsionnykh chekov v Rossiiskoi Federatsii," *Kommersant,* no. 34 (17–24 August 1992), 24.

37. "Chek na chernom rynke," *Delovoi mir,* no. 233 (3 December 1992), 1.

38. Besedovali M. Panova and N. Prikhod'ko, "Poluchim privatizatsionnyi chek. Chto dal'she?" *Ekonomika i zhizn',* no. 36 (September 1992), 15.

39. Georgii Tselms, "Kak zhivem, Rossiiane?" *Megapolis-Express,* no. 46 (25 November 1992), 6.

40. Aleksandr Zaichenko, "Property in the Balance," *Delovie lyudi,* no. 27 (October 1992), 3. See also Valilii Seliunin, "Tret'ia popytka," *Izvestiia,* no. 211 (22 September 1992), 1, 3.

41. Seliunin, "Tret'ia popytka."

42. Irina Demchenko, "Privatizatsiia bez vauchera? Teper' eto nevozmozhno," *Izvestiia,* no. 228 (15 October 1992), 2; and Pavel Sorokin, ". . . plius vaucherizatsiia vsei strany," *Delovoi mir,* no. 199 (15 October 1992), 8.

43. "O razvitii sistemy privatizatsionnykh chekov v Rossiiskoi Federatsii," and "O prodazhe za privatizatsionnye cheki zhilishchnogo fonda, zemel'nykh uchastkov i munitsipal'noi sobstvennosti," *Ekonomika i zhizn',* no. 43 (October 1992), 5.

44. Demchenko, "Privatizatsiia bez vauchera?"

45. More than 2,000 large and middle-sized industrial enterprises had been transformed into joint-stock companies by the end of 1992. See Ol'ga Berezhnaia, "Masshtabnaia narodnaia privatizatsiia nachnetsia s Volgograda," *Moskovskie novosti,* no. 4 (24 January 1993), 5.

46. Il'ia Kitaigorodskii, "Vse vesplatnoe stoit dorogo," *Nezavisimaia gazeta,* no. 193 (7 October 1992), 4; and Lora Velikanova, "Anatolii Chubais: 'Do 80 protsentov gosudarstvennoi sobstvennosti—za cheki,' " *Literaturnaia gazeta,* no. 47 (18 November 1992), 10.

47. Ekaterina Vasil'eva, "Vaucher, kak vino: trebuet vyderzhki . . . ," *Delovoi mir,* no. 229 (27 November 1992), 2.

48. Ibid.

49. ITAR-TASS, "Vokrug cheka," *Delovoi mir,* no. 6 (14 January 1993), 5.

50. Berezhnaia, "Masshtabnaia narodnaia privatizatsiia nachnetsia s Volgograda," 5.

51. See, for example, Vladimir Shifrin, "Na chto goden vaucher," *Vecherniaia Moskva* 166 (27 August 1992): 1.

52. See "Programma uglubleniia reform," *Izvestiia,* no. 224 (9 October 1992), 2.

53. Aleksandr Borisov, ". . . plius sploshnaia vaucherizatsiia vsei strany," *Megapolis-Express,* no. 35 (2 September 1992), 3.

54. Grigorii Tsitriniak, "Novaia volna: politiki bez proshlogo," *Literaturnaia gazeta,* no. 3 (20 January 1993), 10.

55. Grigorii Tsitriniak, "Pogranichnaia situatsiia," *Literaturnaia gazeta,* no. 45 (4 November 1992), 10 (emphasis added).

56. "Programma uglubleniia reform."

57. Igor' Karpenko, "Shto my znaem o vauchere," *Izvestiia,* no. 265 (8 December 1992), 2.

58. Nelson, Babaeva, and Babaev, "Perspectives on Entrepreneurship and Privatization in Russia: Policy and Public Opinion," 271–86.

59. Sergei Chugaev, "Oppozitsiia stavit pod vopros sud'bu reform," *Izvestiia,* no. 224 (9 October 1992), 1–2.

60. Anatolii Kostiukov, "Boris El'tsin povernul telegu. Budet li meniat' konei?" *Megapolis-Express,* no. 41 (14 October 1992), 20.

61. Vasilii Kononenko, "Koppektirovka reform: prodolzhenie ili smena kursa?" *Izvestiia,* no. 222 (7 October 1992), 2; and Valerii Vyzhutovich, "El'tsin zakliuchaet soiuz s 'Grazhdanskim soiuzom,' " *Izvestiia,* no. 222 (7 October 1992), 2.

62. Vyzhutovich, "El'tsin zakliuchaet soiuz s 'Grazhdanskim soiuzom.' "

63. Dmitrii Khranovitskii, "Tol'ko s''ezd pokazhet, chego khotiat deputaty: prodolzhat' reformu ili povernut' ee vspiat'," *Izvestiia,* no. 258 (27 November 1992), 1.

64. See, for example, Boris Grushin, "Kogda Rossiiskie lidery mnenii liubiat svoego prezidenta?" *Nezavisimaia gazeta,* no. 8 (16 January 1993), 1–2.

65. "MN Express Poll," *Moscow News,* no. 45 (8–15 November 1992), 2. This national survey included 1,520 people and was conducted October 10–20.

66. "MN Express Poll," *Moscow News,* no. 49 (6–13 December 1992), 2. The national survey included 1,603 people and was conducted November 13–23.

67. "Khod ekonomicheskikh reform v Rossii: vzgliad E. Gaidara," *Izvestiia,* no. 261 (2 December 1992), 1, 3.

68. Vladimir Tikhonov, "Scourge of Monopoly," *Moscow News,* no. 38 (20–27 September 1992), 3.

69. Grigorii Tsitriniak, "Pogranichnaia situatsiia," *Literaturnaia gazeta,* no. 44 (28 October 1992), 11.

70. Egor Gaidar, "A Tunnel Two Years Long," *Delovie lyudi,* no. 22 (April 1992), 19.

71. Quoted in *Delovie lyudi,* no. 29 (December 1992), 33.

72. Nikolai Petrakov, "A Second Stage of Reform . . . ," *Delovie lyudi,* no. 29 (December 1992), 27.

73. Grigory Iavlinskii, "Trust in Reformers and Reforms Has Gone . . . ," *Delovie lyudi,* no. 29 (December 1992), 44.

74. Responses were equally split between those who responded "Difficult to say" and "I won't participate in a referendum."

75. Fourteen percent gave no answer.

76. "Esli by referendum provodilsia segodnia, to prezident poluchil by podderzhku treti izbiratelei," *Literaturnaia gazeta,* no. 1–2 (13 January 1993), 11.

77. Aleksei Levinson, "Ostav'te vse kak est'!" *Izvestiia,* no. 260 (1 December 1992), 2.

78. Ibid.

79. The 1992 figures given here are from the government report "Sotsial'no-ekonomicheskoe polozhenie Rossii v 1992 godu (predvaritel'nye dannye)," *Delovoi mir*, no. 7 (15 January 1993), 6–7.

80. For a discussion of these points, see Otto Latsis, "God s Gaidarom," *Izvestiia*, no. 275 (22 December 1992), 3.

81. Igor' Karpenko, "Pervyi chekovyi auktsion v stolitse," *Izvestiia*, no. 266 (9 December 1992), 1–2.

82. Kononenko, "Koppektirovka reform: prodolzhenie ili smena kursa?"; and Vyzhutovich, "El'tsin zakliuchaet soiuz s 'Grazhdanskim soiuzom.'"

83. Arkady Volsky, "The Middle Road to the Market," *Business in the USSR*, no. 11 (April 1991), 55.

84. "Pravitel'stvo meniat' poka rano, no programmu reform nado korrektirovat'," *Delovoi mir*, no. 225 (21 November 1992), 2.

85. Ibid.

86. Vasilii Nikolaev, "Otkazat'sia ot illiuzii," *Delovoi mir*, no. 198 (14 October 1992), 6.

87. *CDSP*, vol. 43 (1 May 1991), 5; from *Nezavisimaia gazeta* (2 June 1991), 10 (emphasis added).

88. Vasilii Nikolaev, "Otkazat'sia ot illiuzii."

89. *CDSP*, vol. 44 (2 May 1992); from *Nezavisimaia gazeta* (2 June 1992), 10.

90. Anatolii Kostiukov, "Kto ponial zhizn', tot ne speshit," *Megapolis-Express*, no. 46 (25 November 1992), 21.

91. Andrei Lekant, "Vol'skii zhdet do zavtra," *Nezavisimaia gazeta*, no. 221 (17 November 1992), 1; "Trinadtsat' punktov programmy Vol'skogo," *Izvestiia*, no. 217 (30 September 1992), 2; and Arkadii Vol'skii, "Pravitel'stvo meniat' poka rano, no programmu reform nado koppektirovat'," *Delovoi mir*, no. 225 (21 November 1992), 2.

92. Anatolii Kostiukov, "Kto ponial zhizn', tot ne speshit," *Megapolis-Express*, no. 46 (25 November 1992), 21.

93. M. Dobbs, "Pridet i spaset?" *Argumenty i fakty*, no. 34 (September 1992), 3.

94. Åslund, "Shokovaia terapiia v Rossii—mif."

95. Sergei Protasov, "For 'Business' Read 'Party,'" *Delovie lyudi*, no. 25 (July–August 1992), 27.

96. "Programma partii ekonomicheskoi svobody," *Delovoi mir*, no. 232 (2 December 1992), 5.

Chapter 5. "The Smooth Reformist Period Has Ended . . ."

1. Margarita Lemeshko, "Crisis Continues," *Moscow News*, no. 11 (12 March 1993), 5; and Leonid Lopatnikov, "Spad proizvodstva. Mneniia i fakty," *Delovoi mir*, no. 69 (14 April 1993), 7.

2. *Current Digest of the Post-Soviet Press* (hereafter *CDPSP*), vol. 45 (10 March 1993), 6; from *Izvestiia* (6 February 1993), 1.

3. Elaine Scioliono, "U.S. Hopes Yeltsin Will Prevail but Fears He Might

Seize Power," *The New York Times*, vol. 142 (12 March 1993), A1, A6; and Margaret Shapiro, "Congress Curbs Yeltsin's Power," *The Washington Post*, no. 98 (13 March 1993), A1.

4. Shapiro, "Congress Curbs Yeltsin's Power."

5. Celestine Bohlen, "Yeltsin, Defying Congress, Says the Referendum Is On," *The New York Times* (international edition), vol. 142 (13 March 1993), 4.

6. Shapiro, "Congress Curbs Yeltsin's Power," A16.

7. Margaret Shapiro, "Russian Congress Acts Against Yeltsin's Ministers, Targets Media," *The Washington Post*, no. 99 (14 March 1993), A1, A25.

8. Serge Schmemann, "Yeltsin, Asking Aid, Talks of Communist Revival," *The New York Times*, vol. 142 (17 March 1993), A6.

9. "Obrashchenie k grazhdanam Rossii Prezidenta Rossiiskoi Federatsii Borisa El'tsina," *Delovoi mir*, no. 53 (23 March 1993), 1.

10. "Do you approve of the socioeconomic policy carried out by the president of the Russian Federation and the government of the Russian Federation for 1992?"

11. Sergei Parkhomenko, "Vy khoteli referendum? Vy ego imeete! . . . ," *Segodnia*, no. 7 (6 April 1993), 3.

12. Fred Hiatt, "Yeltsin Forces Urge Speedup In Reforms," *The Washington Post*, no. 143 (27 April 1993), A14.

13. See Celestine Bohlen, "Yeltsin, Fresh from His Victory, Is Attacked by Political Enemies," *The New York Times* (international edition), vol. 142 (27 April 1993), A8.

14. Iurii Levada, "Narod o s''ezde i vlasti: pervye vpechatleniia," *Izvestiia*, no. 50 (18 March 1993), 4.

15. "Konflikt vlastei v otsenke gorozhan," *Izvestiia*, no. 61 (2 April 1993), 3.

16. In 1991 he captured 57.3 percent of the vote.

17. "Moscow Evening News," 28 April 1993.

18. Iurii Levada, "Shto nyne lezhit na vesakh," *Izvestiia*, no. 77 (24 April 1993), 4. For a similar interpretation by economist Otto Latsis, provided *after* the referendum, see "Itogi referenduma obiazyvaiut prezidenta deistvovat' bystro i reshitel'no," *Izvestiia*, no. 78 (27 April 1993), 1.

19. Leon Trotsky, *The Russian Revolution: The Overthrow of Tzarism and the Triumph of the Soviets*, ed. F.W. Dupee (Garden City, NY: Doubleday Anchor Books, 1959), x.

20. "Opros obshchestvennogo mneniia v Rossii," *Izvestiia*, no. 16 (28 January 1993), 2.

21. Veronika Kutsyllo, "Presidentskaia kampaniia nachinaet napominat' predvybornuiu," *Kommersant-Daily*, no. 87 (13 April 1993), 6.

22. "If Voters Reject Yeltsin, He'll Quit," *The Washington Post*, no. 131 (15 April 1993), A20.

23. In the IMF's terminology, "repurchases" of a member country's soft currency in exchange for hard currency.

24. See Alexei V. Mozhin, "Russia's Negotiations with the IMF," Stockholm Institute of East European Economics, working paper no. 52 (1992).

25. "Osnovnye napravleniia ekonomicheskoi politiki Rossiiskoi Fede-

atsii," *Kommersant,* no. 9 (24 February–2 March 1992), 22.

26. Quoted in *Delovie lyudi,* no. 29 (December 1992), 33.

27. Mozhin, "Russia's Negotiations with the IMF," 2.

28. Jeffrey D. Sachs and Peter Boone, "Strengthening Western Support for Russia's Economic Reforms," mimeo (28 December 1992), 1.

29. Jeffrey D. Sachs, "The Grand Bargain," in *The Post-Soviet Economy: Soviet and Western Perspectives,* ed. Anders Åslund (New York: St. Martin's Press, 1992), 213–14.

30. Ibid., 210.

31. Ibid., 215.

32. Britain, Canada, France, Germany, Italy, Japan, and the United States.

33. "Goriachee kreslo," *Megapolis-Express,* no. 19 (6 May 1992), 12.

34. "Ekonomicheskaia strategiia pravitel'stva Rossii," *Biznes, banki, birzha,* no. 14 (22 March 1992), 2 (emphasis added).

35. Marshall I. Goldman, "Yeltsin's Reforms: Gorbachev II?" *Foreign Policy,* no. 88 (Fall 1992), 90.

36. Jeffrey D. Sachs, "Russian Sachs Appeal: The G7 Has One Last Chance," *The International Economy* 7 (January/February 1993), 51–52.

37. Fred Hiatt, "The $6 Billion Russia Never Got to Spend," *The Washington Post,* no. 86 (1 March 1993), A12.

38. Aleksandr Shal'nev, "Rossiiu ne poimut, esli ona voz'met obiazatel'stva i opiat' ikh ne vypolnit," *Izvestiia,* no. 21 (4 February 1993), 1, 3.

39. Ibid., 3.

40. Fred Hiatt, "Western Effort to Aid Ailing Russia Is Seen as Collapsing," *The Washington Post,* no. 86 (1 March 1993), A1.

41. Elaine Sciolino, "To Show Support, Clinton Will Meet with Russian," *The New York Times* (international edition), vol. 142 (19 March 1993), A5.

42. Craig Whitney, "Europe Cautiously Supports Yeltsin," *The New York Times* (international edition), vol. 142 (22 March 1993), A9.

43. Paul Blustein, "Russian Brings Ideas to Key Talks on Aid," *The Washington Post,* no. 99 (14 March 1993), A25.

44. Paul Blustein, "G–7 Nations to Rush More Aid to Russia," *The Washington Post,* no. 100 (15 March 1993), A16.

45. See Daniel Williams, "Aid to Russia Approved by G–7 Nations," *The Washington Post,* no. 132 (16 April 1993), A1, A18.

46. Steven Greenhouse, "Group of Seven Urges Yeltsin to Push His Reforms," *The New York Times* (international edition), vol. 142 (30 April 1993), A6.

47. Ibid. (emphasis added).

48. Anders Åslund, "A Critique of Soviet Reform Plans," in *The Post-Soviet Economy,* 169.

49. Lipton and Sachs, "Prospects for Russia's Economic Reforms," in *Brookings Papers on Economic Activity,* no. 2, ed. William C. Brainard and George L. Perry (Washington, DC: Brookings Institution, 1992), 246.

50. Jeffrey D. Sachs, "The Road to the Market: If Yeltsin Can Stay the Course on Economic Reform, Russia Will Prosper," *The Washington Post,* no. 113 (28 March 1993), C2.

51. A. Meshcherskii, "Rossiia na fone mira," *Argumenty i fakty,* no. 5 (February 1993), 4.

52. Lipton and Sachs, "Prospects for Russia's Economic Reforms," 216–18.

53. Irina Demchenko, "V pol'she udalas' 'nasha' reforma," *Izvestiia,* no. 37 (26 February 1993), 4.

54. Aleksandr Kuranov, "Strasti vokrug biudzheta," *Nezavisimaia gazeta,* no. 30 (17 February 1993), 4.

55. Leonid Kornilov, "Pod ugrozoi rospuska pol'skii seim utverdil zhestkii biudzhet," *Izvestiia,* no. 30 (17 February 1993), 3.

56. John Darnton, "Polish Parliament Rejects Bill to Privatize Industries," *The New York Times* (international edition), vol. 142 (19 March 1993), A3.

57. Jane Perlez, "Plan to Privatize Wins Polish Vote," *The New York Times* (international edition), vol. 142 (1 May 1993), 3.

58. Lipton and Sachs, "Prospects for Russia's Economic Reforms," 246.

59. Ibid., 247.

60. Ammeter-Inquirer, "Poland: Results of a Survey of Economic and Political Behavior," Studies in Public Policy Number 201 (Glasgow: Centre for the Study of Public Policy, University of Strathclyde, 1992), 19.

61. Tat'iana Sokolova, "Bally i krony," *Radikal,* no. 39 (October 1992), 15.

62. Iurii Ershov, "Pol'skii variant," *Delovoi mir,* no. 23 (6 February 1993), 4.

63. Organisation for Economic Co-operation and Development, *OECD Economic Surveys: Poland 1992* (Paris: OECD, 1992), 10.

64. Organisation for Economic Co-operation and Development, and the Centre for Co-operation with the European Economies in Transition, *Industry in Poland: Structural Adjustment Issues and Policy Options* (Paris: OECD, 1992), 12.

65. See B.J. McCormick, *Hayek and the Keynesian Avalanche* (New York: St. Martin's Press, 1992), 148.

66. Anders Åslund, "Prospects for a Successful Change of Economic System in Russia," Stockholm Institute of East European Economics, working paper no. 60 (November 1992), 1.

67. Roman Frydman, Andrzej Rapaczynski, and John S. Earle, *The Privatization Process in Central Europe* (New York: Central European University Press, 1993), 40.

68. A summary of Bulgaria's economic reform program is provided in ibid., 3–37.

69. Georgii Bovt and Natal'ia Kalashnikova, "Natsional'naia valiuta pomozhet vyvesti torgovliu iz krizisa," *Kommersant-Daily,* no. 32 (2 February 1993), 3.

70. Nikolai Ermolovich, "Otnosheniia MVF s riadom stran Vostochnoi Evropy rezko oslozhnilis'," *Izvestiia,* no. 6 (14 January 1993), 3.

Chapter 6. New Money, New Business

1. Egor Gaidar, "Rossiia i reformy," *Izvestiia,* no. 187 (19 August 1992), 3.

2. Aleksandr Khandruev, "Ne tak strashen TsB, kak ego maluiut," *Megapolis-Express,* no. 7 (17 February 1993), 12.

3. *The Current Digest of the Post-Soviet Press* (hereafter *CDPSP*), vol. 44 (2 September 1992), 1; from *Komsomol'skaia pravda* (4 August 1992), 2.

4. *CDPSP*, vol. 44 (2 September 1992), 3.

5. Georgii Matiukhin, "Ekonomicheskie i politicheskie svobody v usloviiakh giperinfliatsii nedostizhimy," *Finansovye izvestiia* (*Izvestiia* supplement), no. 13 (28 January–3 February 1993), 3.

6. Devid Bollz, "Nazhim promyshlennogo lobbi ugrozhaet sorvat' finansovuiu stabilizatsiiu," *Finansovye izvestiia* (*Izvestiia* supplement), no. 13 (28 January–3 February 1993), 2.

7. *O razvitii ekonomicheskoi reformy v Rossiiskoi Federatsii v 1992 g.* (Moscow: Goskomstat Rossiiskoi Federatsii, 1993), 15.

8. Aleksandr Frenkel' and Valerii Galitskii, "Ekonomika Rossii v 1993 godu," *Delovoi mir*, no. 45 (11 March 1993), 10.

9. Jeffrey D. Sachs, "Achieving Monetary Stabilization in Russia in 1993," mimeo (7 March 1993), 1.

10. Georgii Matiukhin, "Segodnia pravitel'stvo ne mozhet effektivno borot'sia s infliatsiei," *Finansovye izvestiia* (*Izvestiia* supplement), no. 9 (7–13 January 1993), 3.

11. *CDPSP*, vol. 45 (10 March 1993), 23; from *Izvestiia* (10 February 1993), 1.

12. *CDPSP*, vol. 44 (2 September 1992), 4; from *Izvestiia* (4 August 1992), 1–2.

13. Elena Kotel'nikova, "Prem'er-praktik obeshchaet snizit' tempy infliatsii," *Kommersant-Daily*, no. 15 (29 January 1993), 3.

14. Erlen Bernshtein, "Kreslo—uzhe ne tochka opory," *Nezavisimaia gazeta*, no. 19 (2 February 1993), 4.

15. Bollz, "Nazhim promyshlennogo lobbi."

16. Vladimir Tikhonov, "Vlast' i rynok," *Vek*, no. 11 (22–29 October 1992), 6.

17. *CDPSP*, vol. 44 (2 September 1992), 2.

18. Efrem Maiminas, "Traektoriia nashego dvizheniia," *Nezavisimaia gazeta*, no. 21 (4 February 1993), 5.

19. Tikhonov, "Vlast' i rynok."

20. Maiminas, "Traektoriia nashego dvizheniia."

21. "Arkadii Vol'skii: predprinimateliam tozhe nuzhny kredity," *Delovoi mir*, no. 1 (5 January 1993), 1.

22. Artur Vardanian, "Tsentral'nyi bank Rossii provodit antirynochnuiu politiku," *Kommersant-Daily*, no. 53 (24 March 1993), 9.

23. Vasilii Kononenko, "Pravitel'stvo Rossii budet borot'sia za reformy," *Izvestiia*, no. 45 (13 March 1993), 2.

24. Stephen Erlanger, "Russians to Limit Monetary Growth," *The New York Times* (international edition), vol. 142 (11 April 1993), 12.

25. Boris Krotkov, "Nakal strastei i realii situatsii," *Delovoi mir*, no. 46 (12 March 1993), 1.

26. Ibid.

27. Ibid.

28. Kononenko, "Pravitel'stvo Rossii budet borot'sia za reformy."

29. Ibid.

30. A fuller discussion of cooperatives is provided in Anthony Jones and William Moskoff, *Ko-ops: The Rebirth of Entrepreneurship in the Soviet Union* (Bloomington: Indiana University Press, 1991).

31. Lynn D. Nelson, Liliia V. Babaeva, and Rufat O. Babaev, "Perspectives on Entrepreneurship and Privatization in Russia: Policy and Public Opinion," *Slavic Review* 51 (Summer 1992): 278.

32. "O predpriiatiiakh i predprinimatel'skoi deiatel'nosti," *Ekonomika i zhizn'*, no. 4 (January 1991), 16, 17.

33. Valentina Sal'nikova, "Pul's malogo biznesa Rossii," *Delovoi mir*, no. 134 (15 July 1992), 5.

34. Ol'ga Osetrova, "Podderzhit li gosudarstvo predprinimatelia," *Torgovo-promyshlennye vedomosti*, no. 5 (November 1992). See also N. Palkina, "Podderzhka malykh predpriiatii v Rossii," *Ekonomicheskaia gazeta*, no. 39 (September 1992), 16.

35. Ibid.

36. Fedor Rusinov and Mikhail Ioffe, "Rossiiskoe predprinimatel'stvo," *Delovoi mir*, no. 6 (14 January 1993), 12.

37. Diiaz Zamilov, "Nishcheta i blesk malogo predprinimatel'stva," *Delovoi mir*, no. 48 (11 March 1992), 6.

38. Leonid Shinkarev, "Chastnoe delo millionov," *Izvestiia*, no. 6 (14 January 1993), 5.

39. Mikhail Glukhovsky, "Yeltsin's Council Means Business," *Delovie lyudi*, no. 26 (September 1992), 20.

40. Ibid., 21.

41. Igor' Krylov, "Gora rodila mysh'," *Delovoi mir*, no. 240 (12 December 1992), 9.

42. Dmitrii Khrapovitskii, "Predprinimateli Rossii poluchaiut pravitel'stvennuiu podderzhku," *Izvestiia*, no. 64 (7 April 1993), 2.

43. Anders Åslund, *Gorbachev's Struggle for Economic Reform* (Ithaca, NY: Cornell University Press, 1989), p. 140.

44. I.I. Stoliarova and M.A. Sazhinoi, eds., *Sovmestnye predpriiatiia v ekonomike sotsializma* (Moscow: Izdatel'stvo Moskovskogo universiteta, 1991), 121–22.

45. "Postanovlenie Soveta ministrov SSSR: O dal'neishem razvitii vneshneekonomicheskoi deiatel'nosti gosudarstvennykh, kooperativnykh i inykh obshchestvennykh predpriiatii, ob''edinenii i organizatsii" (Decree of the Council of Ministers of the USSR: On the further development of the foreign economic activity of state, cooperative, and other public enterprises, associations, and organizations), *Ekonomicheskaia gazeta*, no. 51 (December 1988), 17–18.

46. Sergei Zamzhitskii, "Kuda podat'sia bednomu SP?" *Delovoi mir*, no. 53 (18 March 1992), p. 5.

47. "Joint Ventures in Trade and Services," *Delovie lyudi*, no. 28 (November 1992), 40.

48. For a concise discussion of this point, see Pekka Sutela, "The Role of the External Sector during the Transition," in *The Post-Soviet Economy: Soviet and Western Perspectives,* ed. Anders Åslund (New York: St. Martin's Press, 1992), 85.

49. "Osnovy zakonodatel'stva ob inostrannykh investitsiiakh v SSSR," *Ekonomika i zhizn',* no. 32 (August 1991), 1.

50. *Current Digest of the Soviet Press* (hereafter *CDSP*), vol. 43 (22 May 1991), 6; from *Pravda* and *Izvestiia* (23 April 1991), 2–3.

51. On the Liberalization of Foreign Economic Activity on the Territory of the Russian Federation. See "Laws on Foreign Economic Activities," *Business in the Ex-USSR,* no. 19 (January 1992), 68.

52. "Ekonomicheskaia strategiia pravitel'stva Rossii," *Biznes, banki, birzha,* no. 14 (March 1992), 1–2.

53. "Ob uskorenii privatizatsii gosudarstvennykh i munitsipal'nykh predpriiatii"; and "Osnovnye polozheniia programmy privatizatsii gosudarstvennykh i munitsipal'nykh predpriiatii v Rossiiskoi Federatsii na 1992 god," in *Vse o privatizatsii v torgovle* (Moscow: Torgovlia, 1992), 47–48; and 48–60.

54. Boris Krotkov, "Nikto ne khotel ustupat'," *Delovoi mir,* no. 29 (13 February 1992), 1.

55. Ibid.

56. Ibid.

57. Private enterprise personnel, however, were more likely to have a positive attitude about foreign investment (47 percent) and less likely to believe that foreigners benefited the most from such activities (36 percent). Attitudes of personnel in private enterprises were not much different from those of state employees.

58. See Violetta Tveritina, "Munitsipal'nye vlasti: v rasprodazhe Rodiny zamecheny ne byli," *Kommersant,* no. 28 (6–13 July 1992), 13; and Ivan Rodin, "Moskovskoe rukovodstvo zhaluetsia: valiutu sdaiut neokhotno," *Nezavisimaia gazeta,* no. 136 (18 July 1992), 6.

59. Vadim Bardin, "Privlekat' inostrannykh investorov v Rossiiu budet spetsial'noe agentstvo," *Kommersant-Daily,* no. 3 (13 January 1993), 4.

60. Leonid Brodskii, "Korporatsiia budet strakhovat' ot politicheskikh riskov," *Kommersant-Daily,* no. 30 (19 February 1993), 10.

61. Vadim Bardin and Dmitrii Kamin, "Parlament golosuet za kontsessii," *Kommersant-Daily,* no. 14 (28 January 1993), 3.

Chapter 7. The Anatomy of Privatization: Structure, Pace, and Scope

1. The July 3, 1991, law was extended and amended on June 5, 1992, but the changes did not affect the privatization structure discussed here.

2. These decisions may be appealed in court or through arbitration.

3. Buyers of privatized enterprises sold at auction have the right to lease

or buy buildings and land that are part of the enterprise one year after their purchase. Alternatively, they are required to lease the buildings and land for at least fifteen years.

4. "Rasporiazhenie no. 770-r ot 13 noiabria 1992 g.," *Moskovskie novosti,* no. 1 (3 January 1993), 14.

5. These shares may be paid for through installments over a three-year period.

6. C. Mikhailov, "O nekotorykh itogakh privatizatsii v 1993 godu," *Ekonomika i zhizn',* no. 14 (April 1993), 15.

7. Elena Kotel'nikova, "Pravitel'stvo po-prezhnemu delaet stavku na vaucher," *Kommersant-Daily,* no. 13 (27 January 1993), 9. Thirty-four percent chose the first variant, 64 percent the second, and 2 percent the third. More than 5,000 large enterprises had begun the privatization process by this time.

8. Just over half of our Moscow DMs were professional bureaucrats and functionaries (52 percent). The other 48 percent had varying backgrounds—as engineers, legal specialists, entrepreneurs, journalists, former enterprise directors, and academicians. Two of every five Ekaterinburg DMs had also been bureaucrats and functionaries, but in Voronezh and Smolensk the percentages were considerably smaller (12 and 33 percent, respectively). In these other cities there was also a diverse mix of backgrounds among DMs.

9. German Broido, "13 chinovnich'ikh iskushenii," *Vecherniaia Moskva,* no. 203 (19 October 1992), 2. A searing and much-discussed article about government corruption was published in June 1992 by Iurii Shchekochikhin ("Strakh," *Literaturnaia gazeta,* no. 24 [10 June 1992], 11).

10. Andrei Grachev, ". . . Plus the Privatization of the Country as a Whole," *Moscow News,* no. 30 (26 July–2 August 1992), 6.

11. *Vecherniaia Moskva,* no. 195 (7 October 1992), 1.

12. Quoted in N. Marinich, "Larisa Piiasheva: 'Mne nikogda ne bylo tak tiazhelo,' " *Vecherniaia Moskva,* no. 127 (3 July 1992), 1–2.

13. Petr Filippov, "Ne prosit' milostei u chinovnika," *Izvestiia,* no. 112 (14 May 1992), 3.

14. Vladislav Belianov, "Rossiiskie predpriiatiia v usloviiakh krizisa," *Delovoi mir,* no. 55 (25 March 1993), 7.

15. The study included 2,000 respondents: See Iurii Levada, "Zhizn' surova, no bol'shinstvo trebuet prodolzheniia reformy," *Izvestiia,* no. 210 (21 September 1992), 2.

16. Efrem Maiminas, "Traektoriia nashego dvizheniia," *Nezavisimaia gazeta,* no. 21 (4 February 1993), 5.

17. Stephen M. Meyer, "The Military," in *After the Soviet Union,* ed. Timothy J. Colton and Robert Legvold (New York: W.W. Norton, 1992), 134.

18. Ibid.

19. Ibid., 136–38. See also Vladimir Rubtsov, "Reformy po-general'ski," *Nezavisimaia gazeta,* no. 17 (29 January 1993), 4.

20. Mikhail Sergeev, "Zapushchen v proizvodstvo samolet dlia neftianikov i shpionov," *Kommersant-Daily,* no. 33 (24 February 1993), 1.

21. "Nizhnii Novgorod: vozrozhdenie russkogo dukha predpri-

nimatel'stva," *Chastnaia sobstvennost'* (*Izvestiia* supplement), no. 7 (31 March 1993), 1. See also "Egor Gaidar: Chtoby ne bylo bednykh . . . ," *Literaturnaia gazeta,* no. 1–2 (13 January 1993), 11.

22. Rubtsov, "Reformy po-general'ski."

23. See Anatolii Velednitskii, "Nam skazali—my progolosovali," *Delovoi mir,* no. 84 (30 April 1992), 2; and Marinich, "Larisa Piiasheva."

24. *Current Digest of the Soviet Press* (hereafter *CDSP*), vol. 42 (9 Janury 1991), 5; from *Izvestiia* (4 December 1990), 1.

25. *CDSP,* vol. 42 (9 January 1991), 2; from *Pravda* (27 November 1990), 1.

26. Wanting to speed up the process, Yeltsin issued a decree on December 27, 1991—two days after the collapse of the Soviet Union—which set March 1, 1992, as the date by which this first stage should be completed.

27. Vasilii Uzun, "Poslednii mesiats," *Izvestiia,* no. 5 (13 January 1993), 4.

28. "O reorganizatsii kolkhozov, sovkhozov i privatizatsii gosudarstvennykh sel'skokhoziaistvennykh predpriiatii," *Vash partner* (supplement to *Ekonomika i zhizn'*), no. 43 (October 1992), 6.

29. Uzun, "Poslednii mesiats."

30. *Current Digest of the Post-Soviet Press* (hereafter *CDPSP*), vol. 45 (17 February 1993), 28; from *Izvestiia* (20 January 1993), 2.

31. Twenty-nine percent were leased.

32. Viktor Nefedov, "Bolee milliona krest'ian v SNG stali fermerami," *Izvestiia,* no. 19 (2 February 1993), 2.

33. Ibid.

34. Liliia Babaeva, "Land: Why No Takers?" *Moscow News,* no. 11 (17–23 March 1991), 10. The survey was conducted in Russia, the Ukraine, Belorussia, and Kazakhstan.

35. *CDSP,* vol. 42 (9 January 1991), 1; from *Pravda* (27 November 1990), 1.

36. V. Starkov, "V. Chernomyrdin: nel'zia zhit', kak na Zapade, rabotaia, kak v Rossii," *Argumenty i fakty,* no. 4 (January 1993), 1.

37. Aleksandr Dymkovets, "Leonid Abalkin: 'Sovmestim li rynok c rossiiskoi obshchinnost'iu?' " *Delovoi mir,* no. 250 (26 December 1992), 6.

38. Vadim Sazonov, "O prevratnostiakh privatizatsii," *Radikal,* no. 10 (March 1992), 15.

39. Aleksandr Zhelestsov and Leonid Kesel'man, "Zemliu—krest'ianam," *Nezavisimaia gazeta,* no. 38 (26 February 1992), 2.

40. Sergei Parkhomenko, "Chastaia sobstvennost' na zemliu stanovitsia real'nost'iu," *Nezavisimaia gazeta,* no. 225 (21 November 1992), 1.

41. The study was conducted by the Center for Public Opinion and Market Research and included 1,630 respondents. See Iurii Levada, "Est' vysshii sudiia—narod . . . ," *Izvestiia,* no. 57 (27 March 1993), 4.

42. Valerii Konovalov, "Pravitel'stvo Chernomyrdina namereno stabilizirovat' sel'khozproizvodstvo v 1993 godu," *Izvestiia,* no. 16 (28 January 1993), 2.

43. Personal discussion with Irina Kuzes.

44. I. Kuleva, "Disproportsii narastaiut," *Ekonomika i zhizn'*, no. 12 (March 1993), 3.

45. See, for example, Valerii Konovalov, "Pravitel'stvo podderzhivaet fermerov," *Izvestiia*, no. 55 (25 March 1993), 4.

46. *CDPSP*, vol. 45 (17 February 1993), 28; from *Izvestiia* (20 January 1993), 2.

47. "O privatizatsii zhilishchnogo fonda v RSFSR," *Ekonomika i zhizn'* (supplement), no. 33 (August 1991), 3.

48. Aleksandr Frenkel', "Ekonomika Rossii v 1993 godu," *Delovoi mir,* no. 45 (11 March 1993), 12.

49. Sazonov, "O prevratnostiakh privatizatsii."

50. But not collective farms.

51. *CDPSP*, vol. 45 (10 March 1993), 22; from *Izvestiia* (12 February 1993), 1.

52. Leonid Mikhailov, "Ot bednogo sotsializma—k bednomu kapitalizmu," *Nezavisimaia gazeta*, no. 233 (3 December 1992), 2.

53. Igor' Karpenko, "A. Chubais: U nas net raznoglasii s V. Chernomyrdinym po programme privatizatsii," *Izvestiia*, no. 10 (20 January 1993), 5; and Valentina Ukhina, "Volgograd prinimaet estafetu u Nizhnego Novgoroda," *Delovoi mir*, no. 10 (20 January 1993), 9.

54. Karpenko, "A. Chubais."

55. Ibid.

56. "Rossiiskaia privatizatsiia: 'narodnaia'—po forme, regional'naia—po soderzhaniiu," *Kommersant-Daily*, no. 67 (13 April 1993), 8.

57. German Galkin, "Chubais nameren provesti v Cheliabinskoi oblasti vserossiiskii chekovyi auktsion," *Kommersant-Daily*, no. 70 (16 April 1993), 4.

58. Ol'ga Bolmatova and Sergei Mitin, "Reformatory uvereny v pobede prezidenta i gotoviatsia k parlamentskim vyboram," *Finansovye izvestiia* (*Izvestiia* supplement), no. 25 (17–23 April 1993), 1.

59. Faina Osmanova, "Chubais v otstavku ne sobiraetsia," *Nezavisimaia gazeta*, no. 76 (23 April 1993), 2.

60. Bolmatova and Mitin, "Reformatory uvereny v pobede prezidenta."

61. Evgeniia Galan, "Privatizatsiia obostrila protivorechiia v pravitel'stve," *Kommersant-Daily*, no. 73 (21 April 1993), 2.

62. Irina Demchenko, "Viktor Chernomyrdin vspominaet Gosplan i obeshchaet skorrektirovat' reformy," *Izvestiia*, no. 62 (3 April 1993), 2.

63. Dmitrii Khrapovitskii, "Kak i u liudei, u vauchera est' nadezhda—na referendum," *Chastnaia sobstvennost'* (*Izvestiia* supplement), no. 8 (7 April 1993), 1.

64. Ibid.

65. "RTSB: privatizatsionnye cheki 11–16 ianvaria," *Delovoi mir*, no. 13 (23 January 1993), 9.

66. Boris Kagarlitskii, "Rossiia posle El'tsina," *Nezavisimaia gazeta*, no. 70 (15 April 1993), 2.

67. Vitalii Tambovtsev, "Khozhdenie vo vlast' kak sposob obogashcheniia," *Nezavisimaia gazeta*, no. 48 (16 March 1993), 4.

68. Aleksandr Vladislavlev, "Nuzhen proryv," *Nezavisimaia gazeta,* no. 70 (15 April 1993), 4.

69. Vitalii Kliuchnikov, "Motivy i lokomotivy," *Nezavisimaia gazeta,* no. 46 (12 March 1993), 4.

Chapter 8. Perspectives from the Work Force

1. First-person usage in this chapter refers to Lynn Nelson. In several cases, names of interviewees and their enterprises have been changed to ensure anonymity.

2. V. Starkov, "V. Chernomyrdin: Nel'zia zhit', kak na Zapade, rabotaia, kak v Rossii," *Argumenty i fakty,* no. 4 (January 1993), 2.

3. Table not shown.

4. Table not shown.

5. In the case of privatized enterprises, after privatization.

Chapter 9. Politics and the Promise of Economic Reform

1. Sergei Fateev, "Nekotorye problemy privatizatsii v Rossiiskoi Federatsii i vozmozhnosti ikh resheniia," *Delovoi mir,* no. 110 (10 June 1992), 5.

2. Andrei Siniavskii, *Soviet Civilization: A Cultural History* (New York: Little, Brown, 1988), 189.

3. Tony Cliff, *Lenin,* vol. 2, *All Power to the Soviets* (London: Pluto Press, 1976), 379.

4. See Alan M. Ball, *Russia's Last Capitalists: The Nepmen, 1921–1929* (Berkeley: University of California Press, 1987), 15.

5. Vladimir Orlov, "Gosudarstvo idet s molotka," *Moskovskie novosti,* no. 2 (12 January 1992), 14.

6. Ibid.

7. Anders Åslund, "Principles of Privatisation for Formerly Socialist Countries," Stockholm Institute of Soviet and East European Economics, working paper no. 18 (1991), 4.

8. "'Demokraticheskaia Rossiia' vozderzhivaetsia ot priamoi konfrontatsii s prezidentom . . . ," *Izvestiia,* no. 274 (21 December 1992), 1–2.

9. Anders Åslund, "The Gradual Nature of Economic Change in Russia," Stockholm Institute of East European Economics, working paper no. 56 (1992), 10.

10. Ibid.

11. Grigorii Tsitriniak, "Pogranichnaia situatsiia," *Literaturnaia gazeta,* no. 44 (28 October 1992), 11.

12. David Lipton and Jeffrey Sachs, "Prospects for Russia's Economic Reforms," paper prepared for the Brookings Panel on Economic Activity,

Washington, DC, September 17–18, 1992, 44.

13. Michael Mandelbaum, "By a Thread," *The New Republic* (5 April 1993), 20.

14. Jeffrey Sachs, "The Road to the Market," *The Washington Post,* no. 113 (28 March 1993), C2.

15. Mandelbaum, "By a Thread," 21..

16. See also "Kompleks mer po stabilizatsii i vyvodu iz krizisa ekonomiki Rossii," *Delovoi mir,* no. 228 (26 November 1992), 2.

17. See, for example, Valerii Vyzhutovich, "Smena nyneshnego sostava Rossiiskogo pravitel'stva oznachala by smenu kursa reform," *Izvestiia,* no. 265 (8 December 1992), 2.

18. Aristarkh Vladimirov, "Prem'er-ministru aplodirovali tol'ko direktora," *Kommersant-Daily,* no. 1 (9 January 1993), 2.

19. John Lloyd, "Poka dela idut kak obychno," *Finansovye izvestiia* (*Izvestiia* supplement), no. 9 (24–29 December 1992), 1.

20. Fred Hiatt, "Russia's New Premier Talks to Legislators Like a Free Marketeer," *The Washington Post,* no. 55 (29 January 1993): A20.

21. Pavel Popov, "Chernomyrdin pokinul Shveitsariiu 'dostoinym pre-emnikom Gaidara,'" *Kommersant-Daily,* no. 17 (2 February 1993), 9.

22. A. Meshcherskii, "Rossiia na fone mira," *Argumenty i fakty,* no. 5 (February 1993), 4.

23. Pavel Popov, "Chernomyrdin pokinul Shveitsariiu."

24. Artem Zaitsev, "Iadro komandy Gaidara ostaetsia v pravitel'stve," *Finansovye izvestiia* (*Izvestiia* supplement), no. 9 (24–29 December 1992), 1.

25. Vera Kuznetsova, "Boris El'tsin poluchil ostorozhnuiu podderzhku rukovodstva RSPP," *Nezavisimaia gazeta,* no. 72 (17 April 1993), 1.

26. Ibid., 2.

27. Margaret Shapiro, "Yeltsin Wins Pact to Keep Reformers," *The Washington Post,* no. 16 (21 December 1992), A14.

28. See Leonid Brodskii, "Perestanovki tol'ko nachalis'," *Kommersant-Daily,* no. 56 (27 March 1993), 3.

29. Ol'ga Bolmatova and Sergei Mitin, "Reformatory uvereny v pobede prezidenta i gotoviatsia k parlamentskim vyboram," *Finansovye izvestiia* (*Izvestiia* supplement), no. 25 (17–23 April 1993), 1.

30. "O finansovo-ekonomicheskoi politike Rossii v 1993 godu," *Izvestiia,* no. 15 (27 January 1993), 5.

31. Aleksandr Slavuk, "Pravitel'stvo vystupaet za kontrol' nad chastnymi predpriiatiiami," *Kommersant-Daily,* no. 33 (24 February 1993), 9.

32. Anatolii Kostiukov, "Chto El'tsinu nado?" *Megapolis-Express,* no. 9 (3 March 1993), 20.

33. Irina Demchenko, "Viktor Chernomyrdin vspominaet Gosplan i obe-shchaet skorrektirovat' reformy," *Izvestiia,* no. 62 (3 April 1993), 2.

34. Kostiukov, "Chto El'tsinu nado?" Kostiukov was writing about the referendum originally scheduled for April 11. His reasoning is obviously ap-plicable, also, to the April 25 referendum.

35. *Current Digest of the Post-Soviet Press* (hereafter *CDPSP*), vol. 44 (6

January 1993), 10; from *Moskovskie novosti* (13 December 1992), 7.

36. Andranik Migranian, "Ot VII s'ezda narodnykh deputatov k referendumu," *Nezavisimaia gazeta,* no. 29 (16 February 1993), 5.

37. Liudmila Telen, "The Play Begins Behind the Scenes," *Moscow News,* no. 50 (13–20 December 1992), 7.

38. Michael Dobbs, "Yeltsin Challenges His Foes in Congress, Calls for Referendum," *The Washington Post,* no. 6 (11 December 1992), 1.

39. Ibid.

40. Ibid., A48.

41. Fred Hiatt, "Attempt to Rein In Yeltsin Fails," *The Washington Post,* no. 96 (11 March 1993), A26.

42. Vladimir Abarinov, " 'Ul'timatum' Andreia Kozyreva," *Nezavisimaia gazeta,* no. 241 (15 December 1992), 1.

43. Serge Schmemann, "The Spotlight, Again, Falls on Yeltsin," *The New York Times* (international edition), vol. 142 (3 April 1993), 4; Fred Hiatt, "Power Struggle Traps Yeltsin," *The Washington Post,* no. 99 (14 March 1993), A24.

44. Sachs, "The Road to the Market."

45. Princeton University's Stephen F. Cohen offered a useful alternative to the predominant theme of the day ("American Policy and Russia's Future," *The Nation* [12 April 1993], 476–83).

46. "ABC of Russia's Revival" (interview with Gennadii Burbulis), *Moscow News,* no. 14 (5–12 April 1992), 6.

47. Kostiukov, "Chto El'tsinu nado?"

48. Migranian, "Ot VII s'ezda narodnykh deputatov k referendumu."

49. "Gavriil Popov: 'Presidential rule is needed, but with guarantees for democracy,'" *Moscow News,* no. 49 (6–13 December 1992), 4.

50. "Lichnoe mnenie," *Megapolis-Express,* no. 11 (24 March 1993), 3.

51. Ibid.

52. Len Karpinskii, "Congress as a Phenomenon of the Political Landscape," *Moscow News,* no. 13 (26 March 1993), 2.

53. Vitalii Tret'iakov, "Pozhaluista, ne delaite bol'she oshibok," *Nezavisimaia gazeta,* no. 56 (26 March 1993), 5.

54. Ibid.

55. *CDPSP,* vol. 45 (24 March 1993), 1–3; from *Grazhdanin Rossii* (February 1993), 6.

56. Anatolii Kostiukov, "Depkorpus Rossii: politicheskaia anatomiia," *Megapolis-Express,* no. 15 (21 April 1993), 23; and "S'ezd parlamentariev i obshchestvo," *Delovoi mir,* no. 63 (6 April 1993), 5. For additional analysis see Sergei Chugaev, "Deputatskie nastroeniia meniaiutsia v zavisimosti ot zanimaemoi dolzhnosti," *Izvestiia,* no. 56 (26 March 1993), 2.

57. Kostiukov, "Depkorpus Rossii: politicheskaia anatomiia."

58. Representing the Radical Democrats and Democratic Russia factions.

59. Representing the Accord for Progress, Left Center/Cooperation, Free Russia, Motherland, and Sovereignty and Equality factions.

60. Representing the Workers' Union, Rising Generation/New Policy, and Industrial Union factions.

61. Lynn D. Nelson and Paata Amonashvili, "Voting and Political Attitudes in Soviet Georgia," *Soviet Studies* 44 (1992), 687–97.

62. Fred Hiatt, "Yeltsin Forces Urge Speedup in Reforms," *The Washington Post,* no. 143 (27 April 1993), A14 (emphasis added).

63. According to Yeltsin's proposal, the chair of the legislature would be first in line to succeed the president.

64. Margaret Shapiro, "Yeltsin Starts Push for New Constitution," *The Washington Post,* no. 146 (30 April 1993), A35.

65. Ibid., A38.

Appendix A. Technical and Supplementary Material

1. The population estimates for these cities are for 1990 and are taken from *Demograficheskii ezhegodnik SSSR: 1990* (Moscow: Gosudarstvennyi komitet SSSR po statistike, 1990).

2. Lynn Nelson.

3. Lynn D. Nelson and Neil W. Henry, "Simultaneous Control and Cross-tabular Presentation with Polytomous Variables: The Case of Religion Predictors," *Journal for the Scientific Study of Religion* 29 (1990): 255–63.

4. Morris Rosenberg, "Test Factor Standardization as a Method of Interpretation," *Social Forces* 41 (1962): 553–61; Ottar Hellevik, "Decomposing Proportions and Differences in Proportions: Approaches to Contingency-Table Analysis," *Quality and Quantity* 18 (1983): 79–111; and James A. Davis, "Extending Rosenberg's Technique for Standardizing Percentage Tables," *Social Forces* 62 (1984): 679–708.

5. Peter R. Cox, *Demography* (Cambridge: Cambridge University Press, 1976), 297–301.

Index

About the Authors

Dr. Lynn D. Nelson is a sociology professor at Virginia Commonwealth University, where his research specialty is Russian politics and society. He held a Fulbright lectureship in the Soviet Union in 1990, and for the past three years he has studied economic reform in Russia with grants from The National Council for Soviet and East European Research (NCSEER), the Center for Institutional Reform and the Informal Sector (IRIS) at the University of Maryland, and the International Research and Exchanges Board (IREX). He has spent nearly half of the past three years in Russia, concentrating his research in Moscow, Ekaterinburg, Voronezh, and Smolensk. In 1987 he was a visiting fellow at Harvard University's Russian Research Center. Results of his recent research have been published in several Western and Russian periodicals, including *Slavic Review*, *Soviet Studies*, *Sotsiologicheskie issledovaniia*, *Literaturnaia gazeta*, *Nezavisimaia gazeta*, *Ekonomika i zhizn'*, and *Moskovskie novosti*.

Irina Y. Kuzes was trained at the Institute of Urban Planning in Moscow, where she conducted research for eight years on problems of urban land use. Her inquiries into coordination problems in urban planning gave her a unique orientation to privatization issues, which have been the focus of her work since 1991. She held an appointment as a visiting researcher at Virginia Commonwealth University during the 1992–93 academic year. She is currently an instructor at the Institute of Architecture in Moscow and a correspondent for the journal *Znanie—sila*. Findings from her research on the subject of Russian economic reform have been published in *Literaturnaia gazeta* and *Moscow News*.

The authors are currently at work on a sequel to the present study.